W9-BVB-871

Advanced Marathoning

SECOND EDITION

Pete Pfitzinger ▪ **Scott Douglas**

Human Kinetics

Library of Congress Cataloging-in-Publication Data

Pfitzinger, Pete, 1957-
  Advanced marathoning / Pete Pfitzinger, Scott Douglas. -- 2nd ed.
    p. cm.
  Includes bibliographical references and index.
  ISBN-13: 978-0-7360-7460-5 (soft cover)
  ISBN-10: 0-7360-7460-0 (soft cover)
  1. Marathon running--Training. I. Douglas, Scott. II. Title.
  GV1065.17.T73P45 2009
  796.42'52--dc22
                            2008041703

ISBN-10: 0-7360-7460-0 (print)   ISBN-10: 0-7360-8203-4 (Adobe PDF)
ISBN-13: 978-0-7360-7460-5 (print)   ISBN-13: 978-0-7360-8203-7 (Adobe PDF)

This publication is written and published to provide accurate and authoritative information relevant to the subject matter presented. It is published and sold with the understanding that the author and publisher are not engaged in rendering legal, medical, or other professional services by reason of their authorship or publication of this work. If medical or other expert assistance is required, the services of a competent professional person should be sought.

Acquisitions Editor: Laurel Plotzke; **Developmental Editor:** Kevin Matz; **Assistant Editors:** Elizabeth Watson and Carla Zych; **Copyeditor:** Patricia MacDonald; **Proofreader:** Darlene Rake; **Indexer:** Nan N. Badgett; **Graphic Designer:** Robert Reuther; **Graphic Artist:** Tara Welsch; **Cover Designer:** Keith Blomberg; **Photographer (cover):** Ryan Pierse/Getty Images (for DAGOC); **Photographer (interior):** Neil Bernstein, unless otherwise noted; **Photo Asset Manager:** Laura Fitch; **Visual Production Assistant:** Joyce Brumfield; **Photo Production Manager:** Jason Allen; **Art Manager:** Kelly Hendren; **Associate Art Manager:** Alan L. Wilborn; **Illustrators:** pp. 76-77 K. Galasyn-Wright, all other illustrations Tom Roberts; **Printer:** United Graphics

Human Kinetics books are available at special discounts for bulk purchase. Special editions or book excerpts can also be created to specification. For details, contact the Special Sales Manager at Human Kinetics.

Printed in the United States of America   10 9 8 7 6 5 4 3 2 1

Human Kinetics
Web site: www.HumanKinetics.com

United States: Human Kinetics
P.O. Box 5076
Champaign, IL 61825-5076
800-747-4457
e-mail: humank@hkusa.com

Canada: Human Kinetics
475 Devonshire Road Unit 100
Windsor, ON N8Y 2L5
800-465-7301 (in Canada only)
e-mail: info@hkcanada.com

Europe: Human Kinetics
107 Bradford Road
Stanningley
Leeds LS28 6AT, United Kingdom
+44 (0) 113 255 5665
e-mail: hk@hkeurope.com

Australia: Human Kinetics
57A Price Avenue
Lower Mitcham, South Australia 5062
08 8372 0999
e-mail: info@hkaustralia.com

New Zealand: Human Kinetics
Division of Sports Distributors NZ Ltd.
P.O. Box 300 226 Albany
North Shore City
Auckland
0064 9 448 1207
e-mail: info@humankinetics.co.nz

To all runners willing to work hard and intelligently

—Pete Pfitzinger and Scott Douglas

Contents

Foreword

Growing up, I was always looking for a challenge. I ran 15 miles for my first run when I was 15, and after that I ran to the top of every mountain in the nearby vicinity. We have a course called the 5,000-foot run that climbs from roughly 6,000 feet to more than 11,000 feet in just over 10 miles. It is brutal, but the sense of accomplishment that comes with conquering it is addictive.

Challenge is what I love most about the marathon. It is the ultimate test. For some runners the draw is simply the distance, and for others it is a matter of speed over the distance, but for all of us the marathon is a test of the will and the spirit.

When I crossed the line at the 2008 Flora London Marathon, with the clock stopping at 2:06:17, I had never been so exhausted in my life. I felt like I was having an out of body experience during the final 200 meters, yet the sensation of having finished the race while leaving every bit of my mind, body, and heart out on the course is something that I hope to replicate over and over again in my career as a marathoner.

As I approach each race, it is satisfying to know that I have been well prepared by my coach, Terrence Mahon, in training and have done everything to the best of my ability, whether it be core strengthening, optimal recovery and nutrition, or nailing a well-placed long run in the training régime.

While reading this second edition of *Advanced Marathoning*, I was constantly nodding my head in agreement with Pete Pfitzinger and Scott Douglas. They echo many of the "secrets" to marathoning that I have picked up from coach T (as we call him) and Olympic medalists Meb Keflezighi and Deena Kastor. I am confident that everyone from the seasoned marathoner looking to improve upon a long-standing personal best to the debut baby will find great wisdom in this systematic, logical, and yet artistic approach to marathoning. I myself was constantly reminded of all the ins and outs that go with achieving success in this sport.

Those of you who are just going for distance will find easy application points that will make your journey much more enjoyable and fun. "Fun" may not be the adjective most commonly associated with the marathon, but the marathon offers the well-prepared runner more enjoyment than any other race out there. In no other race is it possible to feel so good for so long. The racing section of the book will provide many keys to ensure that your 26.2-mile journey is indeed a fun one. Those of you who are going for speed will not only find out how to cycle and structure your workouts but also how to live as we pros live, taking care of the smallest details, which will give you the extra edge on race day to crack that elusive personal best.

I thank Pete and Scott for writing such a helpful aid to the marathoning world. This resource will undoubtedly be credited by marathoners all over the world as they celebrate having prepared and raced to their fullest potential.

—Ryan Hall

Preface

Guidelines for Advanced Marathoning

Welcome to the second edition of *Advanced Marathoning*. The positive reception to the first edition, and the direct feedback about it that we're pleased to regularly receive, only strengthens our belief that there are tens of thousands of readers out there eager to know how to conquer one of running's most challenging races.

The key to simply finishing a marathon isn't a secret: Train long to go long. But what about when you want to race a marathon? Then things aren't so simple.

Besides gaining enough baseline endurance to complete the distance, now your concerns turn to matters such as how fast to do your long runs, what types of interval sessions to do, how to manipulate your diet for maximum performance, how to schedule hard workouts to allow both progress and recovery, and so on. The best answers to these questions aren't so obvious, and they require a solid base of knowledge. You'll acquire that knowledge through this book.

If you've run a marathon and want to move beyond the basics, or if you're an accomplished runner at shorter distances planning a marathon debut, then it's time to graduate to *Advanced Marathoning*. We hope you'll agree that this second edition, with new chapters and expanded, updated information in every chapter, will become one of the most valuable resources in your running library.

Advanced Marathoning

What do we mean by advanced marathoning? Simply this: that many runners aren't content with saying, "I finished." They want to run the marathon as they do shorter races—as fast as possible. That doesn't mean they're going to drop everything in their lives and do nothing but train, but it does mean they're committed to doing their best, taking into consideration such factors as their age and real-world commitments. The runners for whom we wrote this book have goals such as setting a personal best, qualifying for Boston, or running faster than they did 10 years ago.

Competing in the marathon, as opposed to completing the distance without regard for time, requires thorough, intelligent preparation. Being dedicated to improving your marathon performance requires knowing such things as how fast to do your long runs given your goal race pace, how far and how fast your hard sessions should be, what to eat so that you're able to run as fast at mile 25 as at the start, and so on. Advanced marathoning has to be based on more than common sense and running folklore. *Advanced Marathoning*, therefore, is based on sport science.

The training schedules in the second section of this book are based on a simple concept: Research in exercise physiology has revealed that the fastest marathoners have a few key attributes in common. These include an ability to store a large amount of glycogen (the stored form of carbohydrate) in their muscles, an ability to sustain submaximal speeds for prolonged periods, an ability to send large amounts of oxygen to muscles and have their muscles use that oxygen, and an ability to run faster than others using a given amount of oxygen. We know which of these attributes are most important for successful marathoning, and we know what types of training best improve these attributes. Marathon training, then, should be a matter of balancing these types of training with adequate recovery so that your body's ability to sustain a relatively fast pace for 26.2 miles (42.2 km) improves as your goal race approaches.

We could, of course, simply present the training schedules found in the latter part of this book and say, "Just do what we tell you. Trust us." But we think that the more you understand why you're running a given workout, the more motivated you'll be to stick with your training and the better prepared you'll be to assess your progress toward your marathon goal. For that reason, before our training schedules are several chapters that explain the principles of successful marathoning. These chapters explain what is critical for marathon success and why. Digesting the information in them will help you be a better marathoner. Let's look at the contents of the first part of this book.

Your Guide to Understanding the Marathon

Chapter 1 is the longest chapter in this book. We don't expect that everyone will sit down and read it all at once; in fact, you could start on the training schedule of your choice right now and not have to worry that you haven't looked at chapter 1. Eventually, though, you'll want to read this chapter carefully and understand its key concepts because it explains the science we used in constructing the training schedules.

Chapter 1 gives an in-depth examination of the physiological attributes needed for success in the marathon. These include a high lactate threshold, an ability to store a large amount of glycogen in your muscles and liver, a well-developed ability to use fat as fuel, a well-developed maximal oxygen uptake, and good running economy. (Don't worry if any of these concepts are unclear to you—you'll fully understand them and their relation to marathoning after reading chapter 1.) We look at the traits your body must have to run a good marathon, and then we detail how to train to provide the greatest stimulus for these traits to improve.

Understanding the concepts in chapter 1 is critical. Contrary to what some people think, training for a fast marathon doesn't mean simply running as many miles as possible as quickly as possible. Regardless of how inspired you are to run your best marathon, you most likely have to prepare for it while not neglecting those annoying little details such as your job. Your training, then, should provide the biggest return for the time you put into it. After you read chapter 1, you'll know why the targeted training the schedules call for is optimal for marathoning success.

Chapter 2 explains the crucial role that proper nutrition and hydration play in successful marathoning. What marathoners should eat and drink is the subject of much ill-informed discussion—perhaps almost as much as training is. After reading chapter 2, you'll know what marathon training and racing require in terms of fuel and how your diet contributes to meeting your marathon goal. You'll also understand how dehydration can significantly reduce your performance and the strategies you can use to avoid it in training and on race day.

As we said previously, intelligent marathon preparation means more than accumulating repeated days of hard mileage. You'll make more progress toward your goal by doing one of the key workouts described in chapter 1, allowing your body to absorb the benefits of that workout, and then doing another targeted session. In other words, you should allow your body to recover after an especially long or hard run. Chapter 3 shows how to maximize your recovery, including how far and how fast to run in the days following a long or hard session, what to eat and drink to refuel most quickly, and how to monitor your body's signs to stay healthy enough to reap the benefits of your hard work.

If you follow one of the training schedules in this book, your training will contain all the running elements you'll need for a fast marathon. But there are things you can do in your nonrunning hours that can help your overall improvement as a marathoner. In chapter 4, we detail the types of flexibility, core strength, resistance training, and aerobic cross-training activities that will make you the best marathoner. We also describe a few technique drills that will help improve your running form.

What you do in the last few weeks before your marathon can have a profound effect on your finishing time. Because tapering your training before the marathon is both so important and so misunderstood, we've created a new chapter devoted to the topic. In chapter 5, you'll learn how—and why—to reduce your mileage as the marathon approaches and what workouts to do just before the race to reach the start line with the optimal blend of being rested and ready.

The final background chapter details what to do on race day. Chapter 6 discusses race strategy, with section-by-section pacing advice, and presents information on other crucial matters, such as what to eat on race day and how to drink on the run to minimize dehydration.

The Training Schedules

Chapters 8 through 11 apply the principles detailed in chapters 2 through 6 to day-by-day training schedules leading to your marathon. They're preceded by chapter 7, another new chapter in this second edition, which gives in-depth direction on how to follow the training schedule of your choice, including how fast to do each of the key types of workouts.

Chapters 8 through 11 are divided on the basis of weekly mileage. (The training schedules in these chapters, as well as in chapter 12, also describe each day's workout in terms of kilometers. Choose whichever unit of measurement you're more comfortable with.) Chapter 8 contains the schedules that call for the lowest weekly mileage; these peak at 55 miles, or 88 kilometers, per week. Chapter 9 contains schedules that call for 55 to 70 miles (88 to 113 km) per week. Chapter 10's schedules range from 70 to 85 miles (113 to 137 km). The final new chapter in this book, chapter 11, is for the real high-mileage folks—it includes weeks of just more than 100 miles, or 161 kilometers.

The weekly mileage you follow is up to you. Making that decision should be based on your running history, your tendency toward injury above a certain level of mileage, what else will be going on in your life in the months before your goal race, and so on. Regardless of which schedule you follow, it will contain the workouts that will lead to the biggest gains in marathon-specific fitness for that level of mileage.

Chapters 8 through 11 present you with another decision to make. Each chapter contains a 12-week and an 18-week schedule. Although we recommend that most readers follow the 18-week schedule, we realize that sometimes you don't have the luxury of that amount of planning. The 12-week schedules are for these situations, and while they're more compact than is optimal, they nonetheless contain the workouts needed to make significant progress in such a short time.

The schedules are designed to be easy to read, vertically and horizontally. Horizontally, they show you how your mileage and training emphases change as your marathon approaches. This helps you understand your key training goals for a given period. Looking at the schedules vertically enhances that understanding because you can quickly grasp the key workouts in a given week. The schedules specify the purpose of each day's workout. That way you can not only determine what you're trying to achieve on a certain day of the week, but you can also look down through the week to see your most important training goals for that week.

You'll note that the schedules specify what to do every day of the many weeks leading up to your marathon. We realize, of course, that it's the rare reader whose life will so perfectly coincide with such a detailed schedule. Again, looking at the schedules vertically and horizontally will prove helpful because you'll know what types of training are most important for wherever you are on the schedule, so you'll know which workouts to emphasize if you need to juggle a few days around.

Chapter 12 is a bit different from the other training-schedule chapters, and it's for marathoners who themselves are a bit different. Chapter 12 is for multiple-marathon runners who want to run two or more marathons within 12 weeks or less. Following such a schedule usually isn't the way to run your fastest marathon, but it's not our place to say categorically that you should never attempt such a feat. Chapter 12 acknowledges that some runners want to tackle this challenge, and it provides schedules that will maximize your chances of success in the second (or third or fourth) marathon in a given time period. Using the principles behind the other schedules, chapter 12 provides schedules for your best possible marathon 4, 6, 8, 10, and 12 weeks after another marathon.

Now that you know what's in this book and how to use it, let's get going on understanding the basics of successful marathoning.

Acknowledgments

Our thanks go to

- our wives, Christine Pfitzinger and Stacey Cramp, for undying support;
- Laurel Plotzke and Kevin Matz at Human Kinetics for bringing this book to fruition;
- Ryan Hall for writing the foreword;
- the world-class marathoners profiled in these pages for sharing how they've succeeded; and
- Jack Daniels, the late Arthur Lydiard, Bill Rodgers, David Martin, Bill Squires, Joe Vigil, Lorraine Moller, Kevin Ryan, Arch Jelley, and Randy Wilber for their valuable insights into marathon training.

Training Components

Elements of Training

The marathon demands respect. The physiological and psychological demands of the marathon are extreme; therefore you must plan your preparation intelligently and thoroughly.

Unfortunately, *intelligent* and *thorough* aren't the two words that most readily come to mind when thinking about some marathon training programs. Search the Web under "marathon training" and you'll find thousands of well-meaning but only intermittently helpful sites. The training advice on many of these sites is based more on personal anecdotes and handed-down folk wisdom than on exercise science. You'd be hard-pressed to cull through these sites and summarize why they're prescribing the type of preparation they present.

That's too bad because while running a marathon isn't easy, training for it should be relatively simple. Running a marathon requires specific physiological attributes. The task at hand is to run 26.2 miles (42.2 km) as fast as possible. The requirements for this feat in terms of fuel use, oxygen consumption, biomechanical requirements, and even psychological attributes are highly predictable. In this chapter, we look at the physiological demands of the marathon and how to train most effectively to meet those demands.

First we look at the physiological demands, such as having a high lactate threshold and the ability to store large amounts of glycogen in your muscles and liver. Then we look at the types of training that are most effective for improving marathon performance and explain why. Next we investigate how to structure your training so that it progresses logically to your desired end point. Finally, we look at the importance of using shorter races as tune-ups to the marathon. After reading this chapter, you'll see the logic underpinning effective marathon training and will better understand which types of training to emphasize and why.

Marathon Physiology

Successful marathoners have many factors in common. Most of these factors are determined by both genetics and training. Genetics determines the range within which you can improve; training determines where your current abilities fall within that range. In this section, we'll consider the physiological variables necessary for marathon success.

Successful marathoners have these physiological attributes:

- High proportion of slow-twitch muscle fibers. This trait is genetically determined and influences the other physiological characteristics listed here.
- High lactate threshold. This is the ability to produce energy at a fast rate aerobically without accumulating high levels of lactate in your muscles and blood.
- High glycogen storage and well-developed fat utilization. These traits enable you to store enough glycogen in your muscles and liver to run hard for 26.2 miles (42.2 km) and enable your muscles to rely more on fat for fuel.
- Excellent running economy. This is the ability to use oxygen economically when running at marathon pace.
- High maximal oxygen uptake ($\dot{V}O_2$max). This is the ability to transport large amounts of oxygen to your muscles and the ability of your muscles to extract and use oxygen.
- Quick recovery. This is the ability to recover from training quickly.

Remember, no one factor makes a successful marathoner. Frank Shorter, for example, had 80 percent slow-twitch fibers and a $\dot{V}O_2$max of 71.4 ml/kg/min (milliliters of oxygen per kilogram of body weight per minute). In contrast, Alberto Salazar had 93 percent slow-twitch fibers and a $\dot{V}O_2$max of 78 ml/kg/min. More anecdotally, consider that marathon world-record holder Haile Gebrselassie has the sprint speed to have won an indoor world title at 1,500 meters, while Bill Rodgers never broke 2:00 for 800 meters. Still, each was the best in the world at his peak. The combination of these physiological factors, in conjunction with biomechanical variables and psychological makeup, determines marathoning success. Let's look more closely at each of the main physiological factors.

High Proportion of Slow-Twitch Muscle Fibers

Your thousands of muscle fibers can be divided into three categories—slow-twitch, fast-twitch A, and fast-twitch B. The higher the percentage of slow-twitch fibers in your muscles, the greater your likelihood of marathon success. Slow-twitch muscle fibers are naturally adapted to endurance exercise.

They resist fatigue and have a high aerobic capacity, a high capillary density, and other characteristics that make them ideal for marathon running.

The proportion of slow-twitch fibers in your muscles is determined genetically and is believed not to change with training. Although fast-twitch muscle fibers can't be converted to slow-twitch fibers, with general endurance training they can gain more of the characteristics of slow-twitch fibers, especially the fast-twitch A fibers. These adaptations are beneficial because they allow your fast-twitch fibers to become better at producing energy aerobically.

A muscle biopsy is the only method of determining your proportion of slow-twitch muscle fibers. In a biopsy, a small amount of tissue is cut out of your muscle and analyzed. Though it is interesting (and painful), this procedure is pointless—once you know your fiber-type distribution, there's nothing you can do about it. In contrast, you can improve other physiological characteristics with training.

High Lactate Threshold

A high lactate threshold (LT) is the most important physiological variable for endurance athletes. Lactate threshold most directly determines your performance limit in any event lasting more than 30 minutes. Your marathon race pace is limited by the accumulation of lactate (a by-product of carbohydrate metabolism) and the associated hydrogen ions in your muscles and blood. A close relationship exists between your lactate threshold and marathon performance because lactate threshold reflects the rate at which your muscles can sustain aerobic energy production. Successful marathoners typically race at a speed very close to their lactate-threshold pace.

The average runner's lactate threshold occurs at about 75 to 80 percent of his or her $\dot{V}O_2max$. Successful marathoners generally have lactate thresholds of 84 to 88 percent of $\dot{V}O_2max$; elite marathoners tend to have lactate thresholds of about 88 to 91 percent of $\dot{V}O_2max$. This means that elite marathoners can use a larger proportion of their maximal aerobic capacity before lactate starts to accumulate in their muscles and blood.

Lactate is produced by your muscles and is used by your muscles, heart, liver, and kidneys. The lactate concentration in your blood represents a balance between lactate production and consumption. Even at rest, you produce a small amount of lactate. If your blood lactate were measured right now, you would have a lactate concentration of about 1 millimole. As you increase your effort from resting to walking to easy running, your rates of lactate production and lactate consumption increase, and your blood lactate concentration stays relatively constant. When you run harder than your lactate threshold, however, your lactate concentration rises because the rate of lactate clearance can no longer keep up with lactate production.

When you accumulate a high level of lactate, the hydrogen ions associated with lactate production turn off the enzymes used to produce energy

Brian Sell

Fastest Marathon: 2:10:47
Marathon Highlights:
Third place, 2008 U.S. Olympic
Trials; Ninth place, 2005 World
Championships

© Andy Lyons/Getty Images

Brian Sell should be an inspiration to every runner out there who is willing to believe that great things are possible through sheer hard work.

In high school, his best 3,200-meter time was a mediocre 10:06, more than a minute slower than the best scholastic runners in the U.S. Yet a decade later, Sell was able to average under 5:00 per mile for a marathon. As he said after placing fourth at the 2006 Boston Marathon, "I started thinking about how I just ran 26 miles faster than I could run two miles in high school. I just hope that people look at it and say, 'Hey, if this yahoo can do it, then I can do it too.' It's just a matter of putting the miles in and working. It's not so much how much talent you have."

Obviously, to have become an Olympic marathoner, Sell was born with above-average genetics for distance running. But that innate ability only really started to surface in 2004, by which time he had already been averaging well over 100 miles per week for years. After leading the 2004 Olympic Marathon Trials for 19 miles but then fading to 12th, Sell could have been excused for thinking he wasn't meant to run at the elite level. Instead, he got back to work—upping his mileage to 160 miles per week in marathon buildups—and continued to progress, making the 2008 Olympic team ahead of runners such as former world-record holder Khalid Khannouchi and 2004 Olympic silver medalist Meb Keflezighi.

Although few, if any, readers of this book are going to be able to handle repeated weeks of 160 miles, all can draw inspiration from Sell. First, consider his dedication to and faith in simply getting out the door and putting in the miles. How many other runners of Sell's caliber in high school might potentially be 2:10 marathoners today? Put another way, how do you know how good you can be until you try?

Second, think about Sell's ability to handle such high mileage. Being able to put in the training necessary to run a good marathon is itself a form of talent. Although you may not consider yourself blessed with a lot of "natural talent," as judged by your ability to run a really fast 5K, you might very well have Sell's ability to hold up to and absorb a lot of miles, which should translate to faster marathons. Again, how will you know until you try?

Finally, Sell is part of the Brooks-Hanson training group. They meet for distance runs most days and do almost of all their long runs and hard workouts together. Sell credits the group with pulling him through tough physical and emotional times in his training. You, too, can benefit from finding regular training partners who share your goals and are of roughly your speed.

and may interfere with the uptake of calcium, thereby reducing the muscles' ability to contract. In other words, you can't produce energy as quickly, so you're forced to slow down. This explains why you run the marathon at an intensity just below your lactate threshold.

With the correct training, adaptations occur inside your muscle fibers that allow you to run at a higher intensity without building up lactate. The most important of these adaptations are increased number and size of mitochondria, increased aerobic enzyme activity, and increased capillarization in your muscle fibers. These adaptations all improve your ability to produce energy using oxygen.

Increased Number and Size of Mitochondria

Mitochondria are the only part of your muscle fibers in which energy can be produced aerobically. Think of them as the aerobic energy factories in your muscle fibers. By fully utilizing your ability to produce energy without accumulating high levels of lactate, lactate-threshold training increases the size of your mitochondria (i.e., makes bigger factories) and the number of mitochondria (i.e., makes more factories) in your muscle fibers. With more mitochondria, you can produce more energy aerobically and maintain a faster pace. This is a relevant adaptation for marathoners because more than 99 percent of the energy needed for running a marathon is produced aerobically.

Increased Aerobic Enzyme Activity

Enzymes in your mitochondria speed up aerobic energy production (i.e., increase the rate of production in your aerobic energy factories). Lactate-threshold training increases aerobic enzyme activity; this adaptation improves the efficiency of your mitochondria. The more aerobic enzyme activity in your mitochondria, the faster you are able to produce energy aerobically.

Increased Capillarization of Muscle Fibers

Oxygen is necessary to produce energy aerobically. Your heart pumps oxygen-rich blood to your muscles through a remarkable system of blood vessels. Capillaries are the smallest blood vessels, and typically several border each muscle fiber. With the correct training, you increase the number of capillaries per muscle fiber. With more capillaries per muscle fiber, oxygen is more efficiently delivered where it's needed. Capillaries also deliver fuel to the muscle fibers and remove waste products such as carbon dioxide. A more-efficient delivery and removal system provides a constant supply of oxygen and fuel and prevents waste products from accumulating in your muscles as quickly. By providing oxygen to the individual muscle fibers, increased capillary density allows the rate of aerobic energy production to increase.

High Glycogen Storage and Well-Developed Fat Utilization

Glycogen is the form of carbohydrate stored in the body, and carbohydrate is the primary fuel used when racing a marathon. The two ways to ensure that glycogen stores last throughout the marathon are to train your body to store a large amount of glycogen and to train your body to conserve glycogen at marathon pace.

A large supply of glycogen in your muscles and liver at the start of the marathon enables you to work at a high rate throughout the race without becoming carbohydrate depleted. During the marathon, you use a combination of carbohydrate and fat for fuel. When you run low on glycogen, you rely more on fat, which forces you to slow down because fat metabolism uses oxygen less efficiently. With the correct training, your muscles and liver adapt to store more glycogen. Design your training so that toward the end of certain workouts, you run very low on glycogen; this provides a stimulus for your body to adapt by storing more glycogen in the future.

Because your body can store only a limited supply of glycogen, it's an advantage to be able to use as much fat as possible at marathon race pace. Successful marathoners have developed their ability to use fat; this trait spares their glycogen stores and helps ensure that they make it to the finish line without becoming glycogen depleted. When you train your muscles to rely more on fat at marathon race pace, your glycogen stores last longer. In the marathon, that means that "the wall" moves closer and closer to the finish line and eventually disappears. (The concept of "the wall" is really a reflection of improper marathon preparation and pacing.) Later in this chapter, we'll look at how to train to improve glycogen storage and fat utilization. In chapter 2, we'll examine how your diet affects these vital processes.

Excellent Running Economy

Your running economy determines how fast you can run using a given amount of oxygen. If you can run faster than another athlete while using the same amount of oxygen, then you're more economical. This concept is similar to the efficiency of an automobile engine—if a car can travel farther using a given amount of gasoline, then it's more economical than another car.

Running economy can also be viewed as how much oxygen is required to run at a given speed. If you use less oxygen while running at the same speed as another runner, then you're more economical. If you know how much oxygen a runner can use at lactate-threshold pace, as well as that athlete's running economy, you can generally predict marathon performance fairly accurately. In fact, a classic study by Farrell and colleagues found that differences in pace at lactate threshold predicted 94 percent of the variation in racing speed among distance runners (Farrell et al. 1979).

Running economy varies widely among runners. While testing elite runners in the laboratory, Pete has found differences of more than 20 percent in running economy among athletes. Obviously, a large advantage exists in being able to use oxygen as economically as possible during the marathon—your aerobic system supplies nearly all of the energy for the marathon, and oxygen is the main limiting factor in the rate of energy production by the aerobic system.

For example, say two athletes with identical lactate-threshold values of 54 ml/kg/min are racing at a pace of 5:55 per mile (per 1.6 km). Although it seems that they should be working equally hard, this often isn't the case. If Stacey has an oxygen requirement of 51 ml/kg/min at that pace and Christine requires 57 ml/kg/min, then Stacey will be comfortably below lactate threshold and should be able to maintain a 5:55 pace. Christine will steadily accumulate lactic acid and will need to slow down. Stacey has a faster pace at lactate threshold because she uses oxygen more economically to produce energy.

The primary determinants of running economy appear to be the ratio of slow-twitch to fast-twitch fibers in your muscles, the combined effect of your biomechanics, and your training history. The proportion of slow-twitch muscle fibers is important because they use oxygen more efficiently. One reason that successful marathoners tend to be more economical than slower marathoners is because they generally have more slow-twitch muscle fibers. Runners with more years of training and more miles "under the belt" also tend to have better running economy, possibly due to adaptations that gradually allow fast-twitch muscle fibers to have more of the characteristics of slow-twitch fibers.

Running economy is also related to the interaction of many biomechanical variables, but no single aspect of biomechanics has been shown to have a large impact on economy. We don't know, therefore, how to change biomechanics to improve economy. One of the problems is that it's impossible to change one biomechanical variable without affecting others.

High Maximal Oxygen Uptake ($\dot{V}O_2$max)

Successful marathoners have high $\dot{V}O_2$max values. This means they're able to transport large amounts of oxygen to their muscles, and their muscles are able to extract and use a large amount of oxygen to produce energy aerobically.

The average sedentary 35-year-old man has a $\dot{V}O_2$max of about 45 ml/kg/min, while the average 35-year-old male runner has a $\dot{V}O_2$max of about 55 ml/kg/min. A locally competitive 35-year-old male marathoner tends to have a $\dot{V}O_2$max in the range of 60 to 65 ml/kg/min, whereas an elite male marathoner would tend to be in the range of 70 to 75 ml/kg/min. Although successful marathoners tend to have high $\dot{V}O_2$max values, they typically aren't as high as the $\dot{V}O_2$max values found in elite 5,000-meter runners, whose maxes can reach as high as 85 ml/kg/min. Women's $\dot{V}O_2$max values tend to be about 10 percent lower than those for men because women have higher essential body fat stores and lower hemoglobin levels than do men.

The primary factors in increasing $\dot{V}O_2$max appear to be related to improvements in the ability to transport oxygen to your muscles. This ability is related to four factors: your maximal heart rate, the maximal amount of blood your heart can pump with each beat, the hemoglobin content of your blood, and the proportion of your blood that is transported to your working muscles.

Your maximal heart rate is determined genetically. In other words, it doesn't increase with training. Successful marathoners don't have particularly high maximal heart rates, so it isn't a factor in determining success.

The maximal amount of blood your heart can pump with each beat is called your stroke volume. If the left ventricle of your heart is large, then it can hold a large amount of blood. Blood volume increases with training, resulting in more blood being available to fill the left ventricle. If your left ventricle is strong, then it can contract fully so that not much blood is left at the end of each contraction. Filling the left ventricle with a large amount of blood and pumping a large proportion of that blood with each contraction result in a large stroke volume. Stroke volume increases with the correct types of training. In fact, increased stroke volume is the main training adaptation that increases $\dot{V}O_2$max.

The hemoglobin content of your blood is important because the higher your hemoglobin content, the more oxygen can be carried per unit of blood and the more energy can be produced aerobically. Some successful marathoners train at high altitude to increase the oxygen-carrying capacity of their blood. Other than by training at altitude (or through several illegal methods, such as taking synthetic erythropoietin, known as EPO), the hemoglobin concentration of your blood won't increase significantly with training.

We've talked about the amount of oxygen per unit of blood and the amount of blood that your heart can pump. The other factor that determines the amount of blood reaching your muscles is the proportion of blood transported to your working muscles. At rest, just more than 1 liter of blood goes to your muscles per minute. During the marathon, approximately 16 liters of blood are transported to your muscles per minute. When you're running all out, it's more than 20 liters per minute. Much of this increase is due to increased heart rate and stroke volume, but redistribution of blood to your muscles also contributes. At rest, approximately 20 percent of your blood is sent to your working muscles; during the marathon, it rises to roughly 70 percent. With training, your body becomes better at shutting down temporarily unnecessary functions, such as digestion, so that more blood can be sent to your working muscles.

Quick Recovery

Successful marathoners are able to recover quickly from training. This allows them to handle a larger training volume and a higher frequency of hard training sessions than those who recover more slowly. The ability to recover quickly is related to genetics, the structure of your training plan, your age, lifestyle factors such as diet and sleep, and your training history. (The 30th 20-miler of your life will probably take less out of you than your first one.)

Runners vary in how many workouts they can tolerate in a given time. Recovery runs are an important element of your training, but they must be handled carefully. If you do your recovery runs too hard, you run the risk of overtraining and reducing the quality of your hard training sessions. This is a common mistake among distance runners, particularly marathoners—many runners don't differentiate between regular training runs and recovery

■ Head Games

"Mind is everything; muscle, pieces of rubber. All that I am, I am because of my mind." So said Paavo Nurmi, the Finn who won nine Olympic gold medals at distances from 1,500 meters to 10,000 meters. Although he wasn't a marathoner, Nurmi knew the need for psychological strength in distance running.

Most of this chapter deals with the physiological attributes that most directly determine your marathoning success. Traits such as your lactate threshold and $\dot{V}O_2$max can be measured; if we were to gather 10 readers of this book and run them through a series of laboratory tests, we could reasonably predict their order of finish in a marathon.

What we couldn't so easily measure and predict, though, would be which of those runners would come closest to reaching their physiological potential. That's where the mind comes in. Just as there are wide variations among runners in attributes such as percentage of slow-twitch muscle fibers, so too are there great ranges in the less-quantifiable matter of what we'll call, for lack of a better word, "toughness." We all know midpack runners who have a reputation for thrashing themselves in races; at the same time, most followers of the sport could name a few elite runners who often seem to come up short when the going gets tough.

Despite being unmeasurable in a scientific sense, mental toughness can be improved. In fact, it's one of the few determinants of marathon performance that you can continue to better after even 20 or more years of running. Maturity, years of training, and some positive reinforcements along the way can enhance such necessary weapons in the marathoner's arsenal as perseverance and willingness to suffer in the short term for long-term gain.

Nurmi also said, "Success in sport, as in almost anything, comes from devotion. The athlete must make a devotion of his specialty." Having a challenging but reasonable marathon goal provides you with the necessary object of devotion. Intelligent, thorough preparation for that goal—such as that provided in the training schedules in this book—provides the confidence to attack that goal. Do the right training, and both your body and your mind will benefit.

runs. The purpose of your regular training runs is to provide an additional training stimulus to improve your fitness; the purpose of your recovery runs is to help you recover from your last hard workout so that you're ready for your next hard workout.

Recovery runs improve blood flow through the muscles; this process improves the repair of damaged muscle cells, removes waste products, and brings nutrients to your muscles. These benefits are lost, however, if you do recovery runs so fast that you tire yourself out for your subsequent hard training sessions. In addition, by doing your recovery runs slowly, you use less of your glycogen stores, so more glycogen is available for your hard training sessions. Optimizing your diet to enhance recovery is discussed in chapter 2. Recovery runs and other strategies to improve your recovery are discussed in depth in chapter 3.

How to Train to Improve the Key Physiological Attributes

Now that we've discussed the physiological requirements for successful marathoning, let's look at the components of training that improve the key physiological variables and how to do each type of session most effectively in your marathon preparation. Of the six physiological variables we've discussed, all but muscle fiber type improve with the appropriate training. In this section, we'll look at how to train to improve your lactate threshold, ability to store glycogen and utilize fat, running economy at marathon pace, and VO_2max. We'll also consider a specialized training session that integrates the various aspects of your training. In chapters 2 and 3, we'll look at strategies to enhance your recovery from this targeted training.

Improving Your Lactate Threshold

The most effective way to improve lactate threshold is to run at your current lactate-threshold pace or a few seconds per mile faster, either as one continuous run (tempo run) or as a long interval session at your lactate-threshold pace (cruise intervals or LT intervals).

These workouts make you run hard enough so that lactate is just starting to accumulate in your blood. When you train at a lower intensity, a weaker stimulus is provided to improve your lactate-threshold pace. When you train faster than current lactate-threshold pace, you accumulate lactate rapidly, so you aren't training your muscles to work hard without accumulating lactate. The more time you spend close to your lactate-threshold pace, the greater the stimulus for improvement.

Lactate-threshold training should be run at close to the pace that you can currently race for 1 hour. For serious marathoners, this is generally a 15K

© Todd Bigelow/Aurora Photos

Tempo runs let you spend more time close to your lactate-threshold pace and provide a greater stimulus for improvement.

to half marathon race pace. Slower runners should run closer to a 15K race pace on tempo runs; faster runners should run closer to a half marathon race pace. This should be the intensity at which lactate is just starting to accumulate in your muscles and blood. You can do some of your tempo runs in low-key races of 4 miles (6 km) to 10K, but be careful not to get carried away and race all out. Remember that the optimal pace to improve lactate threshold is your current LT pace and not much faster.

A typical training session to improve lactate threshold consists of a 15- to 20-minute warm-up, followed by a 20- to 40-minute tempo run and a 15-minute cool-down. The lactate-threshold workouts in this book mainly fall within these parameters, although most of the schedules include one longer tempo run in the 7-mile (11 km) range. LT intervals are typically two to five repetitions of 5 minutes to 2 miles (3 km) at lactate-threshold pace with 2 or 3 minutes between repetitions.

For runners competing in shorter races, tempo runs and LT intervals are both excellent ways to prepare. For marathoners, however, tempo runs are preferable to LT intervals. After all, the marathon is one long continuous run, and tempo runs simulate marathon conditions more closely. There's both a physiological and a psychological component to the advantage of tempo

What's Your Lactate Threshold?

The most accurate way to find out your lactate threshold is to be tested at the track or in a sport physiology lab. During a lactate-threshold test in a lab, you run for several minutes at progressively faster speeds until your lactate concentration increases markedly. The tester measures the lactate concentration in your blood after several minutes at each speed by pricking your finger and analyzing a couple of drops of blood. A typical lactate-threshold test consists of six increasingly hard runs of 5 minutes each, with 1 minute between runs to sample your blood. By graphing blood lactate concentration at various running speeds, physiologists can tell the pace and heart rate that coincide with lactate threshold. You can then use this information to maximize the effectiveness of your training.

The lower-tech method to estimate lactate threshold is to use your race times. For experienced runners, lactate-threshold pace is very similar to race pace for 15K to the half marathon. Successful marathoners generally race the marathon 2 to 3 percent slower than lactate-threshold pace.

In terms of heart rate, lactate threshold typically occurs at 82 to 91 percent of maximal heart rate or 77 to 88 percent of heart rate reserve in well-trained runners. (Heart rate reserve is your maximal heart rate minus your resting heart rate.) Instructions on finding your maximal heart rate can be found later in this chapter.

runs. The extra mental toughness required to get through a tempo run when you may not be feeling great will come in handy during a marathon.

Improving Glycogen Storage and Fat Utilization

Your ability to store glycogen and use fat for fuel tends to improve with the same types of training. Pure endurance training stimulates these adaptations and increases the capillarization of your muscles. For marathoners, the primary type of training to stimulate these adaptations is runs of 90 minutes or longer. Your total training volume, however, also contributes. That's one reason to include two-a-day workouts and relatively high weekly mileage in your training program.

Long runs are the bread and butter of marathoners. For all marathoners, including the elite, the marathon distance is a formidable challenge. To prepare to race 26.2 miles (42.2 km) at a strong pace, train your body and mind to handle the distance by doing long runs at a reasonable pace.

A long run also provides psychological benefits. By running long, you simulate what your legs and body will go through in the marathon. When your hamstrings tighten 23 miles (37 km) into the race, for example, it helps to have experienced a similar feeling in training—you'll know you can shorten your stride a few inches, concentrate on maintaining your leg turnover, and keep going. More generally, you'll have experienced overcoming the sometimes overwhelming desire to do anything but continue to run.

During your long runs, you encounter many of the experiences—good and bad—that await you in the marathon.

No scientific evidence will tell you the best distance for your long runs as you train. However, a clear trade-off exists between running far enough to stimulate physiological adaptations and remaining uninjured. If you regularly do runs longer than 24 miles (39 km), you'll become strong but slow because you won't be able to run your other hard workouts at as high a level of quality. You'll also increase your risk of injury because when your muscles are very fatigued, they lose their ability to absorb impact forces, greatly increasing your risk of muscle strain or tendinitis.

Experience suggests that steadily building your long runs to 21 or 22 miles (34 or 35 km) will maximize your chances of reaching the marathon in top shape while remaining healthy. Experienced marathoners who are not highly injury prone should include one run of 24 miles (39 km) in their preparation.

Long runs shouldn't be slow jogs during which you just accumulate time on your feet. The appropriate pace for a specific long run depends on the purpose of that run within your training program. The most beneficial intensity range for most of your long runs is 10 to 20 percent slower than your goal marathon race pace. (A few of your long runs should be done at your goal marathon pace—the rationale for these sessions is explained later in this chapter.) If you use a heart monitor, your long-run pace should be roughly in the range of 74 to 84 percent of maximal heart rate or 65 to 78 percent of your heart rate reserve. This will ensure that you're running with a similar posture and are using similar muscle patterns as when you run at marathon pace.

■ When Are Long Runs Too Long?

My experience as a runner and coach indicates that long runs greater than 22 miles (35 km) take much more out of the body than do runs in the range of 20 to 22 miles (32 to 35 km). I occasionally included runs of 27 to 30 miles (43 to 48 km) in my marathon preparations and believe that I ran slower in my marathons because of those efforts.

The only time I really got carried away with long runs was in preparing for the 1985 World Cup Marathon in Hiroshima. The previous year, I had won the Olympic marathon trials in 2:11:43; 3 months later, I placed 11th at the Olympics. I figured that training even harder would bring even greater success. During a 4-week period, I did two very hilly 27-milers and a 30-miler in New Zealand, and I ran them hard, trying to drop my training partners, Kevin Ryan and Chris Pilone.

The World Cup Marathon was on a lightning-fast course. I was very strong but had little speed, and I finished 18th. Although my time of 2:12:28 was satisfactory, the conditions were excellent, and I blew my best opportunity to run 2:10.   —Pete Pfitzinger

If you do long runs much slower than this, you risk being unprepared for the marathon. Slow long runs reinforce poor running style and do a poor job of simulating the demands of the marathon. If you run long runs too fast, of course, you risk leaving your marathon performance out on your training loops because you'll be too tired for your other important training sessions. Using the suggested intensity range of 10 to 20 percent slower than marathon goal pace, table 1.1 lists suggested long-run paces for a wide range of marathoners.

The first few miles of your long runs can be done slowly, but by 5 miles (8 km) into your long run, your pace should be no more than 20 percent slower than marathon race pace. Gradually increase your pace until you're running approximately 10 percent slower than marathon race pace during the last 5 miles (8 km) of your long runs. In terms of heart rate, run the first few miles at the low end of the recommended intensity range, and gradually increase your effort until you reach the high end of the range during the last 5 miles (8 km). This makes for an excellent workout and provides a strong stimulus for physiological adaptations. These workouts are difficult enough that you should schedule a recovery day the day before and 1 or 2 days after your long runs.

If you do long runs in this intensity range, a 22-mile (35 km) run will take approximately the same amount of time as your marathon. By running for the length of time you hope to run the marathon, you also provide psychological reinforcement that you can run at a steady pace for that amount of time.

Where the training schedules call for a long run the day after a tune-up race, you should run at a more casual pace. After a Saturday race, your Sunday long run should be at a relaxed pace because you will be tired and have stiff muscles, which increases your likelihood of injury. Start these long

TABLE 1.1

Sample Long-Run Paces

Marathon goal pace	Early part (20% slower than goal pace)	Latter part (10% slower than goal pace)
5:00 per mi	6:00 per mi	5:30 per mi
5:30 per mi	6:36 per mi	6:03 per mi
6:00 per mi	7:12 per mi	6:36 per mi
6:30 per mi	7:48 per mi	7:09 per mi
7:00 per mi	8:24 per mi	7:42 per mi
7:30 per mi	9:00 per mi	8:15 per mi
8:00 per mi	9:36 per mi	8:48 per mi

runs like a recovery run. If your muscles loosen up as the run progresses, increase the training stimulus by increasing your pace to about 15 to 20 percent slower than marathon race pace.

The total volume of your training also improves your ability to store glycogen and use fat, and it reinforces some of the other positive training adaptations, such as increased capillarization. There is some benefit, therefore, in doing relatively high mileage. The best marathoners in the world train from 110 to 170 miles (177 to 274 km) per week.

More is only better to a point, however. You have a unique individual current mileage limit that is dictated by your biomechanics, past training, injury history, shoes, running surface, diet, and various other life stressors. (For starters, most of those people running 150 miles [241 km] a week don't commute to a 50-hour-per-week job.) The challenge in pursuing marathoning excellence is to find the mileage range that you can handle without breaking down.

Also, although racing performance improves with increased mileage, the incremental improvement decreases the more mileage you do. In *Daniels' Running Formula* (2005), renowned coach and physiologist Jack Daniels, PhD, explains the principle of diminishing return: "Adding more and more mileage to your weekly training does not produce equal percentages of improvement in competitive fitness" (page 13). Increasing from 70 to 90 miles (113 to 145 km) per week, therefore, will not improve performance as much as increasing from 50 to 70 miles (80 to 113 km) per week, but it may produce a benefit nonetheless.

Although you have an individual current mileage limit, this limit changes over time. The mileage that contributed to your shin splints 5 years ago will not necessarily cause problems for you again. You need to be a good detective and figure out the causes of your past injuries. Many runners say, "I tried high mileage once years ago, and I just got tired and hurt," and they permanently return to what they consider to be their safe mileage range. They don't consider that in the ensuing years their bodies may well have gained the ability—and their minds the wisdom—to handle higher mileage and to reap the concomitant benefits.

Improving Your Running Economy

An important determinant of marathon performance is running economy at marathon race pace. Although some evidence shows that economy improves with training, no one fully understands the secrets of improving running economy. Various studies have found running economy to improve with weightlifting, biofeedback, relaxation training, hill training, exhaustive distance running, speed work, and long intervals. Jack Daniels (2005) recommends running fast intervals to reduce wasted motion and to train the body to recruit the most effective combination of muscle fibers. A variety of biomechanical factors, such as a narrow pelvis, small feet, and

What's Your Maximal Heart Rate and Heart Rate Reserve?

Throughout this book, we'll prescribe specific intensities for various types of workouts to help you prepare most effectively for the marathon. Heart rate monitors are a useful tool you can use to check the intensity of your training. Training intensity can also be described in terms of speed, but unless you train daily on a track or measured stretch of road or run with a GPS, you don't really know how fast you're training most of the time. Monitoring the intensity of your training in terms of heart rate, however, is simple.

Maximal Heart Rate

The intensity of your runs can be stated relative to your maximal heart rate or as a percentage of your heart rate reserve. Your maximal heart rate is, quite simply, the fastest that your heart will beat during maximal-effort running. The most accurate formula for estimating maximal heart rate is 207 minus .7 times your age. Using this formula, a 43-year-old would have a predicted maximal heart rate of 177 [207 − (.7 × 43)]. Because of the variability between individuals, however, your actual maximal heart rate may be more than 10 beats per minute higher or lower than your predicted maximal heart rate. Using an estimated maximal heart rate, therefore, can lead you to train too hard or not hard enough, so it's better to do a performance test to determine your actual maximal heart rate.

You can find your maximal heart rate quite accurately during a very hard interval session. An effective workout is to warm up thoroughly and then run three high-intensity 600-meter repeats up a moderate hill, jogging back down right away after each one. If you run these 600s all out, your heart rate should be within two or three beats of maximum by the end of the third repeat.

Heart Rate Reserve

Heart rate reserve is an even more accurate way of prescribing training intensities because it takes into account both your maximal heart rate and your resting heart rate. Your heart rate reserve is simply your maximal heart rate minus your resting heart rate, and it reflects how much your heart rate can increase to provide more oxygen to your muscles. By resting heart rate we mean your heart rate when you first wake up in the morning. As an example of calculating heart rate reserve, Scott's current maximal heart rate is 188 and his resting heart rate is 38. His heart rate reserve, therefore, is 188 minus 38, which equals 150 beats per minute.

To calculate the proper heart rates for a workout using heart rate reserve, multiply your heart rate reserve by the appropriate percentage, and then add your resting heart rate. For example, as a highly experienced runner, if Scott wanted to do a lactate-threshold workout at 82 to 88 percent of his heart rate reserve, he would stay in the range of 161 [(heart rate reserve of 150 × .82) + resting heart rate of 38] to 170 [(150 × .88) + 38] beats per minute. This compares closely to using 86 to 91 percent of his maximal heart rate, which would put him in the range of 162 to 171 beats per minute.

The prescribed training intensities used in this chapter and chapters 3 and 7 are summarized in table 1.2. These intensity ranges are appropriate for most experienced marathon runners. Less-experienced runners should generally train at the lower end of the recommended ranges, while elite runners will generally be at the high end of the ranges.

TABLE 1.2

Heart Rate Intensities for Standard Workouts

	Maximal heart rate (%)	Heart rate reserve
$\dot{V}O_2$max (5K pace)	93-95	91-94
Lactate threshold	82-91	77-88
Marathon pace	79-88	73-84
Long/Medium long	74-84	65-78
General aerobic	70-81	62-75
Recovery	<76	<70

Allowing for Heart Rate Drift

During a lactate-threshold session or long run, your heart rate will tend to increase several beats per minute even if you hold an even pace. On a warm day, your heart rate increases even more because of dehydration and as your body sends more blood to your skin to aid in cooling. This phenomenon is discussed in greater detail in chapter 2. The implication for your lactate-threshold sessions and long runs is that you should start these sessions at the low end of the specified intensity zone and allow your heart rate to increase to the high end of the zone during the workout.

On a low-humidity day with temperatures in the 70s (low 20s), increase your zones by two to four beats per minute to gain the same benefits as on a cooler day. On a high-humidity day in the 70s (low 20s) or a low-humidity day in the 80s (high 20s to low 30s), increase your zones by five to eight beats per minute. On a high-humidity day in the 80s (high 20s to low 30s), just take it easy (Lambert 1998).

"faster rotation of shoulders in the transverse plane," have been suggested as contributors to running economy.

According to Don Morgan, PhD, who has conducted a large number of studies on running economy, the most important factor for improving economy may be the number of years (and accumulated miles) that you have been running rather than the specific types of workouts that you do. The mechanism for improvement may be that with training your fast-twitch muscle fibers gain more of the characteristics of the more economical

Increasing Mileage While Minimizing the Risk of Breakdown

As with most aspects of running, there are no guarantees, but the following guidelines will help you increase your mileage without getting injured or overtrained:

- Bite off small chunks. Over a few years, you can double or triple your mileage, but increasing mileage too much at once is almost certain to lead to injury or overtiredness. Unfortunately, there's no scientific evidence indicating how great an increase over a given period is safe. A commonly used, but unvalidated, rule of thumb is to increase mileage by a maximum of 10 percent per week. Jack Daniels (2005) recommends increasing mileage by no more than 1 mile (1.6 km) for each training session that you run per week. For example, if you run six times per week, you would increase your mileage by up to 6 miles (10 km) per week.

- Increase in steps. When charting new territory, don't increase your mileage week after week. That approach is very likely to lead to injury. Instead, increase your mileage 1 week, then stay at that level for 2 or 3 weeks before increasing again.

- Avoid speed work while upping your mileage. Don't increase your mileage during a phase of training that includes hard speed work. Fast intervals put your body under a great deal of stress. Increasing your mileage adds more stress. Save the majority of your mileage increases for base training, when you can avoid intervals.

- Reduce your training intensity. When increasing your mileage, it helps to slightly reduce the overall intensity of your training. By backing off the intensity, you can increase your volume without increasing the strain of training. You can then return the intensity to its previous level before upping your mileage again.

- Not all miles are created equal. When building your mileage, it's particularly important to train on soft surfaces to reduce the accumulated jarring on your body and to wear running shoes that suit your needs and are in good repair.

- Give yourself a break. Don't let mileage become a goal in itself. Aimlessly running high mileage can lead to chronic overtiredness and burnout. Your training should be focused on a target race such as a marathon. When you have run your target race, give your body a break before building your mileage for your next goal.

Pete's Progression

My highest sustained mileage was before the 1984 Olympic trials marathon. With Alberto Salazar, Greg Meyer, Tony Sandoval, and Bill Rodgers in the race, making the Olympic team necessitated no compromises. My previous training had peaked at 125 miles (201 km) per week. At the time, I thought that was all my body could handle.

The trials were held in May. For 8 weeks during January and February, I averaged 143 miles (230 km) per week, with a high week of 152 (245) and a low week of 137 (220). Most of this was run at a fairly brisk pace (5:40 to 6:10 per mile), but I was in base training and didn't need to do much speed work.

After I cut my mileage to 100 to 120 miles (161 to 193 km) per week for the last 2 months before the trials, my legs felt fresh and strong all the time. Having adapted to the higher volume, I was able to do high-quality intervals and tempo runs while still running well over 100 miles (161 km) per week. While that mileage looks daunting to me now, there's little question that January's and February's high-mileage training contributed to the improvement that allowed me to win the 1984 trials.

Besides the physiological benefits, high-mileage training provided me with psychological benefits for the marathon. When I was coming up through the ranks, 2:10 marathoner Garry Bjorklund revealed to me that he was running 160 miles (257 km) per week. When I asked him if that much mileage was necessary, he said, "It's not necessary before every marathon, but you need to do it at least once to know you can." —Pete Pfitzinger

Scott's Schedule

High-mileage training—and its many benefits—needn't be solely the domain of the elite. When I was training most seriously, during the 1990s, I averaged 72 miles (116 km) per week, with a peak of 125 miles (201 km) in a week; in 1993, I averaged 95 miles (153 km) per week for the year. All of this occurred while I usually worked 45 hours a week or more at a regular job and put in additional time as a freelance writer.

For many people, our priorities are reflected in how we spend our time. I enjoy running, and I would rather try to be modestly good at it than to simply accept being mediocre, as I would definitely be without hard training. So to the question "Where do you find the time?" the answer is simply "I make it." I've chosen to have running be one of the few things that I concentrate on, and I allot my time accordingly. (Which means you won't see me at a lot of after-work happy hours.)

For the most part, running a decent amount while living a "normal" life means giving a day's one or two runs as much importance when planning my schedule as I do work and other obligations. Besides setting aside time for running, this also means getting to bed at a decent hour most nights; allowing time for a few good stretching and weightlifting sessions each week; and not cramming my weekends with activities so that I can use these days to recharge physically and mentally.

If you're devoted to getting in the miles, you can almost always find ways to squeeze more time out of your schedule. For example, I've had three jobs where logistics allowed running to or from work at least once a week. For another job with a horrific commute on the Washington, D.C., beltway, the best solution was to run from the office at the end of the workday so that by the time I started driving home, the worst of the traffic was over. On other days, I would leave the house early to beat the morning rush hour and run from the office before work.

Of course, you might have other high priorities in your life besides running. In the months before a marathon, however, it's worth setting some of them aside to concentrate on your training. High mileage and the real world aren't inherently incompatible.

—Scott Douglas

slow-twitch fibers. Morgan speculates, however, that different types of training may improve economy depending on the specific strengths and weaknesses of the individual athlete. This individuality in response may explain why no clear consensus exists on how to improve running economy.

Putting all of the evidence together suggests that your running economy should gradually improve over the years and that there may be ways to help hurry the process along. For marathoners, probably the two most worthwhile ways to try to improve running economy are increasing mileage over time so that your fast-twitch fibers gain the positive characteristics of slow-twitch fibers and running short repetitions (80 to 120 meters) fast but relaxed.

Running short repetitions quickly but with relaxed form—strides—may train your muscles to eliminate unnecessary movements and maintain control at fast speeds. These adaptations may translate to improved economy at marathon pace. Along with improved running form, you'll gain power in your legs and trunk that may also contribute to improved running economy. Because these intervals are short and are performed with sufficient rest between them, lactate levels remain low to moderate throughout the workout. As a result, they won't interfere with your more marathon-specific workouts.

A typical session is 10 repetitions of 100 meters in which you accelerate up to full speed over the first 70 meters and then float for the last 30 meters. It's critical to remain relaxed during these accelerations. Avoid clenching your fists, lifting your shoulders, tightening your neck muscles, and so on. Concentrate on running with good form, and focus on one aspect of good form, such as relaxed arms or complete hip extension, during each acceleration.

These sessions aren't designed to improve your cardiovascular system, so there's no reason to use a short rest between accelerations. A typical rest is to jog and walk 100 to 200 meters between repetitions; this allows you to pretty much fully recover before you start the next strider. The most important considerations are to maintain good running form and to concentrate on accelerating powerfully during each repetition. When in doubt, take a little more rest so that you can run each strider with good form.

Improving Your $\dot{V}O_2$max

The most effective running intensity to improve $\dot{V}O_2$max is 95 to 100 percent of current $\dot{V}O_2$max (Daniels 2005). Well-trained runners can run at $\dot{V}O_2$max pace for about 8 minutes. Ninety-five to 100 percent of $\dot{V}O_2$max coincides with current 3,000-meter to 5,000-meter race pace. This coincides with an intensity of approximately 94 to 98 percent of maximal heart rate or 92 to 98 percent of heart rate reserve. Running intervals at this pace or intensity is part of the optimal strategy to improve $\dot{V}O_2$max.

The stimulus to improve $\dot{V}O_2$max is provided by the amount of time you accumulate during a workout in the optimal-intensity range. This fact has implications for how best to structure your $\dot{V}O_2$max sessions. Consider two workouts that each include 6,000 meters of intervals—one of 15 × 400 meters and the other of 5 × 1,200 meters. When you run 400-meter repetitions, you're in the optimal zone for perhaps 45 seconds per interval. If you do 15 repetitions, you would accumulate about 11 minutes at the optimal intensity. When you run longer intervals, you are in the optimal-intensity zone much longer. During each 1,200-meter interval, you would be in the optimal-intensity zone for 3 to 4 minutes and would accumulate 15 to 20 minutes in that zone during the workout. This would provide a stronger stimulus to improve your $\dot{V}O_2$max.

The optimal duration for $\dot{V}O_2$max intervals for marathoners is approximately 2 to 6 minutes. Intervals in this range are long enough so you accumulate a substantial amount of time at 95 to 100 percent of $\dot{V}O_2$max during each interval but short enough so you can maintain the optimal-intensity range throughout the workout. Intervals for marathoners should generally be between 800 and 1,600 meters. The training schedules in this book include some workouts of 600-meter repeats during weeks when your top priority lies elsewhere, such as when the week also calls for a tune-up race.

The training schedules don't include 2,000-meter repeats. Although repeats of this length can provide a powerful boost to $\dot{V}O_2$max, for all but the elite they take more than 6 minutes to complete. That's fine if you're focusing on a 5K or 10K, where $\dot{V}O_2$max is the primary determinant of success. As a marathoner, though, you want to be fresh for the week's more-important endurance workouts, so you don't want your $\dot{V}O_2$max workouts to require several recovery days before and after.

The total volume of the intervals in a marathoner's $\dot{V}O_2$max session should be 5,000 to 10,000 meters, with most workouts in the range of 6,000 to 8,000 meters. Any combination of repetitions of 800 to 1,600 meters will provide an excellent workout. Longer intervals (e.g., 1,200s or 1,600s) make for a tougher workout, physically and psychologically, and shouldn't be avoided.

The optimal amount of rest between intervals is debatable. One school of thought is to minimize rest so that your metabolic rate stays high during the entire workout. This strategy makes for very difficult workouts (which can be good), but you risk shortening your workouts. Another school of thought is to allow your heart rate to decrease to 70 percent of your maximal heart rate or 60 percent of your heart rate reserve during your recovery between intervals.

For the lower-tech crowd, a good rule of thumb is to allow 50 to 90 percent of the length of time it takes to do the interval for your recovery. For example, if you're running 1,000-meter repeats in 3:20, you would run slowly for 1:40 to 3 minutes between intervals.

The $\dot{V}O_2$max sessions in these schedules feature repeats that strike a balance between being long enough to provide a powerful training stimulus and short enough to leave you fresh for your other important workouts of the week. Because $\dot{V}O_2$max training is not the highest priority during marathon preparation, the $\dot{V}O_2$max intervals in the training schedules in chapters 8 through 12 are run at 5,000-meter race pace. This coincides with the lower end of the optimal heart rate range, approximately 93 to 95 percent of maximal heart rate or 91 to 96 percent of heart rate reserve for most marathoners. Running your $\dot{V}O_2$max intervals in this intensity range reduces the recovery time required before your next hard workout. (Be sure to use

■ Don't Max Out Your $\dot{V}O_2$max Workouts

Two related mistakes that marathoners sometimes make in training are running intervals too fast and running intervals too frequently. Let's consider why you should avoid these errors.

Running Intervals Too Fast

A common mistake among marathoners is to do speed work too hard. The idea that running your intervals harder will make you run better is appealing, and it seems logical. It's also incorrect. Running your intervals faster than the optimal zone will do two things—build up a high degree of lactate in your muscles and shorten the duration of your workout. Both of these effects are counterproductive for marathoners.

The marathon is an aerobic event. More than 99 percent of the energy you use in the marathon is supplied by your aerobic system. As you saw earlier in this chapter, during the marathon, you run slightly below your lactate-threshold pace; therefore, you don't accumulate much lactate in your muscles and blood. In fact, when lactate levels are measured at the end of a marathon, they are only slightly above resting levels.

There's no reason, then, for marathoners to do training that builds up high levels of lactate, such as intervals run at 1,500-meter race pace or faster. Running intervals at this pace produces high levels of lactate and improves your ability to produce energy using the glycolytic system (what you probably think of as running anaerobically) and to buffer high levels of lactate. None of these adaptations is relevant to the marathon. Running intervals much faster than 3,000- to 5,000-meter race pace also produces a smaller stimulus to improve your $\dot{V}O_2$max.

Running $\dot{V}O_2$max Sessions Too Frequently

Another common mistake among marathoners is trying to include too many $\dot{V}O_2$max sessions in their marathon training programs. As discussed previously in this chapter, the most important adaptations for marathon success are a high level of endurance, a fast pace at lactate threshold, and the ability to store a large quantity of glycogen in the muscles and liver. $\dot{V}O_2$max sessions are definitely a secondary consideration for a marathoner. Intervals require large amounts of physical and psychological energy, which can be better used doing more specific marathon training. $\dot{V}O_2$max sessions have their place in marathon preparation, but they should be included sparingly.

an accurate assessment of your current 5K pace, namely, a race run under optimal conditions, not a hilly course on a hot day.)

Integrated Training: Training at Marathon Race Pace

Your goal for the marathon is to be able to maintain your goal race pace for 26.2 miles (42.2 km). The physiological demands of this task require a high lactate threshold, an excellent capacity to store glycogen, a well-developed ability to burn fat, and so on. Each of the various types of training that we have discussed so far focuses on improving a specific aspect of your physiology for the marathon. Now we'll discuss a type of training that integrates the various physiological attributes as specifically as possible for the marathon race.

Long runs at marathon race pace directly prepare you for the demands of the race. The principle of specificity of training states that the most effective way to prepare for an event is to simulate that event as closely as possible. The closest way to simulate a marathon, of course, is to run 26.2 miles (42.2 km) at marathon pace. Unfortunately (or perhaps fortunately), long runs at marathon pace are very hard on the body. If you run too far at marathon pace, the required recovery time will negate the benefits of the effort. Similarly, if you do long runs at marathon pace too often, you will greatly increase your likelihood of self-destructing through injury or overtraining.

The training programs in this book include up to four runs in which you'll run 8 to 14 miles (13 to 22 km) of a longer run at goal marathon race pace. These runs are the most specific marathon preparation you'll do. The intention is to stress your body in a similar way to the marathon, but to limit the duration so that your required recovery time is held to a few days. On these runs, use the first few miles to warm up, then finish the run with the prescribed number of miles at marathon race pace. In addition to the physiological and psychological benefits these runs impart, they're an excellent opportunity to practice drinking and taking energy gels at race pace.

Where should you do your marathon-pace runs? Races of the appropriate distance are ideal—you'll have a measured course, plenty of aid stations, and other runners to work with. As with doing tempo runs in races, though, be sure to limit yourself to the day's goal and run them no faster than is called for.

If you can't find a race of suitable length in which to do your marathon-pace runs, try to run at least part of them over a measured course so that you can get feedback about your pace. A reasonable way to check pace is to do 1 or 2 miles in the middle of a road-race course that has markers painted on the road. Similarly, many bike paths have miles marked, or you can use a GPS to check your pace. Your entire run needn't be over a precisely calibrated course, but try to include at least a few stretches where you can accurately assess your pace, and then once you have a good sense of what your pace feels like, rely on perceived exertion or heart rate during the other parts of the run.

Given the opportunity for regular splits and frequent fluids, a track would seem to be an ideal locale for marathon-pace workouts, but bear in mind the reason for these runs. The purpose is to simulate marathon conditions as closely as possible. This means running on a road, not doing endless repeats of a 400-meter oval. Learn your goal marathon's topography, and attempt to mimic it on your marathon-pace runs. Many runners do this when preparing for courses with obvious quirks, such as Boston, but the principle applies for all marathons. Pancake-flat courses such as Chicago also take their toll because your leg muscles are used exactly the same way from start to finish.

Wear your marathon shoes when doing at least one of these workouts, even if you'll be racing the marathon in flats. You want to have at least one run of 15 miles (24 km) or so in your race-day shoes to learn whether they provide enough support when you start to tire and whether they give you blisters.

Structuring Your Training Program: Periodization

Now that we've discussed the types of training that help improve marathon performance, the next step is to develop your overall training plan. You need to prepare so that you're at your best on marathon day. Systematically structuring your training to bring you to your desired end point is called *periodization*. The challenge in developing a periodized training plan is to decide how many hard sessions to do, which types of sessions to do, and when to do them.

A useful framework is provided by organizing your training into macrocycles, mesocycles, and microcycles. These concepts are used for preparing training programs in a wide variety of sports and have been used extensively in track and field.

For a marathoner, a macrocycle is the entire training period leading up to the marathon. You'll likely have two macrocycles per year, each consisting of 4 to 6 months. Both of your macrocycles may culminate with a marathon, or you may have one goal marathon for the year and a second macrocycle leading up to a goal race at a shorter distance. Runners doing more than two marathons in a year will probably still have only two macrocycles per year. Multiple marathoners can do only a partial buildup for some of their marathons.

A macrocycle is divided into several mesocycles, each of which has a specific training objective. For a marathoner, a mesocycle may last from 4 to 10 weeks. For example, the first mesocycle in marathon preparation will almost always be a high-volume base training block of at least 4 weeks. As the race approaches, the priorities in your training shift. Each shift in priorities is reflected in a new mesocycle.

Each mesocycle is divided into several microcycles. A microcycle is a series of days that make up a shorter block of training. Microcycles can be anywhere from 4 days to 2 weeks long. Often, the most effective training pattern is a microcycle of 8 to 10 days. Because we realize that the rest of your life revolves around a 7-day week, we've made a practical compromise on the ideal. We'll use the terms *microcycle* and *week* interchangeably in this book. (Just for kicks, see what happens next Friday at the office when you say to a coworker, "Boy, I thought this microcycle would never end.")

Let's consider a runner whose annual training plan centers around two marathons per year. She would train for the marathon for 12 to 18 weeks culminating in the race, followed by 5 to 8 weeks to recover before starting focused training for the next target race. This indicates a minimum of 17 weeks for a marathoner's macrocycle.

Now, let's consider the training objectives in preparation for the marathon. The macrocycle will generally be divided into five mesocycles (table 1.3). The first mesocycle will focus on increasing mileage and improving pure endurance. This will likely be the longest mesocycle in the program. The second mesocycle will focus on improving lactate threshold, with further improvement of pure endurance as a secondary objective. The third mesocycle will focus on race preparation and will include tune-up races. The fourth mesocycle will include a 3-week taper and the marathon. The fifth and final mesocycle in a marathoner's macrocycle will consist of several weeks of recovery.

Each 7-day microcycle will typically consist of three hard training sessions. This is the maximum number of hard sessions that most distance runners can respond to positively. A few runners can handle four hard sessions per week, and some runners can handle only two. Considering that there are at least five categories of hard training sessions that you can do, it takes a good deal of intelligent planning to come up with the optimal training program for you. The training schedules in this book are structured around

TABLE 1.3

Typical Marathoner's Macrocycle

Mesocycle	Primary objective
1	Increasing mileage to improve pure endurance
2	Improving lactate threshold
3	Race preparation
4	Taper and the marathon
5	Recovery

five mesocycles per macrocycle and generally include three hard training sessions per microcycle.

Tune-Up Races

Training provides a variety of stimuli that lead to adaptations that improve your marathon performance. Training also gives you the confidence that comes with setting and achieving challenging training goals. However, training doesn't completely prepare you for the marathon. An additional component to successful marathoning can be gained only by racing.

Tune-up races are important benchmarks of your fitness and prepare you mentally for the rigors of racing. Because less is at stake, even the toughest workout isn't as mentally demanding as a race. After all, in a race, when you're competing against other runners, there's a fine margin between relative success and relative failure. Similarly, in a race you're committed to finish (or you should be) whether you're having a good day or a lousy day; in a workout, if things aren't going well, you can always stop early with your pride relatively intact. The all-out aspect of racing provides a mental hardening that's necessary to run a good marathon. When runners do no premarathon tune-up races, they have greater anxiety leading up to the marathon.

Tune-up races serve two purposes. First, they provide feedback on your fitness, reducing an element of uncertainty about your marathon preparation. Second, they make you go through the nerves of racing, helping to reduce anxiety in the last few days and hours before the marathon. When you're at your limit in the marathon, feeling tired, wondering whether you can hang on even though there are still 10 miles (16 km) to go, it helps to have been through the demands of racing at shorter distances. Even though the ultimate test (the marathon) is crueler, the preparation gained from shorter races is priceless.

By tune-up races, we mean all-out efforts, not races in which you give less than your best, such as races you use as the setting for a tempo run or marathon-pace run. Tune-up races can vary in length from 8K (5 mi) to 25K, depending on their training purpose. Races of 5K or shorter are less specific to marathon success, and races of 30K or longer require too much recovery.

Tune-up race distances can be divided into two categories. Races of 15K to 25K take at least 5 days to recover from, and you must place them strategically in your training program. These races provide the greatest physiological and psychological benefit. Therefore, prepare for these races with a mini-taper of 4 to 6 days. You can't afford to taper any longer than 6 days because the tune-up race isn't your primary goal, and you need to keep training for the marathon. A tune-up race of 15K to 25K really represents a training block of at least 10 days, consisting of 4 to 6 days of tapering, the race itself, and several days' recovery before the next hard training session.

The second category of tune-up race distances is 8K to 12K. These races take less out of you and require less tapering and fewer recovery days than races of 15K or longer. You can approach tune-up races of 8K to 12K in two ways. First, you can train through them and treat them as an all-out effort done while fatigued. This will provide an excellent training stimulus as well as a mental challenge that will help steel you for the marathon. Racing when tired, however, brings the danger of believing that your finishing time and place represent your current fitness level. If you typically race 10K in 32:00 but run 33:10 in a tune-up race, you could interpret the result as meaning you're not in shape, and you might start to train harder or become discouraged. It's important to put the result in the context of the situation.

The other way to approach a tune-up race of 8K to 12K is to do a mini-taper and give yourself a couple of recovery days. This is the appropriate approach if you're using the race to assess your fitness level or as a confidence booster leading up to the marathon. Table 1.4 indicates how close to a tune-up race you can do a hard workout without going into the race fatigued. Although you won't see the benefits of the workout in this week's race, you should be recovered enough so the workout doesn't detract from your race performance.

Tempo runs are the easiest to recover from because they don't break down the body as much as other forms of hard training. Long runs require at least 4 days of recovery to put in a good race effort, although replenishing glycogen stores generally requires only 48 hours. Interval workouts put the body under the most stress and require the longest time to recover from.

Now you know what physiological traits are needed to run a good marathon and how to train to improve those traits. More so than with any other popular distance, though, success in the marathon depends not only on what you do to your body but also on what you put in your body. Proper nutrition and hydration are critical when training for and running a marathon. They're the subjects of the next chapter.

TABLE 1.4

Balancing Hard Workouts and Tune-Up Races

Type of workout	Minimum no. days before tune-up race
$\dot{V}O_2$max interval	5
Tempo run	4
Long run	4

Nutrition and Hydration

This chapter looks at two critical but often misunderstood factors in marathon preparation and racing—nutrition and hydration. Why are these matters critical? Because the two factors that typically conspire to make you slow in the last few miles of the marathon are glycogen depletion and dehydration. By understanding the role of nutrition for marathon preparation and racing, you can develop strategies to optimize your marathon performance.

This chapter discusses the importance of staying well hydrated and how to prevent dehydration, the roles of carbohydrate and fat as the primary fuels for endurance exercise and how to prevent glycogen depletion, the role of protein for endurance athletes, the need to maintain normal iron levels, and nutrition considerations for racing the marathon. Understanding the information in this chapter is an essential component of your marathon preparation.

The Importance of Hydration

Staying well hydrated is vital to successful marathoning during training and racing. Becoming dehydrated negatively affects your running performance and also slows your ability to recover for the next workout. Your blood and other fluids help remove waste products and bring nutrients to tissues for repair. Replacing lost fluids as quickly as possible after running, therefore, will speed your recovery.

Let's take a look at the physiology of dehydration. When you sweat, the following chain of events occurs:

- Your blood volume decreases, so
- less blood returns to your heart; therefore,
- the amount of blood your heart pumps with each beat decreases, so
- less oxygen-rich blood reaches your working muscles; therefore,
- you produce less energy aerobically, and
- you must run at a slower pace.

These effects are magnified on a hot day because one of your body's major responses to hot weather is to increase cooling by sending more blood to the skin to remove heat from the body; this process means that even less blood returns to the heart to be pumped to the working muscles. The result is a higher heart rate for a given pace and an inability to maintain the same pace as on a cool day. Looked at in another way, dehydration also reduces your body's ability to maintain your core temperature because less blood is available to be sent to your skin, and your sweat rate decreases. Struggling to maintain a fast pace on a hot day becomes more dangerous as you become progressively more dehydrated and can lead to heatstroke.

The need to drink during the marathon is obvious. But staying well hydrated is also important during training. Don't rely just on your thirst—your body's thirst mechanism is imperfect. Marathoners sometimes become chronically dehydrated without realizing it. Interestingly, this seems to happen most often in the winter, when the need to drink isn't as obvious. But whenever you're running high mileage, you need to replace your body's fluid losses daily, even if you're training in conditions of –10 degrees Fahrenheit (–23 degrees Celsius). (Fun fact: One reason you can get dehydrated while running even in extremely cold weather is because some bodily fluids are lost when you burn glycogen.)

Dehydration isn't all bad. When you become dehydrated from exercise, you provide a stimulus for your body to adapt to similar situations in the future by conserving more of what you drink after. The resulting expansion of your blood volume is a positive adaptation. The positive aspects of dehydration are true only up to a point—beyond a moderate amount of dehydration, you sacrifice performance during training, increase your recovery time, and increase your risk of heat-related illness.

That "moderate amount of dehydration" is usually surprisingly small. Studies have found that dehydration of 2 percent of body weight leads to about a 4 to 6 percent reduction in running performance. Ed Coyle, PhD, a former competitive runner and now professor of exercise physiology at the University of Texas at Austin, has provided evidence that even a small amount of dehydration causes a decrease in running performance. This is because any reduction in blood volume will reduce the amount of blood returning to your heart.

During high-mileage runs or runs in hot weather, it's important to stay hydrated. Carry drinks with you or place drinks in planned positions along your route before you begin the run.

It's not unusual to lose 3 pounds (1.4 kg) of water per hour when running on a warm day. At this rate, during a 2-hour run you would lose about 6 pounds (2.7 kg). For a 140-pound (63 kg) runner, this represents more than a 4 percent loss in body weight and an 8 to 12 percent decrement in performance. The effect increases as the run progresses, so this runner wouldn't be any slower the first few miles but would likely slow by up to a minute per mile by the end of the run. Staying well hydrated, then, can be the difference between training hard enough to provide a strong stimulus for your body to improve or just going through the motions in training.

How Much to Drink

For any marathoner training in warm conditions, preventing dehydration must be a high priority. How much you need to drink to stay well hydrated during your marathon preparation depends on a number of factors, including the heat and humidity, your body size, how much you're training, and how much you sweat.

Your baseline fluid needs when you're not training are about 4 pints (1.9 L) per day. On top of that, you need to add your fluid losses from training and other activities. Weigh yourself before and after running and calculate how much weight you lost, then drink with the objective of bringing your weight back up to normal. Becoming fully hydrated typically requires drinking one and a half times the amount of weight you lost—the extra amount is required because some of what you drink will quickly wind up as urine, necessary to rid your body of waste products. So, for example, if you lost 3 pounds (1.4 kg) during a training run, you would need to drink about 4.5 pounds (2 kg) of fluid (4.5 pints; 2.1 L) during the next several hours to be sure you're fully rehydrated. (If your postrun beverage contains sodium, you'll retain more of the fluid you take in.)

If you add 4.5 pints (2.1 L) to make up for the fluid lost during training to the 4 pints (1.9 L) you require as a baseline, that makes a total fluid requirement of 8.5 pints (4 L) for the day in this example. This is a large amount of fluid, and consuming this much during the day requires a strategy, particularly for those with normal jobs. Keeping a water bottle at your workstation is a must. You'll regain fluids most effectively if you discipline yourself to drink regularly throughout the day. Try to avoid waiting until shortly before training to replace your fluids—you can't rush the process, and so you'll go into your workout either bloated from too much fluid ingested too quickly or dehydrated from not having enough fluid.

Interestingly, although it's important to drink throughout the day, recent research has found that drinking more fluid less frequently, compared with drinking the same total volume spread out in smaller, more frequent intakes, speeds gastric emptying (from your stomach to your intestines). That is, drinking, say, a pint of water all at once at the beginning of the hour should result in greater gastric emptying than drinking that same pint divided among 4-ounce servings every 15 minutes. The key is not to overload your system, because that will slow gastric emptying. If you feel bloated and have intestinal distress after drinking a large amount of fluid at once, you've probably exceeded what your system can tolerate at once.

How much you should drink during your race is discussed under "Marathon Race-Day Nutrition and Hydration" later in this chapter.

What to Drink

Water and carbohydrate-replacement drinks that contain sodium are excellent for maintaining hydration during running. The advantage of replacement drinks with 4 to 8 percent carbohydrate is that they're absorbed as quickly as water and also provide readily usable energy. The carbohydrate can help your performance during workouts lasting longer than 1 hour. The exact carbohydrate concentration that's best for you will depend on your stomach's tolerance and how warm it is during training and during your marathon. On a cool day, you may want to use a carbohydrate content of 6 to 8 percent, whereas on a warm day, when fluid is more critical than extra carbohydrate, you may want to stay in the 4 to 6 percent range. Sports drinks should also contain between 250 and 700 mg of sodium per liter to enhance glucose and water absorption and improve fluid retention.

■ Alcohol and Caffeine

Most running books just tell you to avoid alcohol and caffeine. That's neither realistic nor helpful advice for the majority of people who regularly enjoy coffee, tea, beer, wine, or spirits. The real issue is determining how much of these beverages you can drink before they have a significant effect on your running performance.

Alcohol

Alcohol (ethyl alcohol) primarily affects your brain. One or two drinks temporarily lead to reduced tension and relief from stress. In the short term, they will also increase dehydration. According to the most recent position statement on hydration from the American College of Sports Medicine, over the course of 24 hours the initial dehydration is offset by less urine output, and the diuretic effect of a small amount of alcohol is negated. Where to strike the balance? The night before your marathon, reduced tension is a good thing, but as discussed earlier, any amount of dehydration is detrimental to running performance. With this in mind, it's best to limit yourself to one or, at the most, two beers or one glass of wine the night before the marathon. Take in enough extra fluid to make up for the dehydrating effect of the alcohol. Drink an extra ounce (30 ml) of water for each ounce of beer and an extra 3 ounces (90 ml) of water for each ounce of wine that you drink. The same guideline holds for the night before a long run.

After training or racing, wait until you're reasonably well rehydrated to enjoy a postrun potable. Imbibing while you're still dehydrated from running will slow your recovery. And right before training or racing, well, let's not go there.

Caffeine

In its 2005 consensus on hydration, the American College of Sports Medicine wrote, "Caffeine ingestion has a modest diuretic effect in some individuals but does not affect water replacement in habitual caffeine users, so caffeinated beverages (e.g., coffee, tea, soft drinks) can be ingested during the day by athletes who are not caffeine naïve." In other words, if you're used to it, moderate ingestion of caffeine does not increase urine output more than a similar amount of water (Armstrong et al. 2005).

If you are not used to caffeine, there may be a mild diuretic effect in the short term, but then a compensatory mechanism results in your holding on to more water over the ensuing 24 hours. This means there is no significant diuretic effect from a cup of coffee or tea, and a cup of coffee or tea on the morning of the race is fine. In fact, if you're used to having a cup of coffee each morning, abstaining from coffee could have a detrimental effect on your performance because of the withdrawal effects of caffeine deprivation.

In 2005, WADA, the World Anti-Doping Agency, took caffeine off its list of banned substances. Several studies have found performance-enhancing benefits from caffeine ingestion, several others have found no effect of caffeine ingestion on endurance performance, and at least one study found caffeine ingestion to be related to reduced performance. The differences in these results may be partly explained by differences in individuals' responsiveness to caffeine and the nuances of the study designs.

(continued)

Alcohol and Caffeine   *(continued)*

Extrapolating from run-to-exhaustion studies in the lab, the likely benefit of taking caffeine is in the range of 1 to 2 percent (perhaps 20 to 50 seconds in a 10K or 90 seconds to 4 minutes in a marathon). Caffeine may not work as well during races as in lab tests because one of its effects is an increase in epinephrine (adrenaline) levels, which are also stimulated by the excitement of competition, so the caffeine effect may be reduced during a race.

The effects of caffeine that may boost performance for marathoners are a glycogen-sparing effect, an increase in the release of calcium in muscle fibers, and stimulation of the central nervous system. Ingesting caffeine mobilizes fatty acids that allow you to use more fat and less glycogen at a given pace, meaning your glycogen stores last longer. Instead of your hitting the wall at 23 miles (37 km) because of glycogen depletion, caffeine ingestion could theoretically allow your glycogen stores to last the full marathon distance.

The primary effect of caffeine in improving endurance performance may be stimulation of the central nervous system, which increases alertness and concentration. There is intriguing evidence that central nervous system stimulation reduces perception of effort so that a given pace feels easier.

Our view is that runners should use caffeine only if they are already trying every other legal option to improve running performance. This includes training hard and intelligently, having an excellent diet, and working to optimize all the other lifestyle factors that influence running performance. If you are doing everything else right, and your personal ethics permit it, then a low dose of caffeine may allow you to gain a small improvement in performance.

The side effects of caffeine include headaches, dizziness, anxiety, nervousness, gastrointestinal distress, and heart palpitations. Caffeine is also a mild laxative, which can be particularly inconvenient during a race.

Athletes vary widely in their sensitivity to, and tolerance of, caffeine, so you are an experiment of one. If you do not regularly consume caffeine, you will likely be more sensitive to the effects. If you decide to use caffeine for your marathon, practice using it during your longest training run to see how your body responds.

Attempting to do high-mileage or high-intensity training in hot weather is a physiological challenge that requires you to be flexible with your training schedule. By planning your training, you can minimize the impact of hot weather. Start each workout fully hydrated by making rehydration a priority after the previous day's run. Run at the time of day when the weather is the least taxing on your body. On a hot, humid day, slow your pace from the outset rather than waiting until your body forces you to slow.

Hope You Like Carbohydrate

The main fuels for endurance exercise are carbohydrate and fat. Protein also provides a small amount of energy. Carbohydrate supplies the majority of energy during exercise, and fat supplies the bulk of the remainder. If you want to run 26.2 miles (42.2 km) at a good pace, you had better like carbohydrate foods because they'll be the mainstay of your diet during day-to-day training and especially in the few days before the marathon.

Even if you're a gaunt marathoner, your body has a large stockpile of energy in the form of fat. A 140-pound (63 kg) runner with a body-fat level of 6 percent still carries around 8.4 pounds (3.8 kg) of fat. Each pound of fat supplies 3,500 calories of energy, so this individual has more than 29,000 calories stored as fat.

For the purposes of fast marathoning, of course, what matters are your carbohydrate, not fat, stores, and your carbohydrate reserves are much more limited. If you do a good job of carbohydrate loading, you can store about 2,000 to 2,500 calories of glycogen (the body's storage form of carbohydrate).

When you run, your body burns a mixture of carbohydrate and fat. The harder you run, the higher the proportion of carbohydrate you use; the slower you run, the higher the proportion of fat you use. During walking, more than half of the calories you burn are provided by the breakdown of fat. As your pace increases, you use proportionately less fat and more carbohydrate. An easy recovery run may be fueled by 65 percent carbohydrate and 35 percent fat. If you race the marathon, approximately 75 to 90 percent of the fuel you use is supplied by the breakdown of carbohydrate. For those jogging the marathon, the proportion of carbohydrate used would be somewhat lower.

Carbohydrate is a more efficient energy source than fat. The breakdown of fat requires more oxygen per calorie released than does carbohydrate. Because fat doesn't produce energy aerobically as efficiently as carbohydrate does, you can't run as fast burning just fat. Your body uses several strategies to keep you from running out of carbohydrate stores. One of these strategies is to use relatively more fat as your carbohydrate stores become low. Anyone who has hit the wall knows the joys of this "strategy." A problem with glycogen depletion is that there aren't warning signs that it's going to occur until it's too late. When you need to slow suddenly in a marathon, the culprit is probably glycogen depletion, not dehydration, which tends to affect you more gradually.

You can prevent carbohydrate depletion by glycogen loading. Glycogen loading (also known as carbohydrate loading) is the practice of manipulating your diet and training to increase your glycogen stores.

Marathoners can almost double their muscle glycogen stores by doing a long run 7 days before a race, then eating a low-carbohydrate diet for 3 days, followed by a high-carbohydrate diet (70 to 80 percent of calories from carbohydrate) for the 3 days before the race. The long run depletes your body's glycogen stores, and the 3 days of low carbohydrate intake keep them low. This triggers a mechanism in your body to store as much glycogen as possible. When you eat a high-carbohydrate diet during the last 3 days before the marathon, therefore, your body stores an extra supply of glycogen.

This classic approach to glycogen loading has fallen out of favor as we've learned more about tapering for marathons. Carbohydrate depletion recently has been shown to suppress the immune system, so the classic glycogen depletion and loading regimen increases your risk of getting sick when you can least afford it. Also, a 20-miler (32 km) 1 week before your marathon carries too much risk, in the form of lingering fatigue or soreness, for the benefits it brings to your carbohydrate loading. (Besides, what marathoner wants to avoid carbohydrate for 3 days?)

The good news is that glycogen stores can be elevated to similar levels without the long run and low-carbohydrate phases of the original glycogen-loading diet. All you need to do is eat a normal diet up until the last 3 days before the race and taper your training program to about half your normal training load. Then eat a high-carbohydrate diet the last 3 days and do a short, slow run on those days. Your body will store glycogen to almost the same level as if you did the whole regimen of glycogen depletion and loading.

Rice, pasta, bread, sweet potatoes, pancakes, bagels, potatoes, corn, and raisins are excellent sources of carbohydrate. Many of the world's best marathoners eat rice for their prerace meal because it provides plenty of carbohydrate and is easy to digest. Expect to gain a couple of pounds and feel slightly bloated when you glycogen load because your body stores 2.6 grams of water for every gram of glycogen. The added weight is just extra fuel to help get you through the marathon, and the stored water will help prevent dehydration as the marathon progresses.

If you eat a normal runner's diet, with about 60 percent of your calories from carbohydrate, you probably store about 1,500 to 2,000 calories of glycogen in your muscles. If you glycogen load, however, your muscles have the capacity to store between 2,000 and 2,500 calories of glycogen. Each mile (1.6 km) that you run burns about 90 to 140 calories, depending on your weight and metabolism, and 75 to 90 percent of those calories are supplied by carbohydrate. If you do a great job of loading, you'll have just about enough glycogen for the marathon.

Glycogen loading is also important before your long runs. Make sure to eat a high-carbohydrate diet the day before your long run so that you have plenty of fuel to go the distance. Carbohydrate loading before your long runs will help ensure that you have high-quality long runs, which will increase your confidence for the marathon.

How Much Carbohydrate Do You Need in Your Daily Training Diet?

Your daily carbohydrate requirement depends on your weight and how much you're training. If you're averaging an hour to an hour and a half of training per day, you need approximately 7 to 8 grams of carbohydrate per kilogram (3 to 3.5 g/lb) of your body weight per day. If you're training for

2 hours or more per day, you need approximately 9 to 10 grams of carbohydrate per kilogram (4 to 4.5 g/lb) of body weight per day.

As an example, say Gary is running 80 miles (129 km) per week and weighs 154 pounds (70 kg). His average daily training time is about 80 minutes. Gary's daily carbohydrate requirement is 490 to 560 grams (70 × 7 to 70 × 8). Each gram of carbohydrate supplies 4.1 calories, so Gary's calorie supply from carbohydrate should be 2,000 to 2,300 per day.

Tips to Replenish Your Glycogen Stores

With a typical runner's high-carbohydrate diet, you probably have enough glycogen to get you through a 20- to 22-mile (32 to 35 km) run or a hard interval workout. After a long run or a long interval workout, therefore, your glycogen stores are depleted. It typically takes 24 to 48 hours to completely replenish your glycogen stores. When you do two long or hard workouts in a row, therefore, you risk going into the second workout with partially filled glycogen stores, becoming depleted, and having a bad workout. The frequency with which you can train hard is determined by your recovery rate between workouts, and this will be increased greatly by replenishing your glycogen stores quickly.

Here are strategies you can use to increase your rate of glycogen replenishment.

- Don't wait. Your body stores glycogen at a faster rate during the first hour after exercise, so have a carbohydrate drink with you when you finish your long runs or other workouts. Bring along some easy-to-digest carbohydrate foods as well. To speed glycogen resynthesis, take in about 1 gram of carbohydrate per kilogram of body weight (a little under half a gram per pound) in the first 15 minutes after the workout, and another gram per kilogram of body weight during each of the following 3 hours.

- Increase your intake of carbohydrate. After a glycogen-depleting workout, increase your carbohydrate intake to approximately 10 grams per kilogram of body weight (4.5 g/lb) during the next 24 hours.

- Eat high–glycemic index foods. The glycemic index of a food is determined by the effect it has on your blood glucose level. High–glycemic index foods cause a large increase in blood glucose levels, whereas low–glycemic index foods have a lesser effect. During the first few hours after a workout, your glycogen stores will be replenished more quickly if you eat high–glycemic index foods, such as potatoes, rice cakes, bread, bagels, and crackers.

Nancy Clark's Sports Nutrition Guidebook and *Endurance Sports Nutrition* by Suzanne Girard Eberle are excellent and extensive resources for more information on nutrition for endurance athletes.

The Role of Protein for Marathoners

Conventional wisdom indicates that strength-trained athletes such as weightlifters need lots of extra protein to build muscle but that the protein needs of endurance athletes are the same as for sedentary folks. Over the past 15 years, however, studies have clearly shown that endurance athletes have elevated protein needs. As a marathoner, your body needs protein to repair damaged muscles, to make red blood cells to deliver oxygen to your muscles, to make mitochondria in your muscles to produce energy aerobically, to maintain a strong immune system, and to make enzymes and hormones that keep your body functioning normally.

Sedentary individuals need about .8 to 1.0 gram of protein per kilogram of body weight per day (.35 to .45 g/lb per day). Endurance athletes have elevated protein needs because of their greater wear and tear on muscle tissue and red blood cells, need for more mitochondria, and so on. Several formulas are used for calculating the protein needs of endurance athletes, but a typical guideline is 1.2 to 1.7 grams of protein per kilogram of body weight (.55 to .75 g/lb of body weight) per day (Eberle 2007). Table 2.1 presents daily protein requirements for marathoners.

Chances are that most marathoners meet or exceed their protein requirements through a typical American diet. Runners who are vegetarians or who greatly restrict their meat intake may not meet their protein needs. If you're a vegetarian, it's not difficult to meet your protein requirements, but it does require some knowledge and planning.

Eating too much protein can also have negative consequences for your running performance. If you eat too much protein, you may not be consuming enough carbohydrate, so such a diet would reduce your energy levels. Your body would use the excess protein as energy by removing the amino groups and oxidizing the resulting carbon skeleton. This process requires the removal of waste products, which stresses the kidneys and can lead to dehydration.

TABLE 2.1

Daily Protein Requirements for Marathoners

Weight (lb)	Weight (kg)	Protein required (g/day)
100	45	55-75
120	55	66-90
140	64	77-105
160	73	88-120
180	82	99-135
200	91	110-150

The Importance of Iron

Iron is vital to running performance. Despite this importance, many runners don't monitor their iron levels. Even many physicians don't understand the complete role of iron for endurance athletes.

Iron is necessary for producing hemoglobin in your red blood cells. Oxygen attaches to hemoglobin for transport in your blood to your muscles. If your hemoglobin level is low, less oxygen reaches your muscles, which means your muscles can't produce as much energy aerobically. The result is that your $\dot{V}O_2$max and lactate threshold are reduced, and you can't maintain as fast a pace. In addition, iron is a component of many other substances in the body, such as enzymes in your muscle cells that affect aerobic energy production, so low iron levels may cause low energy levels by altering the composition of these other substances.

For many years, top athletes and coaches have recognized the benefits of a high red blood cell count; this awareness has led to the illegal practices of blood doping and using synthetic erythropoietin (EPO) to increase red blood cell count. EPO is a hormone the body produces naturally that determines the body's level of red blood cell production. When EPO levels rise through natural means or through injection of synthetic EPO, red blood cell production and hemoglobin levels increase. The result is that the runner can produce more energy aerobically and, therefore, maintain a faster pace.

Though a few athletes try to artificially achieve a high red blood cell count, the typical marathoner needs to ensure that she or he doesn't have a low red blood cell count or low iron stores. Low iron levels may be the most prevalent nutrition deficiency in Western marathoners. With iron-deficiency anemia, your iron stores are gone and your hemoglobin level is reduced. With iron depletion, on the other hand, your iron stores are low but not gone, and your hemoglobin is still normal. Although anemia is more detrimental, both of these conditions can negatively affect your running performance.

Why Do Marathoners Tend to Have Lower Iron Levels?

Runners tend to have lower iron levels than do sedentary folks for many reasons: increased blood volume, low iron intake, foot-strike hemolysis, iron loss through sweat and urine, and iron loss through the gastrointestinal (GI) system. For marathoners, the iron losses tend to be higher than for those doing shorter races, primarily because of higher training volumes. Let's look at each of these factors.

Increased Blood Volume. Endurance athletes have more blood than do normal people. This adaptation allows the stroke volume of the heart to increase, which allows $\dot{V}O_2$max to increase. This is a good thing. The iron in a runner's red blood cells, therefore, is diluted in a greater volume of blood. If the runner's red blood cell mass doesn't increase as much as the blood volume, then hemoglobin concentration will decrease and may incorrectly indicate an iron deficiency. This is a natural phenomenon that any sports doctor will recognize but that your local general practitioner may not.

Low Iron Intake.   Many endurance athletes have low iron intakes. Low iron intake can be a problem for vegetarians and runners who eat red meat less often than once a week. The typical high-carbohydrate, low-fat, low-cholesterol runner's diet often includes little or no red meat. Red meat contains heme iron, which is more easily absorbed than plant sources of iron. Runners who don't eat meat can obtain sufficient iron through dietary sources but only by carefully selecting their foods. Enette Larson-Meyer's book, *Vegetarian Sports Nutrition,* is a good resource for more information on proper nutrition for vegetarian athletes.

Foot-Strike Hemolysis.   Foot-strike hemolysis is the breakdown of red blood cells when the foot hits the ground. Foot-strike hemolysis is potentially a problem for marathoners who run high mileage on asphalt or are heavier than most runners.

Iron Loss Through Sweat and Urine.   A relatively small amount of iron is lost through sweat and urine, but for high-mileage runners training in hot, humid conditions, this iron loss may add up. For marathoners living in the south or training through the summer in preparation for a fall marathon, sweat may be a significant source of iron loss. More research is needed to determine the magnitude of iron losses in sweat.

Iron Loss Through the GI System.   Loss of iron through the GI tract (primarily the stomach or large intestine) is a problem for some marathoners. In a study following 11 runners over a competitive season, GI bleeding was evident in 17 of 129 stool samples after training and in 16 of 61 stool samples after racing. The bleeding is fairly minor each time, but there may be a cumulative effect over years of running.

All the preceding factors in combination make it important for marathoners to monitor their iron intake and their iron levels. The highest risk occurs in premenopausal female runners, whose iron intake often doesn't meet their needs.

How Do You Know if You Have Low Iron?

If you have low iron, first, you'll be dragging. Your heart rate may be elevated, and your enthusiasm for running will have sunk. These symptoms tend to come on gradually, however, so you may not suspect that you have low iron levels until they've had a large impact on your training. You can confirm your suspicions only with a blood test. You should find out your hemoglobin level (the iron in your red blood cells) and your serum ferritin level (your body's iron stores).

Normal hemoglobin concentration ranges from 14 to 18 grams per deciliter (g/dl) of blood for men and 12 to 16 g/dl of blood for women; for an endurance athlete, the lower end of normal should be extended by about 1 g/dl because of his or her larger blood volume. For a male marathoner, then, a hemoglobin level between 13.0 and 13.9 g/dl could be considered in the low end of the normal range and would be similar to a level of about 14.0 to 14.9 g/dl for an untrained man who doesn't have a marathoner's elevated blood volume. Similarly, a female marathoner with a hemoglobin level between 11.0 and 11.9 g/dl would have a lower than optimal level that would be similar to a level of about 12.0 to 12.9 g/dl for an untrained woman.

Normal reference serum ferritin levels are 10 to 200 nanograms per milliliter (ng/ml) for women and 10 to 300 ng/ml for men. Conflicting schools of thought exist on the relationship between ferritin levels and running performance. One opinion is that ferritin levels aren't directly related to performance, but if your ferritin level falls, eventually your hemoglobin and performances will decline too. Low ferritin, therefore, can be viewed as an early warning sign.

The other school of thought is that ferritin reflects the iron stores the body can use to make enzymes for oxidative energy production; therefore, they have a direct impact on performance. The optimal level of serum ferritin seems to differ among individuals. Dick Telford, PhD, of the Australian Institute of Sport, has found that the performance of some runners seems to be affected when their ferritin levels drop below 50 ng/ml, whereas others perform fine if their ferritin levels remain above 25 ng/ml. Telford says that even with iron supplementation, some runners have difficulty raising their ferritin levels above 50 ng/ml.

David Martin, PhD, who has been in charge of testing elite distance runners for USA Track and Field since 1981, says that in his experience with runners, training and racing performances are usually affected when ferritin levels drop below 20 ng/ml. When those athletes increase their ferritin levels above 25 ng/ml, they experience a rapid turnaround in performance. These experiences indicate that a ferritin level between 25 and 50 ng/ml may be normal or low depending on your individual physiology, but a ferritin level below 25 ng/ml is a definite red flag for a runner.

How Much Iron Do You Need?

According to the National Academy of Sciences' 1989 recommended daily allowances (RDAs), premenopausal women need about 15 milligrams of iron a day, whereas men and postmenopausal women require 10 milligrams of iron a day. Iron requirements haven't been established for high-mileage runners, so all that can be said with confidence is that marathoners need at least the RDA. As with any mineral, too much iron can be a health hazard. In fact, the typical American man is more likely to get an iron overload than to be iron deficient.

How Can You Prevent Iron Depletion?

As with other running problems, such as injuries, the best strategy is to avoid low iron in the first place. Good food sources of iron include liver, lean meat, oysters, egg yolk, dark green leafy vegetables, legumes, dried fruit, and whole-grain or enriched cereals and bread.

Dr. E. Randy Eichner, chief of hematology at the University of Oklahoma Health Sciences Center, offers these tips to prevent iron deficiency:

- Eat 3 ounces (90 g) of lean red meat or dark poultry a couple of times a week.
- Don't drink coffee or tea with meals because they reduce iron absorption.
- Eat or drink foods rich in vitamin C with meals to increase iron absorption.
- Use cast-iron cookware (particularly for acidic foods such as spaghetti sauce).

Although these recommendations may seem like subtle changes in diet, they can have a powerful effect on your iron levels. For example, you'll absorb three times as much iron from your cereal and toast if you switch from coffee to orange juice with breakfast. Both Eichner and Martin recommend taking iron supplements, in the form of ferrous sulfate, ferrous gluconate, or ferrous fumarate, only if necessary after making the recommended dietary changes.

Supplements and Other Ergogenic Aids

Ergogenic aids are substances that may enhance athletic performance. In *The Ergogenics Edge*, Melvin Williams, PhD, classifies ergogenic aids as nutritional aids (e.g., vitamins, minerals, protein supplements, carbohydrate supplements, bee pollen, and ginseng), pharmacological aids (drugs such as anabolic steroids and amphetamines), or physiological aids (e.g., human growth hormone, EPO, creatine, and glycerol) (Williams 1998). Most supposed ergogenic aids have no scientific evidence to support their use and will do nothing to improve your running performance.

The multimillion-dollar supplement industry is poorly regulated, with the result that many unsubstantiated claims are made. The advent of unregulated Internet sites pushing supplements with advertisements written as though they're the results of scientific studies has made it even harder for runners to know what works. It doesn't help when famous athletes endorse these products. The manufacturer tells the athlete wonderful things about the supplement, and the athlete gets paid to build credibility for the product by repeating those wonderful things. As a result, many people waste money on products that neither harm nor help performance.

Taking supplements that you know little about also carries a risk, as they may contain harmful or illegal substances. For example, many athletes who failed drug tests for the steroid nandrolone in the 1990s claimed that small amounts of the substance or of a precursor of nandrolone must have been in one of the supplements they were taking. (Of course, almost everyone who fails a drug test claims the result is false.)

Are there any legal pills you can pop that will help your running performance? The answer is yes, and the list is short. We could spend page after page discussing the supplements that don't work. In *The Ergogenics Edge*, Williams discusses 61 types of supplements and drugs that claim to improve athletic performance. Thirty-nine of those claim to improve aerobic endurance, which, if true, would improve marathon performance. Imagine how fast you would run if you took all 39! In reality, you would be a lot poorer and would still need to eat a healthy diet to get the nutrients you need. Let's look at supposed ergogenic aids by category.

Nutritional Aids

The many nutritional supplements available on the market can be put into the following four categories:

1. Those that have been clearly shown to enhance endurance performance
2. Those that lack evidence from well-controlled scientific studies that they enhance endurance performance
3. Those that enhance performance only if you have a nutrition deficiency
4. Those that require more research

Category 1 includes only carbohydrate supplements and fluid. We have already discussed these topics in depth.

Category 2 includes almost all nutritional supplements that make miraculous claims, including ginseng, bee pollen, and various herbs and plant extracts.

Category 3 includes most vitamins and minerals that have an established RDA. If you fall below the RDA for a prolonged time, you'll develop a nutrition deficiency that could inhibit your running performance and your ability to recover. All of the vitamins and minerals you need can be obtained from foods. Vitamin and mineral supplements are expensive, and relying on them for your vitamin and mineral needs is simply an admission that the quality of your overall diet is poor.

Within category 4, evidence exists that antioxidants can help marathoners and other endurance athletes. Antioxidants work by neutralizing oxygen free radicals, which are formed during aerobic metabolism. Free radicals damage cell membranes and other parts of muscle cells. Antioxidant supplementation, therefore, reduces the damage caused by free radicals. Antioxidants may also help maintain immune function after strenuous exercise. The most commonly used antioxidants are beta carotene (precursor to vitamin A), vitamin C, vitamin E, and selenium.

Studies on the benefits of antioxidant supplementation have had mixed results—some show links between antioxidant supplementation and reduced muscle damage, whereas others show no benefit. Similar mixed results have been reported for the role of antioxidants in maintaining immune function. In one study, runners who took 600 milligrams of vitamin C a day for 3 weeks had more than 50 percent fewer head colds after the Comrades ultramarathon than did runners taking a placebo.

As more evidence accumulates, it's prudent to take only moderate doses of antioxidants. Large doses of one vitamin or mineral may lead to decreased absorption of other nutrients, decreased immune function, or both. For example, studies have found that very high doses of vitamin E, vitamin D, or zinc reduce immune function.

New substances and combinations of substances are being introduced to the market each week, almost all of which will be of no benefit to your athletic performance.

Pharmacological and Physiological Aids

Of the pharmacological and physiological ergogenic aids that have been shown to have a positive effect on athletic performance, almost all have been banned by the International Olympic Committee and many other sporting bodies. Within the realm of legal pharmacological or physiological ergogenic aids, the only ones that may provide benefits for an endurance athlete are moderate amounts of caffeine or glycerol.

The effects of caffeine were discussed earlier in this chapter. That leaves glycerol, a product that our bodies produce naturally. Glycerol supplementation increases total body water stores. This may be an advantage for a warm-weather marathon because if you start the race with more stored fluid, then it should follow that the effects of dehydration will be postponed until later in the race. Although several sports drinks on the market contain glycerol, it's still open to debate whether glycerol leads to enhanced performance during warm-weather competitions. (Glycerol supplementation isn't advisable for shorter races in cool conditions because the weight of the extra fluid you carry would be detrimental to performance.)

Marathon Race-Day Nutrition and Hydration

So you've followed the advice in this chapter and eaten properly and stayed well hydrated throughout your months of preparation. Guess what—your work isn't done yet. Your strategies for taking calories and fluid on race day can have a strong influence on your marathon performance.

Sammy Wanjiru

Fastest Marathon: 2:05:24
Marathon Highlights:
First place, 2008 Olympics in
Olympic record time (2:06:32);
Second-fastest debut
marathon in history (2:06:39).

© Icon SMI

Sammy Wanjiru is the latest—and most successful—marathoner to merge two powerful elements: Kenyan genetics and a Japanese marathon mind-set. The payoff, at age 21 in just his third marathon, was Kenya's first Olympic gold medal in the marathon.

When he was 15, Wanjiru won a cross country race in Kenya that served as a selection contest for runners who would attend high school in Japan. Once abroad, Wanjiru, who had grown up running half an hour or so per day, was immersed in Japan's running culture. That meant he was soon running twice a day in a group setting, at high volume with an emphasis on long-term aerobic development.

Upon graduating, Wanjiru was contracted to run for one of Japan's corporate teams. Although he was soon world-class, with a world junior record for 10,000 meters (26:41.75) and a world record in the half marathon (58:35), his obligations with the corporate team kept him from the siren of overracing that has undone so much young Kenyan talent. His main responsibility was representing his team in four "ekiden," or marathon-length relay races, a year.

In the ekidens, in which the fields are usually strung out after the first leg, Wanjiru mastered running hard by feel and by himself. Japanese-style training, which has as its cornerstones very long long runs, lengthy tempo runs (20 kilometers or more), and long, threshold-based sessions, such as four 5-kilometer repeats, encourages intuition and independence.

It was no surprise, then, when Wanjiru won his first marathon, Fukuoka, in December 2007, and followed that up with a second-place finish at the 2008 London Marathon. After all, consciously or not, he had been training for the marathon for the last six years. In addition, despite the high mileage, he was fresh—as he said before London, "too many races, not good."

(continued)

Sammy Wanjiru *(continued)*

Wanjiru's victory in the Beijing Olympics was a masterpiece of self-knowledge. Despite the warm, humid conditions, Wanjiru set a fast pace from the start, because he feared that a slow, tactical race would let lesser runners be near him at the finish and outkick him. What to most of the world looked to be a suicidal 2:06 pace was actually a supremely well-judged effort, as Wanjiru ran halves of 1:02:34 and 1:04:02, despite rising temperatures in the latter part of the race. His performance shows what solid training, an excellent sense of perceived effort, and self-confidence can make possible.

Let's assume you've done a good job of glycogen loading during the previous several days and you're well hydrated. Before the race, you want to take in between 200 and 500 calories of mostly carbohydrate to top off your glycogen stores. It's best to ingest these calories 3 to 4 hours before the race. This shouldn't be a big deal for races with late starts, such as New York City, which begins a little after 10 a.m., or Boston, with its 10:00 and 10:30 a.m. wave starts. But for a race such as Chicago, which starts at 8:00 a.m., or Honolulu, which starts at 5:00 a.m. (!), you may have to get up a bit on the early side, eat something, and then try to doze a while longer. (Good luck with that on race morning!) You should also take in about a pint (half a liter) of fluid to replace fluids lost overnight and ensure that you're fully hydrated.

Even if you carefully carbohydrate load for several days leading up to the marathon, you don't have much of a buffer against glycogen depletion. The solution is to take in additional calories during the race.

How much you need to drink during the marathon depends on your body size, the heat and humidity, and your sweat rate. The maximum amount you should drink during running is the amount that can empty from your stomach or the amount that you have lost as sweat, whichever is less. Drinking more than you have lost brings the risk of hyponatremia, which is discussed later in the chapter.

Research has shown that most runners' stomachs can empty only about 6 to 7 ounces (180 to 210 ml) of fluid every 15 minutes during running, representing about 24 to 28 ounces (720 to 840 ml) per hour. If you drink more than that, the extra fluid will just slosh around in your stomach and not provide any additional benefit. You may be able to handle more or less than the average, however, so experiment with how much liquid your stomach will tolerate.

During training, it's relatively easy to stop and drink as much as you want whenever you feel like it. All that's required is a bit of planning and perhaps a few containers strategically placed the night before your long run. During the marathon, however, it's very difficult to drink 6 to 7 ounces (180 to 210 ml) of fluid at an aid station without stopping. In fact, a study by Tim Noakes, MD, and colleagues (2007) found that most runners drink less than 16 ounces (480 ml) per hour when racing. Another study found that runners lose, on average, 3.2 percent of body weight during a marathon. As we saw earlier in this chapter, a loss of more than 3 percent of body weight can lead to a significant loss in performance. Many serious marathoners, therefore, run the marathon slower than their potential because of the effects of progressive dehydration during the race.

Drinking 28 ounces (840 ml) per hour of a 4 percent solution will supply 32 grams of carbohydrate, whereas an 8 percent solution will supply 64 grams of carbohydrate. Each gram of carbohydrate contains 4.1 calories, so you'll be taking in 130 to 260 calories per hour. If you run the marathon in 2:45, therefore, you'll take in about 350 to 700 calories during the race. During the marathon, a typical 140-pound (63 kg) male burns about 100 calories per mile. Of those 100 calories, about 80 are supplied by carbohydrate and the remaining 20 by fat. The carbohydrate you consume during the race, therefore, supplies enough carbohydrate fuel to last an extra 4 to 9 miles (6 to 14 km)! Even if you take in only half this amount, you'll substantially increase your chances of reaching the finish without running out of glycogen.

An alternative method of taking in carbohydrate during the marathon or your long runs is to use energy gels. Energy gels are convenient because they come in small packets that you can carry with you. Depending on the brand you choose, each gel packet contains between 80 and 150 calories of carbohydrate. Energy gels are the consistency of pudding. You must follow gels with a couple of sips of fluid to wash them down, and you should take in approximately a cup of fluid afterward to help absorb the gel. The best time to take an energy gel is shortly before an aid station. As always, don't wait until race day to try an energy gel because it takes practice to get the water intake right and to feel comfortable running after taking a gel. Practice taking gel packets while running at marathon race pace.

Avoiding Hyponatremia

If you run the marathon in more than 3 hours on a warm day and drink large amounts of plain water during the race, you are at risk of hyponatremia. This is a condition caused by unusually low sodium levels in your blood; a large proportion of your body fluid is replaced with water, thereby reducing your body's sodium content. There is some evidence that women have a moderately higher risk of developing hyponatremia than do men. The symptoms of hyponatremia include weakness, nausea, disorientation, seizures, and coma. Hyponatremia typically occurs only toward the end of ultramarathons or Ironman triathlons, but it can occur in the marathon on warm days for slower runners who consume only water. The simple way to avoid hyponatremia during a hot-weather marathon is to consume fluids containing at least 250 milligrams of sodium per liter and to not drink more than you have lost as sweat.

Can You Take in Enough Fluid During the Race to Prevent Dehydration?

The answer to this question is straightforward: Compare the amount of fluid you consume during the marathon with the amount you're likely to lose. On a cool day, you'll likely lose 2 to 3 pounds (.9 to 1.4 kg) of water per hour during the marathon, whereas on a hot day the figure is 3 to 4 pounds (1.4 to 1.8 kg) per hour and can be up to 5 pounds (2.3 kg) of fluid per hour when the temperature gets above 80 degrees Fahrenheit (27 degrees Celsius). We already estimated that a typical runner's stomach can absorb about 28 ounces (840 ml) per hour, which is a little bit less than 2 pounds (.9 kg). On a cool day, therefore, you can just about balance your fluid losses with fluid taken in during the marathon. On warm or hot days, you'll incur a steady, progressive fluid deficit, and the farther you run, the greater your fluid deficit will be.

How to Drink on the Run

It's imperative, then, to practice drinking while running at close to marathon race pace until you get good at it. It makes sense to slow a bit at the aid stations, but if you're competitive, you won't want to lose time to the runners around you. By practicing drinking on the run, you can greatly improve your proficiency at this skill.

If you're an elite runner, you can usually arrange to have squeeze bottles at the aid stations along the course. This is optimal but obviously not readily available to everyone. Non-elites can help themselves by choosing marathons where friends or family members can meet them regularly along the way and give them bottles. Still, the majority of marathoners must master the paper cup.

A convenient way to practice drinking from cups is the round-and-round-the-track method—simply set up some cups at the local track and practice drinking every couple of laps. The advantage of the track is convenience. The disadvantage is that, if you're running intervals, you'll be breathing so hard that you'll get to experience the dubious thrill of getting water up your nose. Of course, if you can master drinking at faster than marathon race pace, then drinking during the marathon will be a snap.

Another convenient way to practice drinking on the run is the road-loop method. Back your car to the end of the driveway, put a few cups of the beverage you'll drink during the marathon on the back of your car, and head out for a repetitive loop run, grabbing a cup every time you pass your car.

Race-Day Technique

If volunteers are handing out fluids during the race, try to make eye contact with one and point at the cup so that you don't surprise him or her. (If the cups are on a table, eye contact with the cup generally won't help.) If volunteers are offering both water and a sports drink, begin yelling your preference as you approach the aid station so that the right volunteer hands you a cup.

Slow slightly and try to move your arm back while you grab the cup so that you don't hit the cup with your full running speed. Squeeze the top of the cup closed so that all of the liquid doesn't slosh out, and take a swig. This will help prevent fluid from going up your nose when you tip the cup up to drink. The trick is to breathe normally. Always take a couple of normal breaths between swigs. When you're done drinking, accelerate back to race pace.

Unless you're an elite marathoner, the best strategy on a warm and humid day is to stop and drink at the aid stations. Water stops in a marathon are often every 5K or every 2 miles, so there are about 8 to 12 stops. If you stop for 10 seconds at each station, you'll add about 1 to 2 minutes to your time. If you run through the stops while drinking, you'll slow a little anyway,

© AP Photo/Steven Senne

Grabbing water on the run can be tricky. Unless you're an elite marathoner, the best strategy on a warm and humid day is to just stop for a few seconds and drink at the aid stations.

so stopping isn't going to add much time, and stopping helps ensure that you take in enough fluid to fight off dehydration. On a warm day, an extra minute or 2 at the water stations can repay you with 10 to 20 minutes gained by the finish of the marathon.

What and when you eat and drink play an important role in how you adapt to training for a marathon. As we've seen, neglecting proper nutrition and hydration will mean not reaping the full benefits of your hard work. The same is true for not paying attention to easy days and other aspects of managing recovery from taxing training. Let's look at what to do to maximize your chance of marathon success during the many hours each week when you're not running long or hard.

Balancing Training and Recovery

As we saw in chapter 1, every time you do a hard workout, you provide a stimulus for your body to improve in some way, such as your lactate threshold, fat-burning ability, VO_2max, and so on. Any one workout, though, provides only a mild stimulus for improvement; it's the sum of your workouts over time that determines the total stimulus to improve a specific component of your fitness. For example, if you do one tempo run in the few months before your marathon, you provide a mild stimulus for your lactate threshold to improve. If you do six tempo runs in 8 weeks, you provide a strong repetitive stimulus for your lactate threshold to improve.

The training stimulus, however, is only half of the formula for performance improvement. To improve, your body must recover from training and adapt to a higher level. By learning to manage your recovery, you'll optimize your training. If you manage your recovery so that you can do hard workouts more frequently or so that the quality of your hard workouts consistently improves, then you'll provide a greater stimulus for your body to improve its capacities.

Recovery from training is important, both from day to day and over the course of your marathon-preparation program. Poor management of your recovery can lead to overtraining, which simply overwhelms your body's ability to respond positively to training. In this chapter, we'll review how to optimize your recovery for marathon success.

Recovery and Supercompensation

One of the realities of running is that if you do a hard workout today, you won't be a better marathoner tomorrow. In fact, tomorrow you'll just be tired. Hard training causes immediate fatigue, tissue breakdown, dehydration, and glycogen depletion. Depending on the difficulty of the training session (and other factors discussed in this chapter), you'll require from 2 to 10 days to completely recover from a workout.

At some point, however, the fatigue of each workout dissipates and you adapt to a higher level. To optimize your training, you need to find the correct balance between training and recovery for you. Training provides the stimulus for your body to adapt, but recovery is when you allow your body to adapt and improve. Well-designed training sessions also provide a stimulus for your body to adapt to a higher level, which is called supercompensation.

Effectively managing your recovery means answering two questions:

1. How many days after a workout do you reap the benefits of that workout?
2. How much time should you allow between hard workouts or between a hard workout and a race?

Let's try to answer those questions.

Turning Genes On and Off

The intensity, duration, and frequency (number of sessions per week) of your training all influence the rate at which your body adapts. The adaptations in hormone levels, fat-burning ability, capillary density, and so on that result from endurance training occur because of repeated training bouts rather than as a result of one workout in isolation. It's as though your body must be convinced that you're really serious about training before it makes the physiological adaptations that let you reach a new level.

The process of adaptation begins with your genes. Training provides stimuli (e.g., glycogen depletion) that turn specific genes on or off. By altering the expression of genes, training changes the rates at which your body makes and breaks down specific proteins. For example, endurance training turns on genes for the production of mitochondrial protein. More endurance training leads to more mitochondria in your muscles so that you can produce more energy aerobically. Your muscles and cardiovascular system adapt over days, weeks, and months to the cumulative effects of your repeated training.

Factors Affecting Recovery Rate

Runners vary greatly in how long it takes them to recover from and adapt to a workout. Differences among runners in recovery time and rate of improvement are determined by genetics, age (you tend to recover more slowly with age), training history, gender (women tend to recover more slowly because of lower testosterone levels), and lifestyle factors. Your genetics determine your predisposition to adapt to training; some of us are programmed to adapt more quickly than others. Lifestyle factors, such as diet, quantity and quality of sleep, general health, and various life stressors (such as work, finances, and relationships), all influence how quickly you recover from and adapt to training. Because so much variation exists among runners in how many workouts they can tolerate in a given period, you shouldn't copy your training partner's running program. Only through experience will you learn how much training you can handle.

As an example, figure 3.1, adapted from Tudor Bompa's *Periodization Training for Sports* (2005), details two runners who do the same workout and experience the same amount of initial fatigue but who recover at different rates. Rachel (represented by the solid line) recovers more quickly than Karen (represented by the dashed line). Rachel will be able to recover from and adapt positively to more high-quality workouts in a given period and will, therefore, improve more quickly than Karen. Rachel would also require a shorter taper before a race than Karen.

Only through trial and error will you know how much training your body can positively adapt to in a given time. Successful marathoning requires that you go through this self-discovery process intelligently and systematically. Determining this balance can be tricky because it can be hard to isolate variables. For example, if your job is now much more stressful than the last time you trained for a marathon, your current rate of recovery might be slower. You must find the correct balance of training stimulus and recovery for your specific circumstances over the long weeks that constitute marathon training.

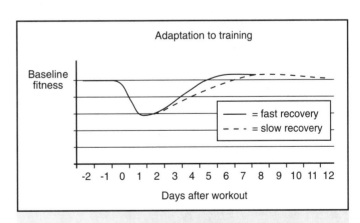

Figure 3.1   **Two runners' rates of recovery.**

Time Required for Recovery and Supercompensation

Unfortunately, the scientific literature doesn't provide clear evidence of the amount of time required to realize the benefits of an individual training session. Personal experience and discussions with many runners and coaches indicate that 8 to 10 days is an adequate amount of time to recover from and reap the rewards of most hard training sessions. Given that any one workout provides only a small fitness benefit—on the order of magnitude of less than 1 percent—but that a workout can cause severe short-term fatigue, it's wise to err on the side of caution and allow enough time to fully recover from training before a race. For the marathon race itself, complete recovery from training is critical for success. Marathon tapering generally requires a full 3 weeks; tapering is the subject of chapter 5.

Table 3.1 shows typical times to reap the benefits of three major types of workouts. The third column indicates typical amounts of time to recover from a workout of each type. For example, the table indicates that you should allow at least 4 days between tempo runs or between a tempo run and a tune-up race. You don't, however, need to allow 4 days between a tempo run and a long run or interval workout. That's because each type of workout uses different combinations of energy systems, so complete recovery from one type of workout isn't necessary before you do another type of workout.

Although you won't see the benefits of this week's workout in this weekend's race, if you do the workout early enough in the week you should recover sufficiently for it not to have a detrimental effect on your race performance. The timelines in Table 3.1 take into account the fact that we often do a tune-up race when the fatigue of previous training is reduced rather than when supercompensation has occurred. You generally can't afford the time required to be optimally rested for tune-up races. Marathoners should allow only enough rest and recovery to obtain optimal results for the marathon itself and possibly for one tune-up race.

TABLE 3.1

Minimum Time Between Hard Workouts and Tune-Up Races

Type of workout	Sample workout	Days before tune-up race or next similar workout
Tempo run	4 mi @ 15K to half marathon race pace	4
Long run	17-20 mi	4
$\dot{V}O_2$max intervals	6 × 1,000 m @ 5K race pace	5

Of the major types of workouts, tempo runs are the easiest to recover from because they don't break down the body as much as the other forms of hard training. Tempo runs are neither fast enough to cause substantial muscle damage nor long enough to totally deplete your muscles of glycogen.

Long runs seem to cause the most variability in recovery time among runners, although replenishing glycogen stores generally requires only 24 to 48 hours. Some runners are able to recover relatively quickly from long runs, whereas others are wiped out for days after one. The variability in recovery time depends on your training history, the genetic and lifestyle factors discussed previously, the type of courses you train on (downhills cause more muscle damage and greater recovery time), and the weather (the same long run in 85-degree F [29-degree C] weather will take longer to recover from than one on a 50-degree F [10-degree C] day).

Interval workouts put your muscles and cardiovascular system under the most stress and generally require the longest recovery time. Later in this chapter, we'll discuss strategies that you can use to speed your recovery.

Regardless of the type of workout involved, the pattern of workout and recovery is basic to effective training. Generally known as the hard/easy principle, this dictates the structure of your training over the weeks and months leading up to the marathon. Let's investigate the rationale for following the hard/easy principle.

The Hard/Easy Principle

Conventional wisdom calls for following the hard/easy principle of training, which is typically interpreted to mean that a hard effort is always followed by 1 or more recovery days. A recovery day may consist of an easy run, a light cross-training session, or total rest. During your marathon preparation, however, it's sometimes best to violate this training pattern and do back-to-back hard days. The appropriate interpretation of the hard/easy principle is that 1 or more hard days should be followed by 1 or more recovery days. Let's investigate the physiological rationale for following the hard/easy principle and look at two situations in which you should do back-to-back hard training days.

Reasons to Follow the Hard/Easy Principle

The hard day/easy day training pattern follows from the physiological dogma of stimulus and response—hard training provides a stimulus for your body to improve, but rest is then needed to allow your body to recover and adapt to a higher level. Three reasons to follow the hard/easy principle are to prevent total glycogen depletion, to prevent illness, and to minimize the effects of delayed onset muscle soreness (DOMS).

Preventing Glycogen Depletion. As discussed in chapter 2, your body can store only a limited amount of glycogen. With a typical runner's high-carbohydrate diet, you probably have enough glycogen to get you through a 20- to 22-mile (32 to 35 km) run or a hard interval workout. It takes about 24 to 48 hours to completely replenish your glycogen stores. When you do two hard workouts in a row, therefore, you risk going into the second workout with partially filled glycogen stores, becoming depleted, and having a bad workout. Although glycogen depletion is potentially a problem on the second hard day, with a bit of planning it needn't be an insurmountable problem. Three hard days in a row, however, would very likely lead to glycogen depletion and a more-prolonged recovery period. By following the hard/easy principle, you give your body time to build up your glycogen stores so you are prepared for the next hard workout.

Preventing Illness. Moderate training makes your immune system stronger. Various studies have found that people who get regular exercise have 20 to 50 percent fewer colds than do sedentary folks. After high-intensity and prolonged exercise, however, the immune system is temporarily suppressed, creating an "open window" during which you're at increased risk of infection. Although immune function varies greatly among individuals, studies indicate that the immune systems of healthy, well-trained runners are typically suppressed only after exercise lasting more than 1 hour at about marathon race pace or faster. Immune system suppression after high-intensity running has been found to last from 12 to 72 hours. Interestingly, there is evidence that immune system suppression is linked to carbohydrate depletion and that restocking carbohydrate quickly may help restore your immune function to full strength in less time. The clear implication is to not do another hard training session until your immune function recovers from the previous hard session or race. Allowing at least one easy day before the next hard workout typically provides enough time for your immune system to return to full strength.

Minimizing the Effects of DOMS. Contrary to many runners' beliefs, high levels of lactate (lactic acid) in your muscles aren't what make you sore for several days after a hard effort. Essentially, all the lactate you produce in a race or workout is eliminated from your body within a few hours. DOMS is caused by microscopic muscle damage that occurs primarily from eccentric (lengthening) muscle contractions, such as when you run downhill. During downhill running, your quadriceps muscles contract eccentrically to resist the pull of gravity and keep your knees from buckling. The resulting muscle damage leads to inflammation, which causes soreness. It takes 1 to 2 days for this process of muscle damage, inflammation, and pain to reach a peak, and the effects can last for up to 5 days. While you're experiencing DOMS, your muscles need time to repair. The damaged muscles are also weaker, so any workout done before the soreness goes away not only will be painful but also will likely not be intense enough to improve your marathon fitness.

The physiology of DOMS favors an approach of 2 hard days followed by 2 easy days, because it takes 1 to 2 days for DOMS to kick in, then it takes another couple of days for the soreness to dissipate. By doing back-to-back hard days, you may sneak in your second workout before soreness and muscle weakness develop. You would then have 2 days to recover before the next hard effort.

When to Do Back-to-Back Hard Days

We've seen several reasons why you should follow the hard/easy principle in your training and that a hard day doesn't always have to be followed by an easy day. A pattern of 2 hard days in a row followed by 2 (or more) recovery days may actually allow you to handle, and recover from, more high-quality training. Let's look at two specific situations in which you should do back-to-back hard days.

During weeks that you race, you need to train but also to rest for the race. In *Daniels' Running Formula*, renowned exercise physiologist and coach Jack Daniels, PhD, recommends back-to-back hard days during race weeks rather than alternating hard and easy days (Daniels 2005).

For example, say you're following a strict hard/easy schedule and have a race on Saturday. If you did a long run on the previous Sunday, then you would run hard Tuesday and Thursday and easy on the other days. Doing a hard session on Thursday, however, doesn't make sense because you would still be tired from that effort for Saturday's race. If, however, you do back-to-back harder workouts on Tuesday and Wednesday, as detailed in figure 3.2, you would still get your hard sessions in but would have an extra day to recover for the race. Although this modification still doesn't provide the optimal amount of time to recover for Saturday's race, it's an intelligent compromise that allows you to get your high-quality training while also racing reasonably well.

Another time when you might do 2 hard days in a row is if your weekly schedule is dictated by the Monday-to-Friday workweek. If you're too busy or fatigued during the week to get in regular high-quality training, then you'll want to take advantage of the weekend and squeeze in 2 hard days. This situation is detailed in figure 3.3. Hard days on Saturday and Sunday followed by recovery days on Monday and Tuesday provide a strong training stimulus and 2 full

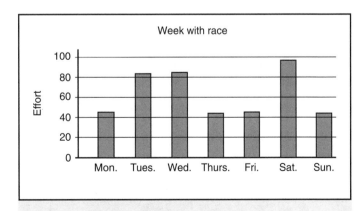

Figure 3.2   **Consecutive hard days during a race week.**

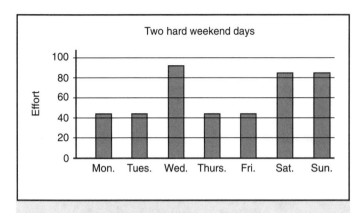

Figure 3.3   **Consecutive hard days on weekends.**

days to recover before the next hard effort on Wednesday. Easy days on Thursday and Friday then leave you well rested for another weekend of hard training. Four of the 5 weekdays become recovery days, and you still get in three hard training sessions per week.

This brings us to the time-honored tradition of racing on Saturday and doing your long run on Sunday. If you race 10K or less, you'll dip into your carbohydrate stores but (assuming that, like most runners, you generally eat a lot of carbohydrate) will most likely not come close to fully depleting your glycogen stores. By eating your normal high-carbohydrate diet, you'll be reasonably topped up with glycogen and ready to handle your long run on Sunday morning. As discussed in chapters 1 and 7, however, after a tune-up race, your long run should be at a more-relaxed pace. If Saturday's race is longer than 15K, however, you'll likely have severely depleted your glycogen stores and may find yourself at less than your best for Sunday's long run. If you race more than 15K on Saturday, skip the long run on Sunday. In that situation, you'll be better off by postponing your long run until you've recovered from the race.

So far, we've considered only the pattern of hard training and recovery within a week. Just as important is the pattern of hard efforts and recovery over the course of your marathon preparation. Week after week of hard training can eventually lead to staleness or overtraining. To adapt optimally, it's best to have several hard training weeks followed by a recovery week. The training schedules in the second section of this book regularly incorporate recovery weeks.

There are several patterns that you can follow. The correct pattern for you depends on how hard you're training, your body's ability to adapt to training, and the sum of other stressors in your life. The most commonly used pattern is 3 hard weeks followed by a recovery week. During the early buildup phase of marathon preparation, some runners can handle 4 high-mileage weeks followed by 1 recovery week. In other cases, 2 hard weeks followed by 1 recovery week is optimal. Again, through trial and error, you'll have to find the pattern that's best for you.

As a general rule, your recovery weeks should include about 70 percent as much training volume as your hard training weeks. For example, if your hard weeks consist of 60 miles (97 km) per week, then you would run about

■ Consecutive Hard Sessions of the Wrong Kind

An old school of thought is to do several hard days in a row "to get used to running on tired legs." Does this idea make sense?

As we've seen, the best way to prepare for marathon conditions is to do high-quality long runs and tempo runs. If you run a 22-miler (35 km) at 40 seconds per mile slower than goal marathon pace, starting relatively fresh, you'll provide a more-specific stimulus to improve your marathon performance than if you start the run fatigued and struggle to run 2 minutes per mile slower than goal marathon pace. At least once every 3 weeks, give yourself the chance to do your long run fresh. You'll feel great on these runs, thereby leading not only to a better effort but also to positive psychological reinforcement.

Doing an interval session or tempo run on tired legs makes no sense whatsoever. The objective of interval training (e.g., 6 × 1,000 m at 5K race pace) is to improve your maximal oxygen consumption. The objective of tempo runs (e.g., 5 mi at 10-mi race pace) is to improve your lactate threshold. If you run these workouts while tired, you'll either do them more slowly than is optimal or you'll have to cut back the volume of the workout (e.g., do fewer intervals or a shorter tempo run). In either case, you'll provide less of a stimulus to improve than if you had started the workout relatively fresh.

42 miles (68 km) during your recovery week. Be sure to reduce the quantity and the intensity of your hard sessions during your recovery week. For example, cut the distance of your long run as well as the pace per mile, and schedule a session of striders rather than a hard $\dot{V}O_2$max session during a recovery week.

Recovery Days (or Easy Days)

So far in this chapter, we've discussed the necessity of incorporating recovery into your training schedule. Following the hard/easy principle, 1 or more hard days are always followed by 1 or more easy days. Easy training days are more appropriately called recovery days because their purpose is to allow you to recover for your next hard effort.

So what constitutes a recovery day? As with most aspects of running, the answer depends on your physiology. Recovery days should be less difficult than hard sessions in the volume (distance) and intensity of training. In some cases, a recovery day should be a day of rest or a day of cross-training.

The most common training mistake marathon runners make is training too hard on recovery days. If you train too hard on a scheduled recovery day, then you'll be a bit tired for your next hard day, and that workout won't go as well as planned. If you're like most runners, you'll be ticked off, and you'll run your next scheduled recovery day a bit harder. So begins a vicious cycle in which your recovery days are done too hard and the quality of your hard days declines. The result is mediocre performances in training and racing. Just as it takes discipline to push through a tempo run when you feel bad, so does it take discipline to train easily when you feel good on a planned recovery day.

The other mistake that marathoners often make is trying to squeeze in too much distance on recovery days. Early in your training program, when the marathon is still more than 8 weeks away, it probably doesn't hurt to add a couple of extra miles to recovery days because the overall intensity of training tends to be rather low. When you're into the last 8 weeks of training, however, you have hard sessions with specific purposes. If you go into your hard days tired from too many slow miles on your recovery days, then your overall progress will be compromised.

Your recovery days shouldn't impose additional training stress on your muscles or your nervous system. You should try, therefore, to minimize the pounding on your legs on those days. Running on soft surfaces on your recovery days will reduce the cumulative impact your legs and back experience over the course of the week. When you consider that your recovery days occur when you're the most tired and when your muscles are the most fatigued and least resilient, it makes sense to take it easy on your muscles on those days. This also implies avoiding hill running on your recovery days, not only because running uphill is likely to require more effort than is optimal for an easy day but also because downhill running tends to induce muscle damage, and you certainly don't want to incur additional muscle damage on a recovery day.

Using a heart monitor is a good way to prevent yourself from training too hard on your recovery days. (See chapters 1 and 7 for information about training by heart rate.) If you keep your heart rate below 76 percent of your maximal heart rate or 70 percent of your heart rate reserve plus your resting heart rate, you'll let your body recover to allow high-quality workouts on your hard training days.

For example, say your resting heart rate is 50 beats per minute and your maximal heart rate is 185 beats per minute. If you train by maximal heart rate, then you would want to keep your heart rate below 141 (185 × .76) on your recovery days. Heart rate reserve is your maximal heart rate minus your resting pulse. In this example, then, your heart rate reserve is 135. If you train using this more-complicated but more-precise method, you would want to keep your heart rate below 144 [resting heart rate of 50 + (135 × .70)] on your recovery days.

The lower-tech way to determine your appropriate recovery training intensity is to run approximately 2 minutes per mile (per 1.6 km) slower than your 10-mile (16 km) to half marathon race pace. For example, if you run the half marathon in 1:18, or just under 6 minutes per mile (per 1.6 km), then your recovery runs should be done at roughly an 8-minute-per-mile (per 1.6 km) pace.

■ Recovery Considerations in the Real World

At his peak, Bill Rodgers used to say that nobody working a full-time job would beat him in the marathon. He knew that even if someone could string together training to match his around the constraints of regular employment, the extra rest and attention to detail that his schedule allowed would give him an edge on race day.

Of course, you're probably not trying to win Boston, nor do you likely have the luxury of quitting your job for the sake of your running. Still, you can hasten your recovery from hard workouts by regularly paying attention to these matters at work.

- **Hydration.** Always have a water bottle at your workstation, and commit to draining it several times a day.
- **Calories.** Keep healthful foods at work so that you can graze throughout the day as opposed to getting so famished that you hit the vending machines in desperation.
- **Posture, part I.** Make sure your computer screen is at eye level and not too far away so that you don't sit with your head tilted and thrust forward all day.
- **Posture, part II.** Even if your computer is set up ideally, it's still easy to sit with a slumped upper body when you're at a desk all day. Sit with your head, shoulders, and hips aligned, and with a slight curve in your lower back. Good posture at work translates into fewer biomechanical woes on the run.
- **Move.** Get up and walk around at least once an hour to lessen the strain on your lower back and hamstrings. If the smokers in your office are allowed to leave their desks throughout the day to tend to their habit, then you should be able to stand and stretch your legs to tend to yours.

In some situations, cross-training is the best type of exercise on recovery days. For marathoners who come out of Sunday long runs feeling beat up, cross-training is the safest option for training on Monday. Your recovery is enhanced by the increased blood flow, but there's no additional pounding on your legs and back. Cross-training is discussed in chapter 4.

Avoiding Overtraining

Overtraining is a danger for any motivated marathoner. In striving to improve your performance, you progressively increase the volume and intensity of your training. At some point, you hit your individual training threshold. When you exceed that threshold, positive adaptation stops, negative adaptation occurs, and your performances in training and racing suffer.

Individual training thresholds vary greatly among runners. Beijing Olympic marathoner Brian Sell handles repeated 150-mile (241 km) weeks, whereas some runners struggle to maintain 40-mile (64 km) weeks. Similarly, some runners can handle 2 hard days of training in succession, whereas others need 3 easy days after each hard workout. Your individual training threshold also changes with time. Sell couldn't always handle such big mileage, but he increased his mileage as his capacity to withstand the stress increased. A detailed training log that you update at least a few times a week will help you discern your limits and how they evolve throughout your running career.

Defining Overtraining

It's important to clarify what overtraining is and isn't. Fatigue for a day or 2 after a hard training session isn't overtraining. In fact, it's a necessary step in the process of recovery and development. When training stress is applied in the appropriate dosage, then you improve at the optimal rate. If your training stress is above the optimal level, you may still improve, but you'll do so at a slower rate. Only above a higher threshold (your individual training threshold) does true overtraining occur.

What's much more common than overtraining is overreaching. Unfortunately, this zone is where many marathoners spend much of their time. Overreaching occurs when you string together too many days of hard training. Your muscle fatigue is most likely primarily from glycogen depletion, and you may simply need time for metabolic recovery. A few days of moderate training combined with a high-carbohydrate diet should quickly remedy the situation. Overreaching can also be caused by dehydration, lack of sleep, or other life stressors on top of your normal training. In all of these cases, your body should rebound in less than a week when the extra stress is removed.

Repeated overreaching eventually leads to overtraining syndrome. The simple explanation for overtraining syndrome is that the combination of training load and other life stressors is greater than the body's ability to recover and adapt positively for a prolonged period of time. The combination of contributing factors and threshold for overtraining syndrome varies greatly among athletes.

The body's response to overtraining may be regulated by the hypothalamus. Located at the base of the brain, the hypothalamus controls body temperature, sugar and fat metabolism, and the release of a variety of hormones; it's essentially your master control center for dealing with stress. When your hypothalamus can't handle the combination of training and other stressors in your life, typical symptoms include fatigue, reduced immune system function, disturbed sleep, decreased motivation, irritability, and poor athletic performance. Chronic inflammatory responses from repeated muscle damage without sufficient recovery have also been hypothesized to contribute to overtraining syndrome.

Overtraining is caused by poor planning and not heeding your body's feedback. In 1998, exercise physiologist Carl Foster, PhD, presented an interesting concept to help avoid overtraining. The concept is based in part on evidence that horses progress after a hard/easy training program but become overtrained when the workload on the easy days is increased. (Stick with us here; this has applications for running.)

The hypothesis is that overtraining is related to both the difficulty of training (the training load) and the "monotony" of training. Monotony of training is a lack of variation in the difficulty of training from day to day. Monotonous training typically consists of 1 moderately hard day after another, whereas varied training consists of a mix of hard days, easy days, and the occasional rest day.

The concept is that training strain is the combined effect of the training load and the training monotony. Foster found that training strain can predict overtraining-related illness and injury, with both load and monotony as contributing factors. This is further evidence that mixing recovery days into your training program is necessary for optimal improvement without breaking down. Again, a good training log can help you here. If you can gain an awareness of the combination of training load and monotony that puts you over the edge, then you can try to adjust these elements for optimal training and optimal marathon performance.

Breaking Out of Overtraining

If you're truly overtrained, you need to take immediate action. The first step is to see a sports physician to check that you don't have an illness that mimics the symptoms of overtraining. The possibility always exists that excessive fatigue is caused by something worse than running. Also ask the physician to check your hemoglobin and ferritin levels to see whether your iron levels are normal (see chapter 2).

Unless you have a particularly severe case of overtraining, 3 to 5 weeks of greatly reduced training should bring your energy level back to normal. It appears that reducing training intensity is more important than reducing training volume in breaking out of overtraining syndrome. Reducing your training intensity so that you're doing only easy aerobic running is the most important step in breaking out of overtraining.

You should, however, also reduce your training volume. The correct amount to reduce your training volume depends on your individual circumstances and how deeply entrenched in overtraining you've become. As a rule of thumb, reducing your mileage by 50 percent should be enough to allow your body to recover. In addition, if you've been training twice a day, it will be necessary to reduce to one training session a day. Your body needs time to recover, and a second workout will slow your progress. For the first several weeks, it's also helpful to have at least 1 day a week off from training.

■ Monitoring Your "Recover-Ability"

Monitoring your body provides valuable information on your adaptation to training, your risk of injury or illness, and your readiness for the next hard training session. There are several good ways to determine when you are overreaching so you can avoid overtraining and remain healthy. You can use this information to improve your recovery by modifying your training schedule.

There are many ways to monitor your recovery, but the simplest measures are often the most useful and the easiest to adhere to. In combination, these measures provide insight into your adaptation to training. Typically, when results on these measures decrease, running performance and recovery deteriorate a few days later. In addition to the details of your training, try recording the following details in your training log, and review your log periodically to find the patterns that predict overtraining, illness, and injury.

- **Weight:** Check your weight at the same time of day each day or several times per week. Decreases in weight over a few days usually indicate dehydration. Decreases in weight over a few weeks can indicate that you are not eating enough calories, have an illness, or are overtraining.

- **Morning heart rate:** Your heart rate when you first wake up in the morning provides an indication of your recovery. It is important to check your heart rate soon after you wake, because it increases as soon as you start thinking about your plans for the day and by about 10 beats per minute when you get up. In addition, waking to an alarm can increase your heart rate and make the data less reliable.

- To find your resting heart rate, therefore, take your pulse immediately upon waking for several days. Your true resting heart rate is the lowest rate you find. If your morning heart rate is more than 5 beats per minute higher than usual, this may be an indication of inadequate recovery or illness. An elevated morning heart rate can be particularly useful in preventing illness, as the increased heart rate is often the first sign that you are not well.

- **Environmental conditions:** Record the temperature and humidity on hot days. Because of increased core body temperature and dehydration, your body undergoes substantially more stress when you run at 80 degrees Fahrenheit (27 degrees Celsius) and 80 percent humidity than at 60 degrees Fahrenheit (16 degrees Celsius) and low humidity. If you train hard or compete on a hot, humid day, the heat you generate can overwhelm your body's ability to eliminate heat, causing your core temperature to climb, which can greatly increase recovery time. Similarly, as discussed in chapter 2, dehydration also increases recovery time. There's great variation in how runners are affected by heat. Your training log will reveal patterns that can help you make needed adjustments during a stretch of hot weather.

- **Hours of sleep:** The number of hours of sleep that you obtain is not particularly important for any one night. Over several nights, however, your quantity of sleep can influence your recovery and ability to adapt positively to training. Your quantity of sleep is one of several measures that, in combination, can explain a lack of recovery and can indicate needed lifestyle changes to help prevent illness or injury.

- **Quality of sleep:** The quality of your sleep is arguably more important than the number of hours. Evaluate the quality of your sleep each night—How soundly did you sleep? Were you awake a lot in the middle of the night? Did you get out of bed feeling refreshed?—and try to be as consistent as possible in your assessment. A reduction in quality of sleep is often associated with overtraining. Reduced sleep quality can also be caused by nonrunning stressors, but the result for your running performance is the same.

- **Diet quality:** Evaluate the overall quality of your diet each day—Were each of your meals balanced? Did you get so hungry that you binged? Did the bulk of your calories come from fresh grains, fruits and vegetables and lean sources of protein?—and try to be as consistent as possible in your assessment. Often, a lack of energy can be traced back to poor diet in the previous few days.

- **Hydration level:** Dehydration has an immediate effect on running performance and slows recovery from training. Evaluate your hydration level each day—Was your urine clear throughout the day? Did you drink small amounts regularly so that you seldom felt thirsty? Did your mouth and throat often feel dry?—and try to be as consistent as possible in your assessment. Your daily weight provides a good indication of your hydration level.

- **Muscle soreness:** It is not unusual for runners to have slightly sore muscles most of the time. An increase in muscle soreness can be due to a hard workout or running downhill. Evaluate your general muscle soreness each day—Were any of your leg muscles much more sore than others? Did your soreness lessen after a few miles of running? Did your soreness seem explainable by your most recent workouts?—and try to be as consistent as possible in your assessment. If increased general muscle soreness lasts more than 4 or 5 days, then it is likely that you are ill or overreaching. Soreness in a specific muscle indicates a potential injury, whereas more-general muscle soreness provides an indication of your recovery and adaptation to training.

- **Energy level:** An assessment of energy level is one of the best indications of recovery from training. Evaluate your energy level each day—Did you have the energy to accomplish your running and daily life goals? Did you feel alert and focused when running or performing a task? Were you willing to undertake activities that required effort, or did you dread them?—and try to be as consistent as possible in your assessment. If your energy level is reduced for more than 3 days, it is important to determine the cause of the reduction. Typical causes of reduced energy levels are lack of carbohydrate intake, training hard too many days in a row, illness, low iron levels, dehydration, and lack of sleep. By reviewing your training log and considering your lifestyle factors, you should be able to identify the likely cause of a low energy level.

(continued)

"Recover-Ability" *(continued)*

■ **Heart rate at a standard pace:** If your heart rate at a set pace is more than about 7 beats per minute higher than usual, then you may not be recovered from your previous training sessions. For example, if your heart rate at an 8-minute-per-mile pace is typically 145 beats per minute, and one day you find it is 155 beats per minute at that pace, then you likely need additional recovery before doing your next hard training session. Heart rate during running at a given pace varies by a few beats per minute from day to day, and it is also influenced by factors such as dehydration and hot or humid conditions, so take this into consideration in evaluating the implications of a higher-than-usual heart rate.

In some cases of overtraining syndrome, a contributing factor is an imbalance between calories consumed and calories used. When you have a caloric deficit for a prolonged period in combination with hard training, your body's hormonal system undergoes modifications that are associated with overtraining syndrome. In this situation, body weight may stay the same or only slightly decrease because your metabolic rate drops as your body attempts to adjust to fewer calories. According to Suzanne Girard Eberle, MS, RD, author of *Endurance Sports Nutrition* (2007), "It appears that the combined effects of chronic dieting and exercise may induce the body to conserve energy (calories) or become more efficient at using the available energy" (page 145). She notes, "Frequent colds, slow recoveries from workouts, nagging injuries, chronic fatigue, and, for women runners, the loss of menstrual periods are the true red flags that you're not consuming enough calories to meet the energy demands of training and racing."

Increasing caloric intake while simultaneously reducing training load will eliminate the caloric deficit and should allow your hormonal system to return to normal.

Techniques to Speed Recovery

In addition to finding the correct balance in your training and optimizing your diet, there are a variety of techniques you can use to enhance your body's rate of recovery. Two traditional aids to recovery from marathon training are hot/cold contrast therapy and massage therapy; compression apparel may also be helpful. Adequate postworkout nutrition and thorough cool-down practices have well-documented recovery benefits.

Hot/Cold Contrast Therapy

Hot/cold contrast therapy was initially most popular in team sports but is now widely used by endurance athletes from a variety of sports. Olympic

Deena Kastor

Fastest Marathon: 2:19:36 (American record)
Marathon Highlights:
Third place, 2004 Olympics;
First place, 2005 Chicago,
2006 London, and 2008 U.S.
Olympic Trials.

© AP Photo/Darron Cummings

Deena Kastor won the 2008 Olympic Marathon Trials more than nine years after she first won a national title (that one being in cross country). In the interim, she set American records at distances ranging from 10,000 meters to the marathon and, most famously, won the bronze medal in the 2004 Olympic marathon.

Other than the broken foot she suffered during the 2008 Olympic marathon, she has remained remarkably resilient despite all those 120-mile weeks. Even more impressive, she has remained as hungry and dedicated as when she was up and coming, despite having achieved enough for two satisfying world-class running careers. How has she managed to stay fresh and focused, and what can the rest of us learn from her on this crucial matter?

Kastor views her training as a full-time pursuit. That means more than just putting in a lot of miles, doing regular core strength workouts, and performing the drills and other activities that challenge her body and mind. It means that, in addition to all the physical work, she places supreme importance on recovery. She's acutely aware that what she does when she is not physically working determines how well she absorbs the benefits of a given session, whether it's a long run on the roads or a strength session in the gym. As a result, she naps almost daily, gets plenty of sleep at night, begins refueling and rehydrating almost immediately after running, and chooses between-workout activities that require little physical or mental strain.

Of course, Kastor is a professional runner—being meticulous about recovery is as much a part of her job as following the economies of developing nations is part of a bond trader's. Most of us can't take daily naps and can't always control what occurs between our runs. Nonetheless, we can—especially during a marathon buildup—eliminate as many outside stressors that drain our physical and mental energy as possible and we can try to get to bed a bit earlier. If this sounds like a lot of sacrifices, take another lesson from Kastor. She says, "We don't make sacrifices. If we truly

(continued)

Deena Kastor *(continued)*

love this sport, and we have these goals and dreams, they're not sacrifices. They're choices that we make to fulfill our goals and dreams."

Having those "goals and dreams" is what has helped Kastor stay so motivated for so long. She excels at selecting as her next major goal one that is most personally meaningful to her. Once she's set the goal, everything else falls into place, and she can honestly view her lifestyle as being filled not with sacrifices, but with choices that help her reach her goal. That same mind-set is available to all marathoners.

marathon medalists Deena Kastor and Meb Keflezighi are known for placing great emphasis on this therapy to speed their recovery.

Contrast therapy should ideally be used within about 20 minutes of running and consists of alternately submerging yourself in hot and cold water, generally using bathtubs or portable tubs at home or facilities at a fitness club. It is an extension of the use of heat and cold for physical therapy for injuries. The hot water is typically about 95 degrees Fahrenheit (35 degrees Celsius), and the cold water is in the range of 50 to 60 degrees Fahrenheit (10-16 degrees Celsius). There is obviously a danger in making the water too cold or too hot. For team sports, the athlete is ordinarily in the hot water two to three times longer than the cold water. For example, a typical protocol is 2 to 3 minutes hot followed by 1 minute cold, repeating the cycle three times. Athletes that Pete coaches find the cold most beneficial and like to alternate 4 minutes in cold water with a 2-minute hot shower. They typically finish with hot water in the winter and cold in the summer.

Here are three practical alternatives for contrast therapy at home:

1. Fill the bathtub with cold water, and alternately soak in the bath for 1 minute followed by a hot shower for 2 to 3 minutes.
2. On a hot day, alternate a cold bath (or a dip in the ocean or a lake) with simply getting out into the warm air.
3. Alternate hot and cold water in the shower. Although showering is not as effective as water submersion, it is far easier and more practical.

There is evidence that hot/cold contrast therapy causes alternating dilation and constriction of blood vessels to improve blood flow, thereby increasing elimination of lactate and other products of hard exercise. Contrast therapy also enhances relaxation, which reduces the metabolic rate and can increase the "perception" of recovery. Other unsubstantiated claims for contrast therapy include reduced inflammation and reduced DOMS.

Massage

Running causes muscle tightness and damage to muscle fibers. Your muscle fibers need time for repair and recovery before they can work optimally again. If you train hard before allowing your muscles to recover properly, then you're likely to have a subpar workout using sore and tired muscles and your risk of injury will increase.

Massage therapy is widely used by competitive marathoners to improve recovery and prevent injury. Unfortunately, it is very difficult to design a scientific study to evaluate the benefits of massage. As a result, there is little scientific evidence but much anecdotal evidence for the benefits of massage therapy for athletes in general, and distance runners in particular.

The established benefits of massage are improved blood flow to the massaged area, enhanced muscle relaxation, improved mobility and flexibility of the muscle and surrounding connective tissue, general relaxation of the athlete, breakdown of scar tissue, and identification of tight areas before they lead to injury. Interestingly, research with horses has shown that massage therapy can increase both range of motion and stride length. These results with horses eliminate the placebo effect, which is one of the problems with massage studies conducted with human subjects, and indicate that, with the correct technique, there can be a performance benefit from massage.

If you can afford massage, anecdotal evidence suggests that it will help you recover more quickly from hard marathon training. To be effective, sports massage should be "pleasantly uncomfortable" (i.e., it shouldn't be gentle). It is beneficial to supplement massage sessions with self-massage on tight muscles that can be easily reached, such as the quadriceps, calf muscles, and feet.

There are many different types of massage therapy, and as with any discipline there are wide ranges in expertise among massage therapists. Since the industry is relatively unregulated, it is best to use a massage therapist who is a member of the American Massage Therapy Association (or a similar national organization in other countries) and has been recommended by other runners, so you can be confident that the sessions will be effective.

Postworkout Nutrition

If you're like a lot of runners, your postworkout routine goes something like this: Stretch, drink water, shower, and get on with the rest of the day. Food? That can wait until you're hungry, right?

Not if you want to feel your best on your next run. The sooner you replenish your glycogen stores by taking in some calories, the quicker you'll recover for the next day's training. The crucial period is the first hour after your run. If you wait until after then, your body's ability to absorb and make glycogen out of what you consume drops by an astounding 66 percent, and you'll likely feel sluggish the next day.

Shoot for consuming 300 to 400 calories during this recovery window. In this time, your body can best make glycogen out of simple sources of carbohydrate—think fruit, smoothies, sports drinks, and sports bars. In addition, research has shown that a little protein—about 1 gram of protein for every 4 grams of carbohydrate—will speed the process of replenishing glycogen.

Compression Apparel

Do compression tights speed recovery? Probably. Over the past few years, compression tights and compression socks have become widely available to wear during training and recovery. Compression apparel applies external pressure to the muscle groups; the most effective products apply graduated pressure, which reduces from the foot or ankle up the leg to the hip. Manufacturers make many claims for the benefits of compression apparel, including improved venous return of blood to the heart, increased lactate flushing, faster muscle repair, and reduced fatigue.

Research on compression clothing is evolving rapidly, but anecdotal evidence suggests that compression tights and knee-high socks are useful for runners both during training and as an aid in recovery. Marathon world-record holder Paula Radcliffe certainly seems to think they work. Even if you don't wear them running, compression socks can help a traveling marathoner during plane flights, as they are particularly useful for reducing stiffness and swollen ankles when flying.

Cooling Down

The purpose of cooling down after a hard run is to help return your body to preexercise conditions. This is the critical first step in managing your recovery from high-intensity training or racing. A thorough cool-down improves your recovery by removing lactate from your muscles and blood more quickly, reducing adrenaline levels, and reducing muscle stiffness, which decreases your likelihood of future injury.

- **Increased Lactate Removal**. After hard intervals or tune-up races, an important role of the cool-down is to remove the lactate that has accumulated in your muscles and blood. Lactate levels decrease more quickly when you do a cool-down run because blood flow is maintained at a higher level, which increases movement of lactate out of your muscles and also increases the rate at which your muscles oxidize the lactate to produce energy.

- **Reduced Adrenaline Levels.** Adrenaline and noradrenaline are hormones that increase the rate and force at which your heart contracts, increase blood pressure, increase your rate and depth of breathing,

■ The Importance of Sleep for Recovery

Getting a good night's sleep is important for recovery and positive adaptation to training. Running generally improves both the quantity and quality of sleep, but overtraining can interfere with sleep patterns. No one knows for sure how exercise leads to improved sleep, but the mechanism may be a change in the balance of sympathetic to parasympathetic nervous system activity. Stimulation of the sympathetic nervous system increases heart rate, blood pressure, metabolic rate, and mental activity, all of which are counterproductive to falling asleep. Parasympathetic activity has the opposite effect. During running, sympathetic activity increases, but endurance training leads to a decrease in sympathetic activity relative to parasympathetic activity when you are not exercising. This alteration in the balance of sympathetic to parasympathetic activity may allow you to fall asleep more quickly and to sleep more deeply.

A change in sleeping habits is an early warning sign of overtraining. The physical and psychological stress of training beyond your individual threshold may stimulate the sympathetic nervous system, leading to irritability and reducing the quality and quantity of sleep. A reduction in sleep is a double-edged sword for a runner because much of the body's recovery and rebuilding occurs during sleep. During preparation for your marathon, you should ensure that you get adequate sleep, or you may experience a decline in performance, have immune system depression, and be more prone to injury.

When you have uncharacteristic difficulty sleeping, you could be training hard too frequently. You may be able to improve your sleep fairly easily by backing off your training and not running too late in the day. The harder you run, the greater the stimulus to your nervous system, so cutting back your training intensity will likely benefit your ability to sleep more than cutting back your mileage.

To improve your sleep pattern, stick with a routine that works for you. Eating dinner and going to bed at approximately the same time each day will help set your body clock, so that your body and mind automatically shut down at the same time each night. In addition, avoid bright lights at night, and avoid caffeinated or alcoholic beverages for several hours before bedtime. Finally, avoid lying down until you are ready to go to sleep so that when you do lie down it provides another signal to ease your mind toward sleep.

and increase the rate at which your muscles break down glycogen. Adrenaline and noradrenaline levels in your blood increase rapidly when you run hard. Adrenaline levels typically decrease to resting levels in less than an hour, but noradrenaline levels can take several hours to return to resting levels. An active cool-down helps get these hormones out of your system, which helps your body recover more quickly.

■ **Reduced Muscle Stiffness.** Cooling down also improves recovery by reducing muscle stiffness. A relaxing cool-down makes the muscles more resilient, which can reduce the risk of injury after a race or hard workout.

Your cool-down should start with easy running for 10 to 20 minutes. (If you're too tired to run, then walk for an equivalent amount of time, or try some easy cross-training.) The optimal clearance of lactate, adrenaline, and so on occurs if you start your cool-down run at about 60 to 75 percent of your maximum heart rate and slow down to a slow jog or walk for the last 5 minutes. After running, your muscles are warm and have very good blood flow, which increases their ability to stretch without injury, so this is the perfect time to gently stretch your muscles.

© AP Photo/Kuni

Because muscles are warm and therefore less susceptible to injury, after a run is a great time to gently stretch.

In this chapter, we look at how ensuring adequate recovery allows you to get the most from your long runs and hard workouts. Successful marathoning, however, often involves more than just running. Just as true recovery days can mean the difference between adequate and optimal progress in your training, supplemental training, such as flexibility work and strength training, can help you get the biggest bang for your marathon-training buck.

Supplementary Training

This chapter focuses on several important aspects of training that can make the difference between mediocrity and marathoning excellence. The chapter discusses five types of supplementary training that often get lumped into the category of cross-training but that really deserve to be treated separately.

First we look at the importance of flexibility for marathon performance and how to improve it. Next we examine core stability training, which is a vitally important but often overlooked aspect of training, particularly for marathoners. Third, we look at whether strength training is beneficial for marathoners and how to incorporate it into your overall training program. Then we describe a few technique drills that can improve your running form. Finally we discuss various forms of aerobic cross-training that will enhance your cardiovascular fitness and reduce your likelihood of incurring injuries.

For the flexibility, core, resistance, and form exercises, we've given a brief explanation of how the exercise in question benefits marathoners. If you have an especially hard time with any of the exercises, you're most likely weak or tight—or both!—in that area. Addressing your most troublesome areas will lead to faster, more enjoyable training and racing. Figure 4.1 provides a diagram of the muscles of the body to use a reference when performing the stretches and exercises in this chapter.

Supplementary work, especially core stability training, form drills, and flexibility exercises, is easy to skip when you're tired and your main training goal is getting in your long runs and tempo runs. These extra sessions, however, will provide refreshing variety to your training. Even more important, by correcting imbalances and weaknesses in your body, they can contribute to better running form. With that improved form, you can train harder and longer at a lower risk of injury, and you will be able to maintain a more-effective running technique throughout the marathon. When scheduling your training, count time for these sessions as an integral part of your marathon preparation.

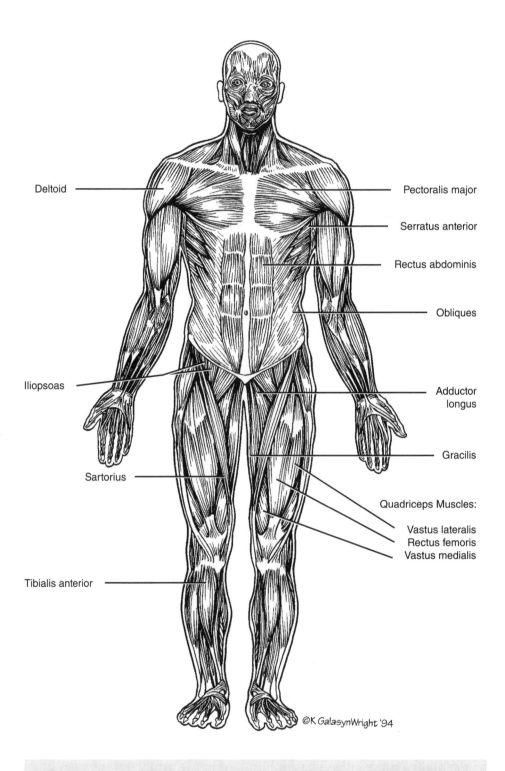

Deltoid

Pectoralis major

Serratus anterior

Rectus abdominis

Obliques

Iliopsoas

Adductor longus

Gracilis

Sartorius

Quadriceps Muscles:

Vastus lateralis
Rectus femoris
Vastus medialis

Tibialis anterior

©K GalasynWright '94

Figure 4.1 Use these diagrams as a reference for locating the muscles worked in the stretches and exercises that are provided in this chapter.

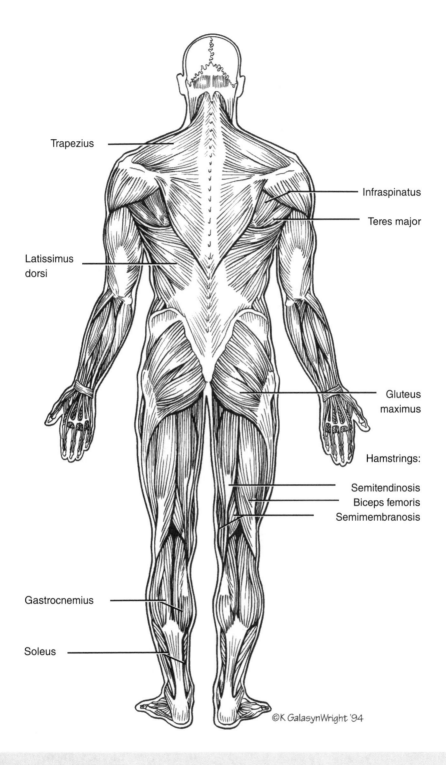

Trapezius

Infraspinatus

Teres major

Latissimus dorsi

Gluteus maximus

Hamstrings:

Semitendinosis
Biceps femoris
Semimembranosis

Gastrocnemius

Soleus

©K GalasynWright '94

Figure 4.1 *(continued)*.

Flexibility Training

Marathon training takes a toll on the body. One of the greatest costs of all that mileage is a loss of flexibility. Improving your natural range of motion can improve your running technique and increase your stride length while reducing your risk of injury.

Tight muscles provide resistance that limits your ability to stride out. Stretching not only increases your muscle length but also improves the length of the connective tissue surrounding the muscle fibers. Your regular stretching routine before and after running helps maintain your flexibility but is unlikely to improve it. To achieve gains in flexibility, include one or two training sessions of at least 30 minutes per week devoted to flexibility exercises or yoga.

Always do your stretching when your muscles are warmed up. A warm muscle stretches more easily and greatly reduces the likelihood of injury while stretching. If you're doing a specific flexibility training session, then walk, jog, or cycle for 5 minutes or so to improve the blood flow in your muscles. If you're doing a normal training run, then warm up for 5 minutes and stretch before starting the run. We know you've probably heard this advice before, and you probably know some good runners in your area who pride themselves on never stretching, but there's no getting around the facts: Even a small amount of stretching before running will improve the flow of your running and help improve your running form. After running, try to allow a minimum of 10 minutes for stretching your major muscle groups.

Stretching should be firm enough to create adequate tension in the muscle, but gentle enough that your muscles can relax. If you stretch aggressively, your muscles will tighten in a protective reflex to prevent straining or tearing of muscle fibers. You need to stretch gently and consistently to obtain improved length in the muscle and surrounding connective tissue.

There are several schools of thought on how long to stretch and how many times to repeat a stretch. The traditional recommendation is to hold a stretch for at least 30 seconds and to do each stretch once or twice. To strike an optimal balance between effectiveness and time-efficiency, we recommend holding stretches for 20 to 30 seconds and repeating each stretch twice.

Be sure to breathe while you stretch. Some runners inadvertently hold their breath while stretching, thereby reducing stretching's effectiveness.

Two important areas for marathoners to focus on are the hip flexors and hamstrings. Your hip flexors (primarily iliopsoas and rectus femoris) are the muscles that lift your thigh relative to your hip. These are some of the strongest muscles in the body, and they tend to become short and inflexible in runners. Improving the flexibility of your hip flexors increases your thigh's ability to move back relative to your pelvis, thereby allowing your stride length to increase.

Tight hamstrings restrict your stride length by preventing your thigh from swinging forward completely. The combination of tight hip flexors and tight hamstrings causes the familiar marathoners' shuffle. Stretching your hamstrings consistently (a slow but steady process) will allow your stride to increase to its natural length.

The following program provides total-body stretches and is recommended if you're serious about improving your flexibility. It's ideal for after your run, or you can do it as a stand-alone session after a few minutes of walking, jogging, or cycling to warm your muscles.

Do each stretch twice. Perform the first repetition with a gentle intensity and the second stretch with a moderate intensity. Don't stretch forcefully. If you don't have time to do the entire program, then select the exercises that work your tightest muscles.

TABLE 4.1

24-Minute Flexibility Program

Exercise	Repetitions	Duration of stretch
1. Bent-leg calf stretch	2 per side	20-30 seconds
2. Straight-leg calf stretch	2 per side	20-30 seconds
3. Kneeling hamstring stretch	2 per side	20-30 seconds
4. Lying hamstring stretch	2 per side	20-30 seconds
5. Quadriceps stretch	2 per side	20-30 seconds
6. Hip flexor stretch	2 per side	20-30 seconds
7. Gluteal stretch	2 per side	20-30 seconds
8. Hip rotation stretch	2 per side	20-30 seconds
9. Swiss ball shoulder and lat stretch	2	20-30 seconds
10. Swiss ball chest stretch	2 per side	20-30 seconds
11. Swiss ball lower back stretch	2	20-30 seconds
12. Downward dog	2	20-30 seconds

Program Notes

- Perform two repetitions of each stretch before moving to the next stretch.
- Breathe normally while stretching; don't hold your breath.
- Don't stretch an area that's painful.

EXERCISE 1: BENT-LEG CALF STRETCH

How many: 2 repetitions of 20 to 30 seconds per side

How it helps: improves flexibility of soleus (deep/lower calf) muscles

How to do it:

Stand an arm's length away from the wall, with your feet shoulder-width apart and toes pointing directly forward.

Slide your right foot back so that your weight is over your left foot, as shown.

Slowly bend your left knee until you feel a stretch in the lower calf muscle.

Repeat on the other side.

EXERCISE 2: STRAIGHT-LEG CALF STRETCH

How many: 2 repetitions of 20 to 30 seconds per side

How it helps: improves flexibility of gastrocnemius (upper calf) muscles

How to do it:

Stand an arm's length away from a wall, with your feet shoulder-width apart and toes pointing directly forward.

Take one step and lean forward so that your hands are flat on the wall as shown.

Keep your back foot flat on the floor and your back knee straight.

Slowly move your hips forward until you feel a stretch in the calf muscle of the back leg.

Repeat on the other side.

EXERCISE 3: KNEELING HAMSTRING STRETCH

How many: 2 repetitions of 20 to 30 seconds per side

How it helps: improves flexibility of hamstring muscles

How to do it:

Kneel on the floor.

Lift one knee and move it out in front of you so that the leg is straight and the heel is on the floor.

Your toes should be pointing forward rather than straight up at the ceiling.

While keeping a slight arch in your lower back and the rest of your back as straight as possible, lean forward until you feel a stretch in your hamstrings.

Repeat on the other side.

EXERCISE 4: LYING HAMSTRING STRETCH

How many: 2 repetitions of 20 to 30 seconds per side

How it helps: improves flexibility of hamstring muscles

How to do it:

Lie on your back on the floor.

Lift one leg up, keeping it relatively straight, and join your hands behind your thigh as shown.

Pull your leg toward you until you feel a stretch in your hamstring muscle.

Repeat on the other side.

EXERCISE 5: QUADRICEPS STRETCH

How many: 2 repetitions of 20 to 30 seconds per side

How it helps: improves flexibility of quadriceps muscles (major muscles that straighten the knee)

How to do it:

Stand near a wall for balance.

Lift your left foot off the floor, bend your left knee, and pull your left heel toward your buttocks as shown until you feel a stretch in the quadriceps.

Don't lean forward or allow your lower back to arch.

Repeat on the other side.

EXERCISE 6: HIP FLEXOR STRETCH

How many: 2 repetitions of 20 to 30 seconds per side

How it helps: improves flexibility of hip flexors (muscles connecting front of hip to trunk)

How to do it:

Start in a kneeling position, and move one leg forward so that your foot is flat on the floor and your front shin is approximately vertical.

While keeping your upper body vertical and head up, move your hips forward as shown until you feel a stretch across the front of your hip.

Repeat on the other side.

EXERCISE 7: GLUTEAL STRETCH

How many: 2 repetitions of 20 to 30 seconds per side

How it helps: improves flexibility of gluteal (butt) and external rotator muscles

How to do it:

Lie on your back on the floor, with knees and hips bent to 90 degrees and feet flat against a wall.

Cross your right ankle over your left knee, and push the inside of your right knee toward the wall as shown until you feel a stretch on the outside of your right hip.

Repeat on the other side.

EXERCISE 8: HIP ROTATION STRETCH

How many: 2 repetitions of 20 to 30 seconds per side

How it helps: improves hip rotation by stretching gluteals and muscles of the lower back

How to do it:

Lie on your back on the floor, with arms out to the side and legs outstretched. Lift one leg off the floor, bending it at the knee and the hip to 90 degrees.

Rotate the bent leg across your body as shown until you feel a stretch in your hip, torso, and lower back.

Use your hand to push the bent leg across your body and toward the floor. Keep your head and shoulders in contact with the floor.

Repeat on the other side.

EXERCISE 9: SWISS BALL SHOULDER AND LAT STRETCH

How many: 2 repetitions of 20 to 30 seconds

How it helps: improves flexibility of shoulders, upper chest, and back

How to do it:

Kneel in front of the Swiss ball, stretch your arms out in front of you, and rest both hands on the ball as shown.

With your upper body horizontal and head looking straight down at the floor, slowly push your chest downward toward the floor until you feel a stretch through your chest, upper back, and shoulders.

EXERCISE 10: SWISS BALL CHEST STRETCH

How many: 2 repetitions of 20 to 30 seconds per side

How it helps: improves flexibility of chest and shoulders

How to do it:

Kneel on the ground with a Swiss ball positioned beside you.

Place one arm on the Swiss ball, and bend your elbow to 90 degrees as shown.

Keep the other arm on the floor to provide balance and support.

Gently push your upper body toward the floor until you feel a stretch through your chest and shoulder.

Repeat on the other side.

This exercise can also be performed with your arm straight.

EXERCISE 11: SWISS BALL LOWER BACK STRETCH

How many: 2 repetitions of 20 to 30 seconds

How it helps: improves flexibility of lower back and abdominal muscles

How to do it:

Sit on the Swiss ball, with your feet flat on the floor.

Slowly roll your hips forward over the ball, and lean back so that you're lying over the ball as shown.

You should feel a gentle stretch in your lower back and abdominal muscles.

Reach above your head only as far as is comfortable.

EXERCISE 12: DOWNWARD DOG

How many: 2 repetitions of 20 to 30 seconds

How it helps: lengthens spine and improves flexibility of shoulders, hamstrings, and calf muscles

How to do it:

Kneel down and lean forward, with your arms outstretched and your hands pressed firmly against the floor (photo *a*).

Slowly lift your hips in the air by straightening your knees until you feel a stretch in your hamstrings (photo *b*). Depending on your level of flexibility, you might not be able to get your legs completely straight.

Keep your back straight and your head down throughout the stretch, as shown.

Rising up and down onto the toes while in the downward dog position alters the stretch in the hamstring and calf muscles.

Core Stability Training

Long-distance running develops muscular endurance in specific leg and hip muscles and is wonderful for your cardiovascular system, but it tends to make some muscles strong and tight while others remain weak. Modern lifestyles, which often consist of sitting for long periods, exacerbate these problems. Core stability training—also called proximal stability training because *proximal* means close to the center of the body—can eliminate these imbalances, thereby preventing injuries and reducing the degree to which your form deteriorates as you fatigue during the marathon. Core stability training consists of strengthening your abdominal, hip, lower back, and gluteal (butt) muscles using a series of exercises. You don't need a gym or machines, just the dedication to stick with the exercises.

When you run, your trunk acts as a fixed base while your legs work as levers relative to that base to propel you forward. If the torso and pelvic muscles that form your fixed base are weak or fatigue quickly, then you can't maintain an efficient body position while running. By improving the strength and muscular endurance of your pelvis and torso, you provide a more-stable base of support for your legs to work from. This improvement will allow you to maintain your stride length throughout the marathon; part of the reason that many marathoners slow as the race progresses is that their stride shortens as they tire.

In addition, runners often have weak abdominal muscles, which allows the pelvis to rotate forward and put more stretch on the hamstrings. This is a less-efficient position for your running and also increases your risk of lower back problems. Proximal stability exercises strengthen the abdominal muscles and work on other stabilizer muscles of the pelvis and trunk. By improving the position of your pelvis, you create a more stable base.

Elite marathoners increasingly incorporate core work into their training. Olympic bronze medalist Deena Kastor and her teammate Ryan Hall, for example, do lengthy sessions every week. The results can be seen both in their low incidence of injury and in their late-race form, which varies little from the form they exhibit in the early miles.

Core stability training should generally be done three times a week. You can do this type of training year-round.

Following are two core strength training programs. The first program contains basic exercises for runners who don't have much experience with core conditioning. The second program (beginning on page 90) is more advanced and includes more-difficult exercises. For optimal results, do one of these programs three times per week. If you don't want to do the whole program, select at least a few from this list that most target your weakest, tightest areas.

TABLE 4.2

Basic Core Strength Session

Exercise	Details
1. Abdominal crunch	20 repetitions
2. Leg pushaway	20 repetitions
3. Swiss ball lying bridge	6 repetitions of 5 seconds
4. Swiss ball superman	12 repetitions
5. Prone hover	4 repetitions of 5-15 seconds

Perform this sequence of exercises twice.

Program Notes

- Perform these five exercises as a circuit. That is, do one set of the first exercise, then move immediately to the second exercise, then the third, and so on. When you have completed the fifth exercise, return to the first exercise and complete a second circuit.

- Rest briefly (15 to 20 seconds) between exercises and 1 to 2 minutes between sets.

EXERCISE 1: ABDOMINAL CRUNCH

How many: 20 per set

How it helps: strengthens anterior abdominal muscles (i.e., "six-pack abs"), which contribute to force production and running speed; increases ability to maintain a level pelvis

How to do it:

Lie on your back, with your knees bent and feet flat on the floor.

Place your arms on the floor by your sides, with palms facing down as shown (photo a).

Push your lower back into the floor.

Lift your head, shoulders, and upper back off the floor.

Slide your arms along the floor, and concentrate on curling your upper trunk as much as possible (photo b).

Slowly return to the start position.

EXERCISE 2: LEG PUSHAWAY

How many: 20 per set

How it helps: improves ability to activate the deep core muscles for better control of the hips and trunk; improves stability and ability to maintain effective running technique

How to do it:

Lie on your back, with your knees bent and feet flat on the floor.

Place your hands on your hips as shown (photo a).

Contract your lower abdominal muscles, and push your lower back toward the floor.

While holding this lower abdominal contraction, make sure you can breathe and speak normally. Don't hold your breath.

Slowly lift one foot off the floor, and raise it until your thigh is vertical (photo b).

Return to the start position, and repeat with the opposite leg.

Your goal during the exercise is to maintain the lower abdominal contraction as you move your legs up and down so that your back does not arch and your hips do not move.

EXERCISE 3: SWISS BALL LYING BRIDGE

How many: 6 repetitions of 5 seconds each per set

How it helps: strengthens hips, lower back, and gluteals to allow full hip extension and a longer stride

How to do it:

Lie on the floor, with your legs up on a Swiss ball and your feet together (photo *a*).

Place your arms flat on the floor by your sides to provide balance.

Raise your hips off the ground as shown so that your body is in a straight line from your shoulders to your heels (photo *b*).

Hold for 5 seconds, lower your body to the ground, rest briefly, and repeat.

EXERCISE 4: SWISS BALL SUPERMAN

How many: 12 repetitions per set

How it helps: strengthens lower back and gluteals; improves balance and coordination, thereby increasing ability to maintain good running posture when fatigued

How to do it:

Lie over the Swiss ball as shown, with hands flat on the floor and feet in contact with the floor (photo *a*).

Lift one arm and the opposite leg off the floor as shown (photo *b*), hold for 2 or 3 seconds, then return to the floor and repeat with the opposite side.

Aim to bring the arm and leg to a horizontal position when you lift them.

EXERCISE 5: PRONE HOVER

How many: 4 repetitions of 5 to 15 seconds each per set

How it helps: engages most core muscles; decreases undesirable lateral midsection movement when running to maintain optimal running technique

How to do it:

Lie facedown, with your weight supported on your toes and forearms.

Your elbows should be shoulder-width apart and directly under your shoulders, and your feet should be slightly apart.

Maintain your head in alignment with your spine. (Don't look ahead or to the side.)

Hold this position for 5 to 15 seconds, drop your knees to the floor, rest briefly, and repeat.

TABLE 4.3

Advanced Core Strength Session

Exercise	Details
1. Abdominal crunch (advanced)	20 repetitions
2. Leg pushaway (advanced)	20 repetitions
3. Staff	6 repetitions of 5 seconds
4. Standing knee hold	12 repetitions
5. Back extension	12 repetitions
6. Side hover	3 repetitions of 10 seconds per side

Perform this sequence of exercises twice.

Program Notes

- Perform these six exercises in a circuit. That is, do one set of the first exercise, then move immediately to the second exercise, then the third, and so on. When you have completed the sixth exercise, return to the first exercise and complete a second circuit.

- Rest briefly (15 to 20 seconds) between exercises and 1 to 2 minutes between sets.

EXERCISE 1: ABDOMINAL CRUNCH (ADVANCED)

How many: 20 repetitions per set

How it helps: further strengthens anterior abdominal muscles (i.e., "six-pack abs"), which contribute to force production and running speed; increases ability to maintain a level pelvis

How to do it:

Lie on your back, with your knees bent and feet flat on the floor.

Place your fingertips on the side of your head, with elbows held out wide and palms facing up as shown.

Push your lower back into the floor.

Lift your head, shoulders, and upper back off the floor.

Concentrate on curling your upper trunk as much as possible.

Slowly return to the start position.

EXERCISE 2: LEG PUSHAWAY (ADVANCED)

How many: 20 repetitions per set

How it helps: improves ability to activate the deep core muscles for better control of the hips and trunk; improves stability and ability to maintain effective running technique

How to do it:

Lie on the floor, with your knees and hips bent at 90 degrees so that your thighs are vertical and your feet are off the ground.

Place your hands on your hips as shown. Contract your lower abdominal muscles, and push your lower back toward the floor (photo a).

While holding this lower abdominal contraction, make sure you can breathe and speak normally. Don't hold your breath.

Slowly lower one foot until the heel touches the floor (photo b).

Return to the start position, and repeat with the opposite leg.

EXERCISE 3: STAFF

How many: 6 repetitions of 5 seconds each per set

How it helps: engages most core muscles; improves coordination between upper body and core muscles to keep shoulders and hips in optimal position to maintain running speed.

How to do it:

Start in the push-up position, with your hands shoulder-width apart.

Lower your body until your elbows are next to your rib cage.

Hold this position for 5 seconds, then push your body back up to the start position.

Rest briefly and repeat.

Try to maintain a flat body position, and don't allow your hips to sag.

EXERCISE 4: STANDING KNEE HOLD

How many: 12 repetitions per set

How it helps: strengthens knee- and ankle-stabilizing muscles and improves single-leg balance; helps reduce wasted motion in running form; increases stride length

How to do it:

Stand with feet shoulder-width apart and arms by your sides.

Lift one foot off the floor, and pull your knee up toward your chest.

Hold this position for 5 seconds, then repeat with the other leg.

EXERCISE 5: BACK EXTENSION

How many: 12 repetitions per set

How it helps: strengthens lower back; increases ability to maintain good running posture when fatigued

How to do it:

Lie facedown on the floor, with your arms straight out in front of you.

Your eyes should be looking at the floor. (This keeps your neck in alignment with your spine.)

Lift your chest and shoulders off the floor as shown, hold for 1 or 2 seconds, then return to the floor and repeat.

EXERCISE 6: SIDE HOVER

How many: 3 repetitions of 10 seconds per side

How it helps: strengthens stabilizing muscles on side, from gluteals through shoulders; helps reduce wasted side-to-side motion

How to do it:

Lie on the floor on your side.

Place the elbow on the floor directly under your shoulder, and place your top hand on your hip (photo a).

Hold your feet together, and align your body in a straight line (from front to back) from your heels to your shoulders.

Lift your hip off the floor and hold (photo b).

Lower to the floor, rest briefly, and repeat on the other side.

Strength Training

Resistance training using weights, bands, or your own body weight can correct muscle imbalances and prevent injuries. We've already discussed core stability training, which is a type of resistance training with a specific purpose. Other types of resistance training will get your arms and shoulders, which don't get much benefit from running, in shape and strengthen your leg muscles. Done correctly, weightlifting can reduce your risk of injury by strengthening the connective tissue, including tendons and ligaments. Weightlifting may even improve your running economy so that you use less oxygen at a given pace.

If done to excess, however, weightlifting will make you muscle-bound, tighten up your muscles, leave you injured, and give you extra bulk that you might not want to be carrying around come the 23-mile mark. Marathoners, after all, want to be the classic vertical hyphen, with no extra baggage—Deena Kastor and Ryan Hall probably don't get asked for help too often on moving day. Resistance training does have a role, however, in a marathoner's overall training program.

To Lift or Not to Lift?

Whether weight training can improve marathon performance is still open to debate; however, it can reduce your likelihood of injury and may improve running economy. The greatest gains for marathoners are obtained by including exercises that strengthen your propulsive and stabilizing muscles. The closer those exercises simulate how you would use those muscles during running, the greater the benefits for your running performance.

If you decide to lift weights, get advice from a coach or trainer who understands that you are weightlifting to improve your running, not to look good at the beach. If you decide to weight train your legs, schedule your weight sessions so that they're not right before or after a hard running workout. If you run before or after work, lunchtime is an excellent opportunity to get in lifting sessions that won't detract from your running.

Lifting for the Long Run

An early study by biomechanists Peter Cavanagh, PhD, and Keith Williams, PhD, found that most runners naturally use the most economical stride length for a given speed (Cavanagh and Williams 1982). This led to the belief that runners shouldn't alter their stride length. That advice is correct for the short term, but that doesn't mean you can't or shouldn't attempt to improve your body to make it a more-effective running machine. Over months and years, you can increase your stride length by improving your strength and flexibility. The gains per stride will be small, but when multiplied over thousands of strides, the benefits can be substantial.

■ What If You Hate to Lift? Hill Training!

If lifting weights isn't for you, then try another form of resistance training—hill training. During hill running, your body weight is the resistance. There is some evidence that running hills can produce improvements in running economy similar to those that occur through "normal" resistance training.

Running uphill requires that your legs propel your body weight upward against gravity. Moreover, they do so under conditions that more closely replicate racing conditions than does even the most well-designed weight machine. Anecdotal evidence for the benefits of hill running comes from the Kenyan and Ethiopian runners of today and goes back to coaching legend Arthur Lydiard and the great New Zealand runners of the 1960s and 1970s. The best runners in the world run hills day after day. Of course, genetic factors separate elite runners from recreational runners, but it certainly appears that hill training is an important element that, unlike your genes, you can influence.

Another advantage of hill running over lifting weights is that you simultaneously build your cardiovascular system. Doing some of your $\dot{V}O_2$max sessions on a moderately steep hill will build muscle strength and power that in theory should improve your running economy and that will definitely build your confidence for a hilly marathon.

© Stacey Cramp

If lifting weights isn't for you, then try hill training. Running hills can produce improvements in running economy similar to those that occur through "normal" resistance training.

Resistance training can improve running performance by increasing the force that your slow-twitch muscle fibers develop. This requires relatively low resistance and high repetitions. Lifting to increase muscle size is counterproductive to endurance (and particularly marathon) performance. During endurance training, you work to increase the capillary density and mitochondrial content of your muscles. When muscle size is increased, the capillary and mitochondrial density of the muscle is reduced. It's important, therefore, that you design your resistance training to avoid gains in muscle size. The program that follows is designed to improve strength specifically for your running without adding unneeded muscle.

Resistance training should generally take place two times a week. With this frequency you will see steady improvements in strength but will not compromise the rest of your training program because of excess fatigue. As discussed previously, core stability training should be done more frequently.

TABLE 4.4

Strength Training Session

Exercise	Details
1. Push-up	10 repetitions
2. Dumbbell lat row	15 repetitions per side
3. Bench dip	15 repetitions
4. Swan	10 repetitions
5. Step-up	15 repetitions per leg
6. Lunge	15 repetitions per leg
7. Squat	20 repetitions
8. Alternate shoulder press	10 repetitions per side
9. Seated triceps press	15 repetitions

Perform this sequence of exercises twice.

Program Notes

- A gentle aerobic warm-up will enhance the safety and effectiveness of this program.

EXERCISE 1: PUSH-UP

How many: 10 repetitions per set

How it helps: strengthens the chest, shoulders, and arms; helps improve arm drive when running powerfully (e.g., hills, finishing kick) and ability to maintain good upper-body form when tired

How to do it:

Start in the push-up position shown, with your toes on the floor and your hands slightly wider than shoulder-width apart (photo *a*).

Bend your elbows and lower your body down until your chest is just above the floor (photo *b*).

Push your body back to the start position.

Don't dip your head toward the floor or allow your hips to sag during this exercise.

Your elbows will move out to the side when performing this push-up.

EXERCISE 2: DUMBBELL LAT ROW

How many: 15 repetitions per side per set

How it helps: strengthens large muscles along side of upper back; improves running posture by balancing strength of the chest and shoulder muscles

How to do it:

Place your right knee on a bench, with your right hand also on the bench to provide balance and support.

Bend forward so that your upper body is approximately horizontal.

Hold a light dumbbell in your left hand, with your arm hanging straight (photo *a*).

Pull the dumbbell upward, with your elbow passing beside your ribs as shown (photo *b*).

Lower the dumbbell back to the start position, and repeat.

EXERCISE 3: BENCH DIP

How many: 15 repetitions per set

How it helps: strengthens shoulders and arms; increases ability to maintain upright running posture when tired

How to do it:

Place your hands on a bench or chair, with your feet flat on the floor and your hips just off the edge as shown (photo *a*).

Lower your hips straight down toward the floor by bending the elbows (photo *b*).

Push back up to the start position, and repeat.

To make the exercise more difficult, move your feet farther away from the bench.

EXERCISE 4: SWAN

How many: 10 repetitions per set

How it helps: strengthens the middle and upper back; improves ability to hold the shoulder blades in correct position, which reduces tendency for upper body to slump forward

How to do it:

Lie facedown, with your arms out to the sides, elbows bent to 90 degrees, and palms facing the floor (photo *a*).

Lift your chest, shoulders, and arms off the floor, and squeeze your shoulder blades together (photo *b*).

Lower back to start position, and repeat.

Look toward the floor at all times.

EXERCISE 5: STEP-UP

How many: 15 repetitions per leg per set

How it helps: strengthens the calves, quadriceps, hamstrings, and gluteals; improves balance and increases the forward power of each stride, increasing stride length

How to do it:

Stand approximately 3 feet (1 m) in front of a bench (or chair or flight of stairs).

Place one foot up on the bench, with the whole of the foot flat on the surface of the bench.

Rise up onto the ball of the foot on your back leg, and keep your head up; this is the start position for every repetition (photo *a*).

Using your front leg as much and your back leg as little as possible, step up onto the bench, and finish in a standing position with feet together (photo *b*).

Try to keep your upper body erect, and don't lean forward more than necessary.

Carefully step back off the box, and repeat with the other leg.

EXERCISE 6: LUNGE

How many: 15 repetitions per leg per set

How it helps: strengthens quadriceps, hamstrings, and gluteals; improves balance between left and right legs; helps develop ability to control the large forces through the legs and maintain form while running downhill

How to do it:

Stand with your feet shoulder-width apart and toes pointing straight ahead.

Hold two light dumbbells (no more than 10 pounds or 5 kilograms) by your sides, and keep your upper body vertical, with your head up (photo *a*).

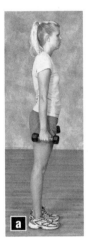

In one movement, take a big step forward, and lower your back knee toward the floor (photo *b*).

Push powerfully back off the front leg so that you return to a standing position.

Perform the next repetition with your other leg.

EXERCISE 7: SQUAT

How many: 20 repetitions per set

How it helps: strengthens lower back, calves, quadriceps, hamstrings, and gluteals; improves ability to keep the knee in good alignment with the hip and ankle, which reduces injury risk and improves running efficiency; also helps develop triple extension (ankle, knee, and hip), which is an important feature of good running technique

How to do it:

Stand with your feet shoulder-width apart and toes pointing straight ahead.

Hold a light dumbbell with both hands under your chin as shown (photo *a*).

Initiate the squat by moving your hips backward as if you were sitting down on a seat.

As you push the hips backward, you'll be forced to lean forward slightly to keep from falling over.

Lower your body without losing your balance until the tops of your thighs are horizontal (photo *b*), then return to a standing position.

During the movement, keep your head up and eyes looking ahead.

Also make sure that your knees are aligned with your feet and stay the same distance apart throughout the exercise.

EXERCISE 8: ALTERNATE SHOULDER PRESS

How many: 10 repetitions per side per set

How it helps: strengthens shoulder and arm muscles; improves ability to maintain a stable upper body while running (minimizes side-to-side sway)

How to do it:

Sit on a bench or chair, with your feet flat on the floor and your back straight.

Hold a light pair of dumbbells overhead, with elbows at approximately 90 degrees (photo *a*).

Push one dumbbell above your head until your arm is nearly straight (photo *b*).

Lower to the start position, and repeat with the other side.

EXERCISE 9: SEATED TRICEPS PRESS

How many: 15 repetitions per set

How it helps: strengthens muscles along back of upper arms; helps maintain relaxed arm action when fatigued

How to do it:

Sit on a bench or chair, with your feet flat on the floor and your back straight.

Hold one light dumbbell above your head with both hands (photo *a*).

While keeping your upper arms vertical, bend at the elbows and lower the dumbbell behind your head as shown (photo *b*).

Return to the start position, and repeat.

Running Form Drills

Your running style is determined by your biomechanics, including the length of your bones, your muscle and tendon flexibility, the strength and endurance of various muscles, and the coordinated contraction pattern of your muscles and the resulting movement of your limbs. Because everyone has a unique physical makeup, there is no ideal or perfect form.

Because running form is determined by your unique makeup, the best way to achieve a more-efficient form is by performing the flexibility and strength training exercises outlined earlier in this chapter. Stride length, for example, is almost always determined naturally by your physiological make-up and is best improved by increasing strength and flexibility. To take another example, excessive forward lean at the waist can be overcome by strengthening the gluteal and abdominal muscles. And trunk instability can be improved through the various core exercises provided in this chapter as well.

But there's something else you can do to improve your form and, therefore, how efficiently you run. You've probably seen sprinters doing various combinations of high-knee running, butt kicks, skipping, and so on. Well, several of these drills are great for distance runners too. First, these exercises can improve your coordination and running form. Second, they lead to gains in strength endurance that can allow you to maintain your stride length throughout a race. Drills up a moderate slope provide even greater resistance. By concentrating on a high knee lift; a complete toe-off; good arm drive; a relaxed neck with the head positioned over the body; relaxed shoulders, arms, and hands; minimal vertical movement (not bouncing with each stride); and an upright posture (not leaning too far forward), you will improve your ability to hold good running form and maximize your running efficiency. When you consider how even a slight flaw in your form will be magnified over the course of a marathon, and when you add the likely scenario of your form, no matter how good, faltering in the last few miles of a marathon, it should be obvious why working to streamline your running technique will help you be a faster marathoner.

When doing drills, the key is to exaggerate various aspects of the running stride and to concentrate on maintaining your form as you begin to fatigue. This attention to various aspects of the running gait will, over time, become ingrained, and pay dividends late in your marathon.

There are endless drills you could do; we've selected four that will significantly help your marathoning. They'll help you maintain your stride length and lessen your ground-contact time, two aspects of running form that can deteriorate with lots of relatively slow marathon training.

You should do drills when you are warmed up but still fresh—there is no use trying to improve your coordination and technique when you are already tired. You'll notice benefits if you do them regularly, at least once, and preferably twice, per week. A good way to easily incorporate drills into your routine is to do them before a session of striders and before harder workouts such as tempo runs and $\dot{V}O_2$max sessions.

Perform the drills as a circuit; that is, do one repetition of each, and then repeat the sequence. Do one repetition of each drill for 15 to 20 meters, and rest before the next one by walking back to the starting point. Visualize yourself completing the drill perfectly.

SKIP MARCH WALK

How to do it:

Begin by walking slowly forward on the balls of your feet using small steps.

Raise one knee to hip level so that your thigh is parallel to the ground.

Rise on the toes of the other foot, straightening your back leg.

Your trunk should be held upright, with your chest out and shoulders back.

Keep your head still and neck relaxed.

Swing your arms forward and back in an exaggerated running motion.

Keep your shoulders, arms, and hands relaxed.

SKIP MARCH RUN

How to do it:

Adopt the same start posture as for skip march walk.

Follow the same movements as for skip march walk, but increase your leg and arm drive to a more-exaggerated skipping motion.

KICKOUT

How to do it:

Walk forward slowly on the balls of your feet.

Raise one knee (photo *a*), and as the knee approaches hip level, straighten the knee to nearly full extension. (Your leg will end up nearly horizontal.)

Allow your momentum to carry your body forward (photo *b*), and hop on your back leg before stepping forward (photo *c*) to repeat with the other leg.

Hold your trunk upright, with your head still and your arms swinging forward in a normal running motion.

As you become more adept at the movement over time, progress from walking to jogging while performing the kickouts.

FAST FEET

How to do it:

In this drill, you run by taking short steps as quickly as possible.

Stay on the balls of your feet at all times, and use a rapid arm movement.

Don't lean too far forward. Try to keep your trunk upright and your head still.

Aerobic Cross-Training

Predictable training errors, such as increasing mileage or adding speed work too quickly, lead to the majority of running injuries. Just as the risk of coronary artery disease can be reduced through regular exercise, so can the risk of running injuries be reduced through modifying risk factors. One way to do this is to reduce pounding on your legs and back by substituting cross-training for a portion of your running.

The primary reason to cross-train is to provide additional cardiovascular fitness without increasing the repetitive wear and tear associated with running. Cross-training indoors can also be useful when the weather or pollution levels prevent you from running outside. Unfortunately, many runners cross-train only when injured and then return exclusively to running as soon as the injury recovers. Sure, cross-training is highly effective for maintaining fitness during times of injury, but that shouldn't be the only time that most runners do it. If you're careful about increases in mileage and intensity, the surfaces you run on, and the like, and you still can't consistently reach the level of weekly mileage you'd like, then you should incorporate cross-training into your training program year-round.

No form of cross-training is a perfect substitute for running because your body adapts very specifically to training. Though you will gain cardiovascular benefits from cross-training, your neuromuscular system will not make similar gains because the movement patterns are different in cross-training activities. That's okay, however, because cross-training should be viewed as a supplement to, not a replacement for, your running. Use cross-training in place of recovery runs and, if necessary, in place of a portion of your general aerobic conditioning. The advantage of using it for recovery training is that the increased blood flow improves your recovery without increasing the cumulative impact forces on your body.

Apples and Oranges?

But won't your racing performances suffer if you replace some of your running with cross-training? The specificity-of-training principle states that your body adapts very specifically to the type of training you do. That's why you won't have much success as a runner by doing all your training on the bike or in the pool. But if the majority of your training is running, you can enhance your running performance by doing other types of aerobic workouts.

Scientific evidence suggests that reasonably well-trained runners can improve their running performance through cross-training, but the improvement is likely to be less than through increased running.

Cross-training activities that work the large muscle groups of the legs (such as cycling, stair climbing, in-line skating, rowing, deep-water running, and cross-country skiing) are most similar to running and should lead to the greatest improvements in performance, whereas activities less similar to running (such as swimming) would likely lead to smaller improvements in running performance.

Although the evidence suggests that cross-training can lead to improved performance in moderately trained or even well-trained runners, no scientific evidence exists concerning cross-training for elite runners, and the specificity-of-training principle likely becomes more critical the higher the level of performance.

For all but the elite, then, it appears that if you increase your training volume by cross-training, you can improve your running performance. The improvement, however, won't be as large as if you had increased your mileage. This point goes right to the heart of the mileage versus injury trade-off. Sure, you would improve more by increasing your running, but you would also increase your risk of injury. The challenge for marathoners is to manage that trade-off by running as much as you can handle before the risk of injury shoots up.

There are many ways to cross-train, including cycling, water running, in-line skating, rowing or kayaking, cross-country skiing, stair climbing, and swimming. Let's look at the pluses and minuses for marathon runners of the various types of cross-training.

Cycling

Cycling offers many options in that you can ride a bike outdoors, use your bike on a wind trainer indoors, or use an exercise bike at home or at a gym. An advantage of cycling is that it works the cardiovascular system while eliminating the impact forces that cause most running injuries. You can therefore add cycling to your training program with little risk of bringing on typical running injuries. An advantage of cycling compared with other cross-training options is that you get to cover ground and feel the wind in your hair, just as in running.

The downsides of cycling are the risk of getting squashed by a car, the large amount of time required compared with running, and the risk of developing a short running stride. The first downside is all too possible, particularly for runners with good cardiovascular fitness but poor bike-handling skills; to keep your heart rate up, you'll likely have to maintain speeds that could put you in danger. In a low-traffic area, cycling outdoors is a great option, but if you're limited to cycling in an urban area without bike paths, then you may want to stay with the more-boring indoor options.

Riding indoors can be a surprisingly satisfying experience because you can concentrate on your workout without distractions or dangers such as traffic lights and cars. Although the maximum time a sane person should sit on a bike indoors is about an hour and a half, when injured, Scott laid claim to the dubious achievement of a 3-hour, 40-minute ride in his garage. (This is what iPods were invented for, right?) During times of injury, an indoor bike can also be used for lactate-threshold training.

Haile Gebrselassie

**Fastest Marathon: 2:03:59
(world record)
Marathon Highlights:
First place, 2006-2008 Berlin,
2005 Amsterdam;
Three fastest marathons in history**

© Icon SMI

Even if he had never run the marathon, Haile Gebrselassie could have been considered the greatest distance runner in history. But once he moved up to the longest Olympic running event and conquered it as well, all doubt was gone—there has never been another runner in the modern era like Gebrselassie. No one can match his range (from a world indoor 1,500 meters title to a world record in the marathon), his accomplishments (nearly 30 world records, from 3,000 meters indoors to the marathon) and his longevity (his marathon world record in 2007 came an astounding 14 years after his first senior world title).

Yet Gebrselassie didn't immediately master the marathon. In his first one as an adult, at London in 2002, he faded over the last few miles to finish a well-beaten third behind Khalid Khannouchi and Paul Tergat. (Debuting in 2:06:35 is hardly a cause for shame, but Gebrselassie was unaccustomed to losing.) "I have to change a lot of things before I can become a good marathon runner," he said at the time. One change he made was to become less of a forefoot runner. Gebrselassie believed that the springy stride resembling a sprinter's that had served him so well on the track was costing him energy over the course of a marathon. He also put greater emphasis on finishing his long runs at marathon race pace.

Gebrselassie returned to the marathon in 2005 with a win at Amsterdam. Starting that year, he ran the fastest time in the world for four years straight, including his 2:03:59 world record at Berlin in 2008.

After all this time, he remains as motivated as ever to train three or more hours a day at altitude. Why? "It's not for money," he says, "because I have enough, and I am making even more with my investments and my businesses. It's simply the thrill of racing." Finding meaningful goals—in Gebrselassie's case, an Olympic gold medal in the marathon and a sub-2:04 clocking—are key to any long career in the marathon.

(continued)

Haile Gebrselassie   *(continued)*

Gebrselassie is steeped in the Ethiopian tradition of near-daily form drills and calisthenics. No doubt his long career and beautiful stride reflect his dedication to them. But even the man whose biography is simply titled "The Greatest" has chinks in his armor. Gebrselassie has been bothered by Achilles tendon problems for much of his career. If he slacks off on doing calf raises and shin-muscle-strengthening exercises, his aches resume. All of us can have healthier, longer running careers if we're diligent about addressing our inherent weak spots with the right stretching and strengthening exercises.

To get a similar workout to running requires about three times as long on a bike. But because the main rationale for recovery runs is simply to increase blood flow through the muscles, you can replace a 30-minute recovery run with about 45 minutes on the bike.

Because cycling is highly repetitive and uses a limited range of motion, it presents a danger of shortening your stride. You can minimize this concern by walking and then running slowly for several minutes after cycling and then stretching your hamstrings, quadriceps, and hip flexors. Also, be sure to keep the bike in an easy-enough gear, with RPMs of at least 90, so that cycling doesn't detract from your running turnover.

Water Running

Unfortunately, a number of running injuries are aggravated by some types of cross-training. Fortunately, with most running injuries, you can safely run in the water. Deep-water running with a flotation vest provides an excellent training stimulus and simulates land running more closely than most other cross-training options. Running in the water is a total-body exercise that works your legs, trunk, and arms and positively stresses your cardiovascular system.

Several studies have verified that runners can use deep-water running to maintain aerobic fitness, lactate threshold, running economy, and time-trial performance for at least 6 weeks. There's little question, then, that water running is an effective method for runners to stay fit.

Water-running technique is an area of some debate. Some coaches insist that you should try to simulate land-running form as closely as possible. Though that's a nice ideal, the most important consideration is to maintain your training intensity to the highest degree possible; if your form needs improvement, so be it.

Regardless of your running form, your stride rate will be slower during water running because of the increased resistance of moving your legs through water. If you try to simulate land running too closely, your stride rate will be even slower. For that reason, don't worry if you don't bring your leg behind your body to the same degree as in land running; just find a happy compromise with decent form and a reasonable rate of leg turnover.

Some athletes move forward while running in the water and (very slowly) do laps during their workouts. Whether you move forward or remain relatively still depends on subtle changes in body position. Try to maintain a relatively upright posture during water running; this posture will work your trunk muscles and result in only a slight tendency to move forward through the water.

You won't be able to achieve as high a heart rate running in the water as when running on land. A study from the Karolinska Institute in Stockholm found that heart rate is 8 to 11 beats per minute lower for the same oxygen uptake when running in the water compared with normal running (Svedenhag and Seger 1992). This study also found that, on average, maximal heart rate is 16 beats per minute lower during all-out water running compared with land running. Lower heart rates during water running are primarily because of the pressure of water on the body; the water pressure makes more blood return to the heart so that more blood is pumped with each heartbeat.

A useful rule of thumb is that heart rates during water running are about 10 percent lower than during land running. For example, if you get your heart rate up to 140 beats per minute in the water, that's roughly equal to 156 beats per minute during normal running. In addition, the temperature of the water affects your heart rate during deep-water running—your heart rate will be lower in cool water and higher in warm water. Interestingly, two studies have found that women have slightly lower heart rates and oxygen consumption than do men during deep-water running. This is thought to be because of women's generally higher body fat content and resultant greater buoyancy as compared with men.

The Karolinska study found that perceived exertion is higher during water running for a given heart rate or level of oxygen consumption. In other words, to get a beneficial workout in the water, you'll feel that you're working harder than during land running. (We can speak from experience that perceived effort at a heart rate of 140 in the water is much higher than for a heart rate of 156 running on land.)

For this reason, if you're injured and replacing land running with water running, you'll need to emphasize interval workouts in the water. If you do only steady water-running sessions, your effort won't be high enough to maintain your fitness. Interval sessions in the water, however, give you brief breaks, both physical and mental, that allow you to work harder and obtain a superior workout. Another plus is that time passes relatively quickly when you're doing intervals, whereas steady water running is terribly boring. A typical 40-minute water-running workout consists of a 5-minute warm-up, followed by 10 repetitions of 45 seconds moderately hard with 15 seconds recovery and then 10 repetitions of 1 minute 40 seconds moderately hard with 20 seconds recovery, and a 5-minute cool-down. Even if you're using water running on your recovery days while marathon training, to get in a halfway decent workout you'll probably need to concentrate on maintaining intensity more than if you were going for an easy run around the block.

In-Line Skating

Advantages of in-line skating for cross-training are that it's fun, it gets you outside with the wind in your hair, and it has some similarities to a running stride. Disadvantages are the time it takes to develop reasonable skill and the safety factor. You may reduce your risk of running injuries by adding in-line skating to your training program, but you could end up with a few scrapes and bruises instead. Once you master it, though, in-line skating can be an effective form of cross-training. After a series of running injuries, Olympic 10,000-meter runner Steve Plasencia successfully used in-line skating to maintain his fitness and reduce his injury risk for several years while continuing to compete at a world-class level. You can use in-line skating for recovery training and general aerobic conditioning.

Rowing

Rowing on the water is a wonderful whole-body exercise that requires a fairly high degree of skill. If you know how to do it, rowing is a great replacement for recovery training and a portion of your aerobic conditioning. Rowing on a machine, such as a Concept II rowing ergometer, is much more forgiving— if your technique is poor, you stay dry. Rowing emphasizes the legs, back, shoulders, and arms. When starting out, ask someone who knows what he or she is doing to show you the correct technique because improper rowing technique can put a large amount of strain on your back.

Cross-Country Skiing

Cross-country skiing is the only form of exercise that provides cardiovascular benefits equal to, or even slightly better than, those associated with running. The whole-body nature of cross-country skiing really works the cardiovascular system, and some of the highest $\dot{V}O_2$max values have been recorded in cross-country skiers.

As with rowing, if you know how to do it, cross-country skiing is pretty much the perfect form of cross-training. Unfortunately, cross-country skiing also requires skill. As can be the case with cycling outdoors, highly trained runners with no experience or little coordination may not be able to go fast enough for long enough while skiing to get in a good workout. As Bob Kempainen famously showed while preparing for the 1992 U.S. Olympic marathon trials, cross-country ski machines are a good option too but are not as much fun as gliding along the snow.

Stair Climbing or Elliptical Training

Stair climbing or elliptical training is hard work and provides a great cardiovascular workout. Unfortunately, the stress of stair climbing is close enough to that of running that the reduction in injuries from substituting stair climbing for a portion of your running may not be that great. For this reason, stair climbing is not recommended during recovery from most running injuries. Elliptical training also works your upper body and has relatively low impact forces, so it can be used while recovering from some running injuries. If you're healthy, stair climbing or elliptical training can substitute for recovery runs or some general aerobic runs.

Swimming

Swimming is a wonderful form of cross-training that works the cardio-vascular system with absolutely none of the jarring stress of running. To get in a decent workout requires some skill, but with a little bit of instruction, even a dyed-in-the-wool marathoner can quickly build up to 30 or 40 laps. Swimming isn't as similar to running as some of the other cross-training options, but if most of your training still consists of running, that doesn't really matter. Swimming is a great way to increase your recovery and your general aerobic fitness without increasing your risk of a running-related injury.

In this chapter, we looked at several types of training that build on the solid foundations of marathon preparation we discussed in chapters 1 to 3. Next, we'll look at how to maximize the gains from all your hard work. Tapering to reach the starting line with the ideal balance of readiness and restedness is the subject of chapter 5.

5

Tapering for Peak Marathon Performance

Training provides the long-term improvements in fitness that are necessary for marathon success. As you're no doubt aware, though, training also tends to leave you a bit tired most of the time. As we've noted, despite much of the popular running literature, this doesn't mean you're overtrained—a moderate amount of residual fatigue is fine during the many weeks of training in preparation for the marathon. The periodic recovery weeks in your training schedule are designed to reduce, but not totally eliminate, the accumulated fatigue of training.

When the marathon approaches, however, you need to cut back your training for a more-prolonged period so that you're optimally rested for the marathon. Tapering your training is critical for reaching the starting line in peak fitness and with maximal energy reserves. The challenge during the last several weeks leading up to the marathon is to find the best balance between continued training to get into the best possible racing shape and resting to eliminate the fatigue of training. In this chapter, we'll look at the best way to strike that crucial balance.

Benefits of Tapering

Put simply, tapering corrects the accumulated wear and tear of training. More specifically, it appears that tapering leads to improvements in running economy (how much oxygen you need to run at a given pace) and muscle strength. As you saw in chapter 1, improvements in running economy have a direct relationship to improvements in marathon race pace, so tapering is money in the bank in improving your marathon performance. In *Lore of*

Running, Fourth Edition, renowned exercise physiologist Tim Noakes, MD, emphasizes that recovery of the shock-absorbing function of the muscles is an important benefit of tapering for marathon runners, which may explain the improvements in running economy. Interestingly, Noakes also suggests that "Perhaps the brain must also be adequately rested to ensure that it can continue to recruit the muscles appropriately once the pain of the marathon becomes increasingly severe" (page 621). Tapering also allows repair of the ongoing microcellular muscle damage from training and full replenishment of the glycogen stores in your muscles and liver, as well as bolstering your immune system.

A review in the *International Journal of Sports Medicine* of more than 50 scientific studies on tapering (Mujika 1998) concluded there's no question that tapering works. Various studies have found improvements in performance or physiological measures of up to 16 percent when athletes taper their training before competition, with most studies finding performance improvements of 3 to 5 percent. In studies with runners, the benefit is generally around 2 to 4 percent, which equates to 3.5 to 7 minutes for a 3-hour marathoner.

So the potential gains from tapering are substantial. What's the most effective way to cut back your training before the marathon?

■ Key Principles for Marathon Tapering

- ■ Begin tapering 3 weeks before your marathon.
- ■ Maintain training intensity.
- ■ Reduce mileage.
- ■ Make recovery days easy, or take days off.
- ■ Optimize recovery strategies with proper diet and hydration.
- ■ Eliminate muscle tightness with stretching, physical therapy, massage, and rest.

How Long Should You Taper?

Several studies investigating the relationship between racing performance at various distances and taper duration concluded that the optimal length of a taper is from 7 days to 3 weeks. For the marathon, the general consensus is to taper for a minimum of 2 weeks, with 3 weeks being optimal. Too short a taper will leave you tired on marathon day, whereas tapering for too long will lead to a loss of fitness. When you consider that any one workout will give you less than a 1 percent improvement in fitness, but that a well-designed taper can provide an improvement in race performance of several percent, it's wise to err on the side of tapering too much rather than not enough. For the marathon, a well-designed 3-week taper will leave you optimally prepared and recovered for the race.

Paula Radcliffe

© Matthew Lewis/Getty Images

**Fastest Marathon: 2:15:25
(world record)
Marathon Highlights:
First place, 2005 World
Championships;
2002, 2003, 2005 London;
2003 Chicago;
2004, 2007, 2008 New York City**

It goes without saying that any world-record holder in the marathon is a supreme athlete. But that doesn't mean that they're all perfect, nor does it mean that they don't make mistakes we can learn from. Although Paula Radcliffe's career includes some very public misfortune, it also includes many positive lessons.

As noted in chapter 6, her two world records in the marathon have been models of optimal pacing; in both performances, she ran first and second halves that were within a minute of each other and ran her fastest miles at the end.

It's also important to note that Radcliffe set her current shorter-distance PRs, such as 30:01 for 10,000 meters, only after becoming a marathoner. This is despite having been a serious runner for more than a decade before running her first marathon in 2002. For many runners, the great aerobic fitness they develop during a marathon buildup can continue to be cashed in after marathon season is over and they've returned to regular road races.

And who wouldn't be inspired by Radcliffe's victory at the 2007 New York City Marathon just nine months after giving birth? Like many women, Radcliffe claims that she felt physically stronger running after pregnancy.

Despite her world records and big-city victories, Radcliffe will also always be known for dropping out of the 2004 Olympic Marathon and sobbing on the curb. Soon after the race, she explained that taking anti-inflammatories for a leg injury had upset her stomach, rendering her unable to fuel properly. Subsequently, she noted that the stress of the event—expectations placed on her by the British press and by herself—had gotten to her. More than any other race, the marathon has the power to overwhelm. Try to remember that you're doing it because you want to (at least

(continued)

Paula Radcliffe *(continued)*

we hope you are!) and that your performance in the race has no bearing on whether you're a contributing member of society or all-around decent person.

There's also a cautionary note in Radcliffe's recent history. After winning New York City soon after giving birth, she was continually beset by injury. Trying to rush back to fitness to get to the start line of a given marathon compounded her bodily woes. In early 2008, a toe injury prevented her from starting April's London Marathon. She then suffered a stress fracture in her thigh while trying to make up for lost time before the Beijing Olympics. She was able to resume running on land only in the month before the marathon there; despite daily cross-training, she simply lacked the running-specific fitness to race for 26.2 miles, and she finished twentythird. After the race, Radcliffe said that if it had been any race but the Olympics, she wouldn't have started. Most of us can be much more flexible in planning our races, so if your training suffers a setback owing to injury or significant illness, be open to the idea of refocusing on another, later marathon.

How Should You Reduce Your Training to Improve Racing Performance?

The scientific evidence indicates that the key to effective tapering is to substantially reduce your mileage while maintaining the intensity of your training. Reducing the amount you run reduces accumulated fatigue to improve your marathon performance, while interspersing efforts that you have been doing throughout your buildup, including $\dot{V}O_2$max intervals and strides, maintains the adaptations that you have worked hard to gain over the past several months. (During your taper, you should do shorter sessions at those paces, so while you're maintaining the intensity of training, you're still reducing the quantity of higher-intensity training.) A tune-up race 2 weeks before the marathon is also a key session for advancing your fitness (and, ideally, providing psychological reinforcement that you're almost ready to roll).

How much you reduce your overall mileage depends on your current training volume, past experience (know thyself), and overall health. In general, older runners tend to require slightly more time to taper than younger runners. Our guidelines for cutting back your mileage, based on research, discussions with elite marathoners and coaches, and personal experience, are as follows:

- Third week premarathon: Reduce mileage by 20 to 25 percent.
- Second week premarathon: Reduce mileage by 40 percent.
- Marathon week (6 days before race): Reduce mileage by 60 percent.

For example, a marathoner whose training peaks at 70 miles (113 km) per week would reduce her mileage by 20 to 25 percent (to 52 to 56 mi; 84 to 90 km) in the third week before the race, by 40 percent (to 42 mi; 68 km) the following week, and by 60 percent (to 28 mi; 45 km) during race week. For race week, the 60 percent mileage reduction is for the 6 days leading up to the marathon.

Three weeks before your marathon is arguably the most important time for a successful taper. This is the week that many marathoners do too much because the marathon still seems a long way off. If you work too hard during this week, however, you may find yourself feeling flat with 2 weeks to go and struggling to rest up as quickly as possible for the race. It's much better physiologically and psychologically to allow your body to start to freshen up during this week. This will put you in a much more relaxed state of mind, feeling that your marathon preparation is on track rather than stressing that all of your efforts are going to be wasted.

Marathoners tend to progressively decrease their training efforts during their marathon taper. That method presents two problems. First, by steadily decreasing training effort over the 3 weeks, they risk a small loss in fitness (adaptations to training are lost at about the same rate that they are gained) before the marathon.

© Human Kinetics

Around three weeks before your marathon is a good time to start your taper, decreasing the intensity and amount of your training.

The larger concern, however, is psychological. The steady-reduction approach doesn't provide any psychological reinforcement. Marathoners generally need reminders that they're still fit, or their confidence may become shaky. The more-effective approach to tapering is to intersperse harder efforts within an overall trend of recovery. Figure 5.1 shows a 3-week marathon taper in which harder efforts are included every few days. This type of taper will leave you fit, rested, and confident for the marathon.

Leading up to the marathon, it is paramount to believe in your training program by adjusting your taper to fit your individual needs. Keep a record of your taper leading up to each of your marathons and how you felt and performed in those races. Over time, you'll be able to identify patterns that will allow you to fine-tune your taper and gain confidence that your taper has given you the maximal edge in performance. For example, many runners prefer a day off quite soon before the marathon. If you've found that works for you, we recommend taking that complete rest day 2 or 3 days before the marathon. It's almost always best to do a light jog the day before the marathon—you'll feel better on race day, you'll have a chance to get a last check on any tight muscles, and perhaps most important, you'll do something other than stare at the walls all day fretting about your race.

Based on the optimal tapering criteria we've just discussed, here's a sample tapering schedule for a marathon (table 5.1). This tapering program is taken from the 18-week training schedule in chapter 9 of this book. By following this schedule, your mileage would have peaked at 70 per week (113 km), and you would have run your last 20-miler (32 km) on Sunday before the start of the taper. Let's go through this schedule day by day to see the rationale for each day's training.

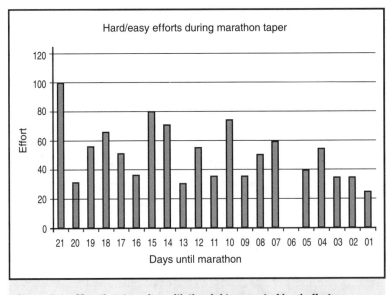

Figure 5.1 **Marathon tapering with the right amount of hard efforts.**

TABLE 5.1

Sample 3-Week Marathon Taper

	WEEKS TO MARATHON		
	2	**1**	**Race week**
Monday	Rest or cross-training	Rest or cross-training	Rest
Tuesday	Recovery + speed 7 mi (11 km) w/ 8 × 100 m strides	General aerobic + speed 7 mi (11 km) w/ 8 × 100 m strides	Recovery 7 mi (11 km)
Wednesday	Medium-long run 12 mi (19 km)	Recovery 4 mi (6 km)	Dress rehearsal 7 mi (11 km) w/ 2 mi @ marathon race pace
Thursday	Recovery + speed 5 mi (8 km) w/ 6 × 100 m strides	$\dot{V}O_2$max 8 mi (13 km) w/ 3 × 1,600 m @ 5K race pace; jog 50 to 90% interval duration between	Recovery 5 mi (8 km)
Friday	Recovery 5 mi (8 km)	Recovery 5 mi (8 km)	Recovery + speed 5 mi (8 km) w/ 6 × 100 m strides
Saturday	8K-10K tune-up race (total 9-11 miles/14-18 km)	Recovery + speed 6 mi (10 km) w/ 10 × 100 m strides	Recovery 4 mi (6 km)
Sunday	Long run 17 mi (27 km)	Medium-long run 13 mi (21 km)	Goal marathon
Weekly volume	55-57 mi/88-92 km	43 mi/69 km	28 mi/45 km (6 days prerace)

Week 1 starts with 2 recovery days to recover from the long run on Sunday. The second day includes eight repetitions of 100-meter strideouts to improve your leg turnover. Wednesday's workout is a 12-miler (19 km) to provide a mild endurance stimulus. Thursday and Friday are recovery days, leaving you well rested for Saturday, when you run your last tune-up race before the marathon. The 8K to 10K tune-up race provides a boost to your fitness that will make marathon pace feel relatively easy, yet it is short enough that recovery will occur quickly. Sunday is a 17-miler (27 km) to again provide a moderate endurance stimulus to help maintain the adaptations, such as increased glycogen storage and blood volume, from your previous long runs.

Week 2 starts with 3 recovery days, with Tuesday including a few strideouts to enhance your leg turnover. Thursday calls for your last workout at close to $\dot{V}O_2$max pace. This is done 10 days before the marathon to allow time for recovery and supercompensation. Friday and Saturday are recovery days, with Saturday again including a few strideouts to enhance your leg turnover. The week ends with a 13-miler (21 km) on Sunday, once again providing the body with a reminder to maintain the adaptations built up over many weeks of long runs.

Marathon week is all easy recovery with the exception of Wednesday. Wednesday is a dress rehearsal for the marathon. Wear the shoes, socks, shorts, and so on that you'll wear in the marathon. This is your last chance to check that everything is right for the race. After an easy 3 miles (5 km), run 2 miles (3 km) at marathon race pace, then 2 more miles easy. You should feel reasonably fresh but will probably not yet feel fully rested. If you have any tight muscles, there's still time to get a massage, stretch, or see a physical therapist to get your legs ready for race day.

By tapering in this way, you'll reach the marathon start line as prepared as possible. Then all that remains is the little matter of covering 26.2 miles (42.2 km) as fast as you can. What pacing and nutrition strategies to use during the marathon to run your best is the focus of the next chapter.

■ Where's the Pasta Feed?

In chapter 2, we discuss the importance of carbohydrate loading for the marathon. It's vitally important that your muscles and liver be optimally stocked with glycogen when you reach the start of the race. Of similar importance is arriving at the starting line fully hydrated. See chapter 2 for in-depth information on these topics.

Tapering Your Other Training

When you start cutting back your mileage, it can be tempting to increase whatever nonrunning training you do. For the most part, try to resist that urge. The various forms of supplementary training we looked at in the preceding chapter have the same general purpose as your running training—to get you to the marathon start line in optimum fitness for racing 26.2 miles (42.2 km). Approach your core, resistance, flexibility, and cross-training as you do your running when the marathon nears. That is, realize that the main work is done, and your goal now shifts to maintaining the gains you made while allowing your body to rest up for race day.

Keep your core and resistance workouts to a minimum in the last 10 days before your marathon, and eliminate them in the last few days. If you're used to cross-training, it's okay to continue gentle versions of your normal activities until a few days before the race. Flexibility training is fine to do right up to race day, but don't go overboard. If you're used to a few 10-minute stretching sessions per week, don't suddenly devote half an hour a day to it in the week before your marathon.

The same goes for form drills. If you're used to doing them, then it's fine to do a short sequence in the week before the marathon. As with flexibility training, the drills will help you feel looser during your taper, which, if nothing else, can provide peace of mind while you're reducing your running. Again, though, don't suddenly add new exercises or increase the amount of drills you do during your taper. The hay is already in the proverbial barn.

Preserving Energy (and Sanity) Before the Marathon

If at all possible, during the last week before the marathon, reduce not just your training but also the amount of stress in your life. Assuming the cooperation of your family, friends, and coworkers, try to do the following:

- Avoid having major deadlines at work or other energy-draining undertakings.
- Wash your hands frequently to lower your risk of catching a cold.
- Get plenty of sleep early in the week.
- Let others do the driving.
- Minimize the amount of time you spend at the prerace expo.
- Save sightseeing for after the marathon.
- Spend a few minutes each day in a quiet spot visualizing a successful race.

Seeing Success

As race day approaches, it's normal to feel anxious. The marathon can seem more like a concept than a reality when it's 10 weeks away, but when it's just a matter of days to go, it can become all too real a presence in your thoughts. That's especially true when you're tapering your training and might be a little more on edge as a result. (And because, if you're like most marathoners, you're worried that all the months of training are quickly evaporating after just a few rest days.)

To keep your mind at ease, practice visualization during your taper. In some of the time that you would usually allot to running, sit or lie in a quiet spot and mentally run through your race. Anticipate potential problems—a twinge in your calf, sudden rain, and so on—and see yourself overcoming them. Also visualize yourself running relaxed in the early stages of the marathon and then running strongly over the final 10K. If you have a time goal for your marathon, repeatedly picture yourself crossing the finish, with the clock showing your goal time.

6

Race-Day Strategy

Your overall preparation for the marathon occurs over several months. During that time, you meticulously plan and diligently train so that you're in peak condition for the race. To do your best, however, you also need to have a plan for the marathon itself. That plan is the focus of this chapter. How much should you warm up for the marathon, and what should that warm-up consist of? How should you handle the first few miles, the first half of the race, the long stretch up to 20 miles (32 km), and the final 6 miles and 385 yards (10 km)? Let's take a look at race-day strategies that help you get everything out of your months of preparation so that you cross the finish line exhausted but satisfied.

Warming Up

Warming up for any race is important. The purpose of a warm-up is to prepare your body to run at race pace. This involves increasing your metabolic rate, your body temperature, and the circulation of blood (and thus oxygen) to your muscles. The warm-up activates your aerobic system to work optimally from the start of the race.

There's a downside, however, to warming up for the marathon. One of the challenges in the marathon is to reach the finish line before becoming glycogen depleted. In chapter 2, we emphasize the importance of carbohydrate loading before the marathon and taking in carbohydrate during the marathon to help ensure that you don't run out of carbohydrate before the finish. But during a warm-up, you burn a mixture of carbohydrate and fat, thereby slightly reducing your glycogen stores. The key, then, is to find the minimum amount of warm-up necessary to prepare your body to handle race pace as soon as the starter's gun is fired so that you save as much of your precious carbohydrate reserves as possible for the 26.2 miles (42.2 km) ahead.

The optimal warm-up for the marathon depends on the level of the marathoner. For beginners, whose main goal is to finish, no warm-up is necessary. They can warm up during the first couple of miles of the race. For more serious marathoners, who will attempt to run the distance significantly faster than their normal training pace, the optimal warm-up consists of two runs of about 5 minutes each, with some gentle stretching in between.

You should start warming up about 30 to 40 minutes before the start of the race. Start your first warm-up run slowly, and gradually increase your pace so that you finish at about 1 minute per mile (per 1.6 km) slower than marathon race pace. Next, stretch for about 10 minutes, including loosening up your shoulders and neck. Follow that with another 5 minutes of running, this time gradually picking up the pace until you reach marathon pace for the final 30 seconds or so. Then stretch a bit more.

That's it. Try to time your warm-up so that you finish no more than 10 minutes before the race starts. If you warm up too long before the race, you'll lose some of the benefits of the warm-up yet will have still used up some of your carbohydrate stores. The ability to time your warm-up like this is an advantage of running a smaller marathon, as compared with a megarace, where you're more likely to be herded to your starting position long before the race begins.

Before the start of the Olympic marathon, the athletes do a bit of nervous jogging around, but almost no one does more than 10 minutes of easy running plus one or two accelerations up to race pace. This is enough of a warm-up for these runners to handle a 5-minute-per-mile pace for the first mile. A similar routine will get you to the starting line prepared to handle your goal marathon race pace.

Your Pacing Strategy

Assuming that you have a time goal for the marathon, how should you go about trying to achieve that time? Some marathoners go out hard and then try to hang on as well as possible in the second half. Others try to run an even pace throughout. A few take it easy early on and then run the second half faster. Let's consider the physiology of the marathon and the implications for your optimal pacing strategy.

In chapter 1, you saw that your marathon pace is very close to your lactate-threshold pace, which is determined by your oxygen consumption at your lactate threshold and your running economy. If you run faster than your lactate-threshold pace, then lactate accumulates in your muscles and blood; the hydrogen ions associated with the lactate deactivate the enzymes for energy production and make you slow down. When you exceed your lactate-threshold pace, you also use more glycogen, so your limited glycogen stores are depleted more quickly than necessary.

These basics of marathon physiology indicate that the best strategy for the marathon is relatively even pacing. If you run much faster than your overall race pace for part of the race, then you'll use more glycogen than necessary and will likely start to accumulate lactate. If you run much slower than your overall race pace for part of the race, then you'll need to make up for this lapse by running faster than the most efficient pace for another portion of the race. The optimal pacing strategy, then, is to run nearly even splits, taking into account the idiosyncrasies of the course you'll be running.

Most runners shouldn't try to run dead-even splits, however, because during the marathon you'll gradually fatigue your slow-twitch muscle fibers and will start to recruit more of your fast-twitch A fibers to maintain your pace. Unfortunately, these fast-twitch fibers tend to be less economical than your slow-twitch fibers in their use of oxygen. Therefore, your running economy will tend to decrease slightly during the race, meaning that your lactate-threshold pace will decrease slightly as well. The result is that your optimal pace will be slightly reduced during the latter stages of the marathon.

For example, if your goal is to run 2:39 for the marathon, then even splits would require you to run 1:19:30 for each half of the race. To run even splits, you would have to increase your oxygen consumption and lactate level as your fatigue level increases during the second half of the race. A more efficient pacing strategy would be to go through halfway in 1:18 to 1:19 because doing so would allow you to slow by 2 to 3 percent during the second half and still achieve your goal. If you ran negative splits for the marathon (i.e., the second half faster than the first half), chances are that you ran more slowly than optimally during the first half of the race and could have had a faster finishing time.

For world-class marathoners, whose genetics and training put them on a higher plane, the optimal pacing strategy is likely a bit different. These select few are so highly trained that they have a lower tendency to recruit less-economical muscle fibers as the race progresses. In addition, they can pick up the pace over the last several miles and gradually accumulate lactate to the finish. For the best marathoners in the world, therefore, the most effective pacing strategy is to run the second half of the marathon at the same pace as, or even slightly faster than, the first half.

Most of the recent world records have followed this model of slightly faster second halves. In setting the world best of 2:03:59 at the 2008 Berlin Marathon, Haile Gebrselassie ran the first half in 62:05 and the second half in 61:54. In setting his first world record at this distance, Gebrselassie ran 2:04:26 at the 2007 Berlin Marathon, with half times of 62:29 and 61:57. Similarly, in her first world record, at the 2002 Chicago Marathon, Paula Radcliffe ran 2:17:18 by running the first half in 69:03 and the second half in 68:15. When

Catherine Ndereba

Fastest Marathon: 2:18:47
(Kenyan record, former world record)
Marathon Highlights:
Second place, 2004 and 2008 Olympics;
First place, 2003 and 2007 World
Championships

Kenya's Catherine Ndereba can reasonably claim to be the best female marathoner in history. In an era of ever-increasing depth in the event, she has repeatedly risen to the highest levels of competition, achieving two Olympic silver medals, two World Championship titles, wins at Boston and Chicago, and, for good measure, at one point a world record. Her sustained excellence is a testament to her consistency and her ability to focus when it counts and to ease off at other times.

Ndereba is remarkable in that her mileage is relatively low for a champion marathoner. She rarely gets above 100 miles per week. Her training is straightforward: during a marathon buildup, she does one long run and two fast sessions per week. Some of her long runs are quite long, as long as three hours—more than half an hour longer than her marathon time. She does most of her long runs at an easy pace so that she can recover quickly from them. (Two massages each week undoubtedly contribute to her recovery.) Like many Kenyans, she does form drills and calisthenics several times a week.

© AP Photo/Tina Fineberg

With this program, Ndereba has remained injury-free. Her consistent training allows her to steadily build her fitness from year to year. There's a lesson there for marathoners whose training often gets interrupted by injury—sometimes it's better to aim for a lower mileage goal and to progress with season after season of good work than to push for spectacular highs and wind up enduring extreme lows.

Not that Ndereba does the same training all the time. Indeed, her strengths include having the faith and discipline to take breaks after key marathons and accepting that she's not going to be in peak form all the time. Ndereba runs shorter races frequently as tools toward her marathon goals, not ends in themselves, and she doesn't worry when her times aren't earth-shattering. For example, three weeks before the 2004 Olympics, she placed fifth at the Beach to Beacon 10K in 32:31. Rather than freaking out afterward because her average speed was not much faster than her marathon PR pace, Ndereba said afterward that she was finishing up her heaviest pre-Olympics training, and that she would feel fresh when it mattered. Her silver medal in Athens proved her right.

In races, Ndereba exhibits the same ability to stay calm in the early stages and dole out her physical and mental reserves when it matters. In the early stages of the 2008 Olympic Marathon, for example, she was always within sight of the large lead pack but never tightly within it. When the moves started, she had the strength to cover them easily and was rewarded with another silver medal. All marathoners can learn from Ndereba's method of patience before pushing.

she set her current world record of 2:15:25 at the 2003 London Marathon, her first half took 68:02, and then she ran the second half in 67:23.

Incidentally, perhaps you'll find it reassuring that even the best runners in the world pay for it when they start a marathon too quickly. At the Dubai Marathon in January 2008, Gebrselassie attempted to break his then 4-month-old world record. En route to a first half of 61:27, he tore through the first 10K in 28:39—fast enough to win most open 10K road races. Even the great Gebrselassie succumbed to such brashness. Well, sort of. He slowed in the last few miles, and his second half of 63:26 was almost 2 minutes slower than his first half, resulting "only" in the third-best time ever, 2:04:53.

Altering Your Strategy Midrace

Although in most cases you should stay with your pacing plan, occasionally the weather or the tactics of other runners merit slightly altering your strategy. If you're running into a headwind, there's a substantial advantage to running in a group of runners and letting others block the wind. Though you may need to do your share in leading the group, you'll still save considerable energy compared with running by yourself into the wind. On a windy day, therefore, you may need to run faster or slower than planned to stay with a group.

Even on a calm day, the best strategy may be to deviate slightly from your goal pace rather than running most of the way by yourself. In a big-city marathon such as Boston, New York, or Chicago, being stuck by yourself isn't a problem. At almost any pace, you'll be among a number of runners, and you can work with them to reach your goal time. In a smaller marathon, however, you have a reasonably high chance of running by yourself for many miles. In that situation, you must make a judgment call as to whether to go a few seconds per mile faster or slower than planned to stay with a group. Although drafting behind other runners will give

■ What Shoes Should You Wear?

Marathoners vary widely in the types of shoes they prefer to race in. On the theory that even an extra ounce adds up over the course of 26.2 miles (42.2 km), some like to wear as light a shoe as possible. On the other hand, some runners figure that during such a long run, they'll need as much cushioning and support as they can get.

Most competitive marathoners should choose their race-day shoes toward the light end of the spectrum. Most shoe companies make a lightweight trainer that works well in the marathon—these are minimalist enough so that you can feel light on your feet but are built up enough in the heel and midsole to provide some protection, especially as you fatigue late in the race.

Most elites, of course, race the marathon in flats. Bear in mind that these runners are usually whippet thin and have excellent biomechanics. Flats have less support and less heel lift than training shoes. The lack of support increases the risk of injury and can make muscles that have to work harder fatigue because of the decreased support. In addition, the lower heel lift puts more strain on Achilles tendons and calf muscles.

In the last few years, many companies have introduced a broader range of racing flats so that marathoners have more choices between the shoes they race 5Ks in and their training shoes, no matter how light the latter are. Usually weighing around 8 ounces (230 g), with a decent amount of cushioning and some heel support, these longer-distance flats are a good choice for marathoners attempting to race the marathon significantly faster than normal training pace. In his world record, for example, Gebrselassie wore the Adidas version of this type of flat. Paula Radcliffe wore Nike's version of a marathon flat in her record. On the other hand, multiple London and New York City champion Martin Lel wears a flat that most average runners wouldn't even dare to do a 5K in. As always, the key is to find what works best for you. Regardless of which shoes you choose for race day, be sure to try them out on tempo runs and at least one of your longer marathon-pace training runs (in addition to the short dress rehearsal run during taper week).

Following are some rough guidelines about the most likely candidates to wear flats in the marathon.

Top candidates for wearing flats in the marathon:

Male	Female
Faster than 2:40	Faster than 2:55
Weighs less than 160 pounds (73 kg)	Weighs less than 140 pounds (63 kg)
History of being relatively injury free	History of being relatively injury free
Good biomechanics	Good biomechanics

you a small energy advantage, most of the benefit of staying with a group is psychological. You don't have to set the pace, and you can relax and go along with the group.

Most runners find it quite difficult mentally to run by themselves for long stretches of the marathon. So what's the trade-off between having company and having to compromise your strategy? A rule of thumb is to deviate from your goal pace by no more than 8 to 10 seconds per mile (per 1.6 km) if you would otherwise be running by yourself during the first 20 miles (32 km) of the race. (Of course, you won't know until afterward whether you would have had to run by yourself.) Running 8 to 10 seconds per mile faster than planned may not sound like much, but this difference in effort can put you over the edge after a couple of miles. The best way to judge whether to pick it up to latch onto a group is by how you feel at the time. If you feel as though you can handle it, then go for it. If your breathing is uncomfortable and you can sense that you're working at a higher intensity than you can maintain until the finish, then relax and let the others go. You may find that the group will soon break up and that you'll once again have others to run with.

During the final 6 miles and 385 yards (10 km), you can afford to be more independent. If no one else is running at the correct pace for you after you've passed the 20-mile (32 km) mark, you need to muster the courage to go it alone. Chances are that forging out will work well psychologically because if you have prepared well and run a fairly even pace, you'll be passing other runners throughout the final miles. Nothing lifts the spirits quite like passing another runner late in the marathon.

If you're racing a marathon in which your specific finishing place is an important consideration (e.g., the Olympic trials), then your pacing strategy will be somewhat determined by the actions of others in the race. If a group of 10 runners break away, then you had better go after them, even if it means running faster than planned. In general, though, it's best to stick close to your race plan and your goal marathon pace.

The First Half

You're finally at the starting line, warmed up, and ready for the task ahead. It's all too easy to get carried away and run the first mile (1.6 km) too fast. A better approach is to run the first mile at, or a bit slower than, your goal pace. Because you won't have done much of a warm-up before the start, your body won't be prepared to go faster than race pace. Also, if you run too fast at the beginning of the race, your body will burn off extra glycogen and accumulate lactate that could negatively affect the rest of your race.

Once the first mile is out of the way, the best strategy during the next few miles is to settle into a good rhythm. Try to run fast but relaxed. Establishing a relaxed running style early in the race will go a long way toward helping you avoid tightening up so that you can maintain your goal pace to the finish. Go through a mental checklist periodically to make sure your shoulders are relaxed, your body is upright, and so on to help you maintain good running style throughout the race.

Take a carbohydrate drink at the first aid station. It's important to drink right from the start rather than wait until you think you need carbohydrate or fluid. Your thirst mechanism isn't particularly closely matched to your hydration level, so waiting until you feel thirsty to drink is a mistake. Similarly, if you wait until you feel tired and light-headed to take in carbohydrate, it will be too little too late. The longer you can postpone dehydration and carbohydrate depletion, the longer you will be able to maintain your goal pace. Taking in carbohydrate and fluid early will help postpone or prevent dehydration or carbohydrate depletion later. As we discussed in chapter 2, a few seconds lost at each aid station can translate into several minutes gained toward the end of the marathon.

Mentally, the first half of the marathon is the time to cruise. Try to save your mental and emotional energy for the second half of the race. All other factors being equal, if there is a group of runners in the lead pack at halfway, the winner will be the one who has cruised along at the back of the pack saving his or her energy for the demands of the second half of the race. Regardless of your ultimate finishing place in the marathon, you should realize that the second half is much harder than the first half; just try to get the first half out of the way at the correct pace without using any more mental energy than necessary.

© Corey Rich/Aurora Photos

It's important to drink right from the start rather than waiting until you feel thirsty. Taking in fluid and carbohydrate early will help postpone or prevent dehydration and carbohydrate depletion later.

▓ When Not to Finish

Most of the time, you should finish the marathon even if you're not running as well as you had hoped. The marathon is a test of endurance. If you casually drop out of a marathon once, it will be all too easy to drop out again. Of course, in certain situations, struggling to finish a marathon may compromise your health or your future marathon success. Here are some legitimate reasons to drop out of a marathon:

- If you're limping, then your running mechanics are thrown off. You'll merely aggravate your injury by continuing.
- If you have a specific pain, and that pain is increasing progressively during the race, then you're doing yourself harm and should stop.
- If you're light-headed and unable to concentrate, you should stop.
- If you're overcome by muscle cramps, a torn muscle, heat exhaustion, or the like, then stop.

On to 20 Miles (32 km)

From the halfway mark to 20 miles (32 km) is the no-man's-land of the marathon. You're already fairly tired and still have a long way to go. This is where the mental discipline of training will help you maintain a strong effort and a positive attitude. It's easy to let your pace slip 5 seconds per mile (per 1.6 km), and then 10 seconds per mile or more, during this stretch. By using all the available feedback on your pace—whether in the form of mile or kilometer splits—you'll know exactly how you're progressing, and you should be able to concentrate and maintain your goal pace during these miles.

Slowing during this portion of the marathon is often more a matter of not concentrating than of not being able to physically maintain the pace. Focusing on your splits gives you an immediate goal to concentrate on. The ability to do a bit of adding in your head while running is a helpful skill. If you're supposed to be running 5:40 per mile, and there are markers every mile during the marathon, then just add 6:00 to your previous mile split and subtract 20 seconds to calculate what your next split should be. If you're 5 seconds too slow, don't try to make up the lost 5 seconds during the next mile; add 5:40 again as your target to get yourself back on track. By focusing on these incremental goals along the way, you'll prevent a large drift in your pace and should be able to stay very close to your goal.

It's not unusual to have a few miles when you just don't feel good. These bad patches are a test of mental resolve. Often these stretches will last a while and then mysteriously go away. For example, you might feel tight and uncomfortable from miles 15 to 17 but then get back in the groove again and feel good to the finish. The key is to have the confidence that you'll eventually overcome this bad patch.

Pete learned this lesson during the 1983 San Francisco Marathon. After working quite hard from 13 to 16 miles, he had a stretch of about 3 miles when his breathing felt out of sync, and he struggled to stay with the other two leaders. Pete kept telling himself to relax and that the other guys might

■ Dropping Out

In my marathon career, I started 18 marathons and finished 16, including 8 victories. Of the two dropouts, one was because of injury and the other was because of stupidity. Both occurred in 1986.

The dropout because of stupidity was the Boston Marathon. This was the first professional Boston Marathon, with lots of media excitement and financial incentives. I ignored my usual race plan of running even splits and got carried away early. During the first 10 miles, Greg Meyer and I exchanged the lead several times. Whenever Greg would take the lead, I would try to take it back.

This was overly aggressive racing for so early in the marathon. Meanwhile, Rob de Castella, who won that day, sat in behind us, probably laughing to himself at the lack of patience of the two Americans. By 12 miles, my breathing wasn't in its usual rhythm, my legs were already pretty beat up, and my intestines were becoming increasingly uncomfortable. During the next mile, I fell off the lead bunch and started to tighten up. Knowing that I had gone too hard too early, I stopped just past the halfway mark and quietly cursed myself. It was a lesson well learned and a mistake I never made again. Note that stupidity doesn't fall under the list of legitimate reasons to drop out of a marathon.

The only positive aspect of dropping out so early was that I recovered fully in about a week. A few weeks later, I used my fitness and frustration to set a personal best of 28:41 for 10,000 meters on the track, and in July I redeemed myself over 26.2 miles by winning the San Francisco Marathon in 2:13:29.

My other dropout was in the 1986 Twin Cities Marathon, which was also the trial race for the next year's world championships. I went into the race with a tight hamstring from stretching too hard after a track workout several weeks earlier. It felt okay early in the race but gradually tightened up in the drizzly 40-degree weather. At 20 miles, I was at the back of the lead pack when the hamstring tightened completely. I couldn't run another step. After walking for about a mile, I gratefully accepted a ride to the finish. That dropout was easier mentally because the decision was out of my hands.

Having had a frustrating year in the marathon, I was determined to get a decent race under my belt as quickly as possible. My physical therapist said that the hamstring wasn't too badly damaged and that I should run easily for about 10 days. With regular massage, it loosened up, and I decided to run the New York City Marathon, which was 3 weeks after Twin Cities. I ran conservatively and gradually moved from 30th place at halfway to finish 9th in 2:14:09. It had been a year of lessons learned.

—Pete Pfitzinger

be hurting, too. Fortunately, he settled back into a comfortable rhythm by 19 miles, felt strong enough to drop the other two runners by the 20-mile mark, and cruised home to victory. If Pete had let himself think negatively during the bad patch and let the other two runners get away, he wouldn't have won that race.

Taking in carbohydrate as often as possible during the second half of the race can help you maintain your mental focus. The only fuel for your brain is glucose (carbohydrate), and when you become carbohydrate depleted, the amount of glucose reaching the brain starts to decrease. If you've carbohydrate loaded, this shouldn't start to affect you until well past the 20-mile (32 km) mark. Taking in carbohydrate during the race and particularly between miles 13 and 20 (km 21 and 32), however, will help ensure that you stay alert and think clearly throughout the race.

The Final 6 Miles and 385 Yards (10 km)

Having made it to 20 miles (32 km), you're at the most rewarding stage of the marathon. This is the part that you have prepared for during your long months of training. This is when your long runs, during which you worked hard over the last stages, will really pay off. Until now, everything required the patience to hold back. Now, you're free to see what you've got. During these final 6 miles and 385 yards (10 km), you get to dig deep and use up any energy that you have left. This is what the marathon is all about. This is the stretch that poorly prepared marathoners fear and well-prepared marathoners relish.

The key from 20 miles (32 km) to the finish is to push as hard as you can without having disaster strike in the form of a cramp or very tight muscles. You will have prepared yourself for this during your long runs, your marathon-pace runs, and, to a lesser extent, your tempo runs. You need to use your body's feedback to determine just how hard you can push. Chances are that, by now, your calf muscles, hamstrings, quads, or some combination of these are on edge and will limit how fast you can go. You need to test the waters a bit and push to what you perceive to be the limit that your muscles will tolerate. This is a progressive meting-out process, in which you can take progressively greater risks as the finish line nears.

Although doing the how-many-miles-to-go math can be daunting early on in the marathon, in this final stage it can help keep you focused. As the finish approaches, telling yourself, "Less than 3 miles to go," or "Just 15 minutes more," can be motivating. If you're struggling a bit toward the end, picture yourself finishing a run on your favorite training loop so that the remaining distance seems more manageable.

If you've been taking in fluid and carbohydrate throughout the race, your muscles should be in pretty good condition. Keep drinking until 25 miles (40 km). Keeping up your blood sugar level will keep you alert so that you can concentrate well to the end. When you see the finish line approaching, give a little more effort so that you run strongly over the line. Show yourself that you have mastered the marathon and are able to kick it in a bit to the finish. Then enjoy the fruits of your labor.

In these first several chapters, we've looked at preparing for and running the marathon from all the necessary angles. Now it is time to put theory into practice. The rest of this book contains training schedules that implement the physiological principles of marathoning. The knowledge gained from this first section of the book, combined with the marathon-specific fitness that following the schedules will bring you, should leave you well prepared for marathon success.

PART
II

Training Programs

7

Following the Schedules

As we note in the preface, many readers want to get right to the training schedule of their choice and start working. That's fine, but before getting too far into your training, you'll want to read this chapter. In it, you'll learn the best way to do each of the types of runs called for in the schedules. You'll also see what to do with your schedule when the almost inevitable roadblocks pop up during your training.

The training schedules in chapters 8 through 12 include the specific workout for each day as well as the category of training for that day. The workouts are divided into the following eight categories: long runs, medium-long runs, marathon-pace runs, general aerobic runs, lactate-threshold runs, recovery runs, $\dot{V}O_2$max intervals, and speed training. Each run is explained here, including how to get the most benefit from a given workout. For an in-depth explanation of the physiological benefit and role of each type of training, see chapter 1.

Long Runs

In the training schedules, a long run is any run of 16 miles (26 km) or longer. The intention of long runs is (obviously) to improve your endurance in preparation for the marathon's 26.2 miles (42.2 km).

To gain the most from your long runs, do them in the correct intensity range. Long runs shouldn't be slow jogs during which you just accumulate time on your feet. As discussed in chapter 1, the appropriate pace for a specific long run depends on the purpose of that run within your training program. The most beneficial intensity range for most of your long runs is 10 to 20 percent slower than your goal marathon race pace. For most marathoners, this pace range coincides with about 74 to 84 percent of maximal heart rate or 65 to 78 percent of heart rate reserve. In this intensity range you find the optimal balance between running hard enough to simulate the muscle patterns and posture you will use at marathon race pace and running moderately enough that you can recover relatively quickly for your other important training sessions.

Start out at the slow end of the range. Gradually pick up the pace so you run the last 5 to 10 miles (8 to 16 km) at about 10 percent slower than your goal marathon race pace. Gradually picking up the pace during your long runs and finishing strongly will also provide positive psychological reinforcement that you're in control of the marathon. To gain the greatest benefit, design your long-run courses to simulate the hill profile of your marathon. (See the section on hill running later in this chapter.) If your long-run course is much hillier than your marathon, then your pace will be somewhat slower.

The schedules also include marathon-specific long runs at goal marathon race pace (discussed later in the chapter) and slower long runs the day after a tune-up race. After a race or hard workout on Saturday, your Sunday long run should be at a relaxed pace because you are likely to be somewhat tired and have stiff muscles, which will increase your likelihood of injury. Start these long runs like a recovery run. If your muscles loosen up as the run progresses, increase the training stimulus by increasing your pace to about 15 to 20 percent slower than marathon race pace.

Medium-Long Runs

A medium-long run is any run of 11 to 15 miles (18 to 24 km). Medium-long runs reinforce the physiological benefits of your long runs. To gain the greatest physiological benefits, the pace for these runs should be similar to the pace for long runs. If you do a hard training session the day before a medium-long run, do the medium-long run toward the slower end of the intensity range.

Avoid the temptation to do your medium-long runs too hard on days when you feel fresh, because this will prolong your recovery time and reduce the quality of your other key workouts. As with long runs, design your courses for medium-long runs to simulate your marathon.

Marathon-Pace Runs

Marathon-pace runs are medium-long or long runs during which you run most of the miles at your goal marathon pace. These runs provide the precise physiological benefit of allowing you to practice the pace, form, and so on of race day. They're also a great confidence booster.

Ryan Hall

Fastest Marathon: 2:06:17
Marathon Highlights:
First place,
2008 U.S. Olympic Trials;
fastest American debut marathon.

It's said that marathoners are made, not born. If so, then Ryan Hall is the proverbial exception that proves the rule.

After all, how many other marathoners ran a 15-miler at altitude as the first run of their life? That was Hall's initiation. After pleading with his father to let him join him on a run, Hall was told he could go along, but only if he made it the whole way. Oh, and no whining. When Hall made it through the run at 9,000 feet in Big Bear Lake, California, it was obvious to his father that his son was meant to run, and run long.

© AP Photo/Frank Franklin II

It took the younger Hall a little longer to figure that out. Even though in high school he regularly did 10-mile runs at a bit slower than 5:00 per mile (again, at altitude), he considered himself a miler. As a collegiate runner at Stanford, his longest serious race on the track was 5,000 meters, and when he made the U.S. team in that event for the 2005 World Championships, his belief that his destiny was in middle-distance running was reinforced. Yet over the next two summers, Hall came nowhere near meeting his expectations in world-class track races.

After a disappointing 2006 outdoor track season, Hall ran the New Haven 20K on Labor Day, winning what was at the time the longest race of his life. The following month, he set an American record of 57:54 for the distance while placing eleventh in the world championships. When he emerged from another three months of altitude training in January 2007, Hall ran a solo 59:43 to win the Houston Half Marathon, becoming the only American to break an hour for the distance and completing his transformation to an elite road racer.

That status has been more than sealed by the first four marathons of his life: an American-debut record of 2:08:24 at London in April 2007; a dominating win at the Olympic Marathon Trials in November 2007, where he ran the second half solo in

(continued)

Ryan Hall *(continued)*

1:02:45 in hilly Central Park; a 2:06:16 at London in 2008; and a tenth-place finish at the Olympics in Beijing.

One key to Hall's success is that he has found the event that best suits his physical and mental make-up. He enjoys and thrives on long runs with solid stretches at marathon race pace. Psychologically, he's more suited to focusing on one race for a long time and then producing a supreme effort than to alternating between training and racing several times a season, as a track racer would do. If you find that, like Hall, you simply like marathon training more than preparing for other events, then that's probably a good sign that the marathon and you are a good match.

Another factor that contributes to Hall's success is the confidence he gains from his training. He runs few, sometimes no tune-up races before a marathon, and instead gauges his fitness from the patterns in his training. As his coach, Terrence Mahon says, "We know more about his marathon preparation from our training runs than from any single race that he could do. Watching how he progresses as a whole in the marathon training buildup allows us to throw out the ebbs and flows, and to see where the average is. If he raced on a day that when he was on a high or a low, then we could get some false data as to how he is really doing, and that could prove confusing." While we advocate a few tune-up races before a marathon, we wholeheartedly agree that the overall quality of your training—especially your marathon-pace runs and tempo runs—is the best way to determine your progress toward your marathon goal.

Related to this focus on the overall pattern is Hall's composure. He says, "One day I will be doing a 13-mile tempo run feeling strong and filled with energy. The very next day I will be doing close to two hours of running (split between two runs) and feel like I couldn't take on a recreational jogger." Rather than despair that the fatigue he felt on the second day meant that he was overtrained or out of shape, Hall recognizes that there will be ebbs and flows during a marathon buildup, both from day to day and week to week. What matters most is accurately assessing the big picture.

Over the past few years, the benefits of marathon-pace runs have become more fully recognized, and we have included more of these sessions in this edition of *Advanced Marathoning*.

Start these runs comfortably, as you would other medium-long or long runs, and then run the last portion at marathon race pace. For example, if the schedule calls for 16 miles (26 km) with 12 miles (19 km) at marathon race pace, gradually pick up the pace during the first 4 miles (6 km), and then run the last 12 miles (19 km) at marathon goal pace. The objective of these runs is to prepare your body as specifically as possible for your upcoming marathon, so design your course to simulate your marathon as closely as possible. For most marathoners, marathon pace coincides with about 79 to 88 percent of maximal heart rate or 73 to 84 percent of heart rate reserve.

General Aerobic Runs

General aerobic runs include your standard, moderate-effort runs of up to 10 miles (16 km). They are slower than lactate-threshold runs, shorter than medium-long runs, and faster than recovery runs. The intention of general aerobic runs is to enhance your overall aerobic conditioning through boosting your training volume; these runs improve your marathon readiness because many of the beneficial adaptations that improve endurance are related to the total volume of your training.

For most runners, the optimal intensity range for these runs is about 15 to 25 percent slower than marathon race pace. Usually, this pace range coincides with about 70 to 81 percent of maximal heart rate or 62 to 75 percent of heart rate reserve. Because the primary purpose of these runs is to increase your training volume, if you're too tired to do a hard training session the next day, then you're doing your general aerobic runs too hard.

Lactate-Threshold Runs

Lactate-threshold runs are tempo runs in which you run for at least 20 minutes at your lactate-threshold pace. This coincides closely with your current 15K to half marathon race pace. For most marathoners, this pace range corresponds with about 82 to 91 percent of maximal heart rate or 77 to 88 percent of heart rate reserve. Tempo runs provide a strong stimulus to improve your lactate-threshold pace, which leads to similar improvements in your marathon race pace. The lactate-threshold sessions are done after a 2- to 3-mile (3 to 5 km) warm-up and should be followed by a 10- to 15-minute cool-down. The tempo runs in the schedules range from 4 to 7 miles (6 to 11 km) long. As an example, if the schedule calls for 10 miles (16 km) for the day and a 5-mile (8 km) threshold run, warm up for 3 miles (5 km), do the tempo run, then cool down for 2 miles (3 km). Slower runners should run closer to their 15K race pace on tempo runs, whereas faster runners should run closer to their half marathon race pace during these workouts.

Recovery Runs

Recovery runs are relatively short runs done at a relaxed pace to enhance recovery for your next hard workout. These runs aren't necessarily jogs, but they should be noticeably slower than your other workouts of the week. The optimal intensity for recovery runs for most marathoners is to stay below 76 percent of maximal heart rate or 70 percent of heart rate reserve. On a subjective basis, on recovery runs you should feel as if you're storing up energy rather than slowly leaking it. You should finish the run refreshed. Going too hard on recovery days—when your body is most tired—means you'll be more tired than you should when it counts later in the week.

Try to find flat courses for your recovery runs, but if your recovery runs include some hills you will need to extend the range by a few beats per minute on the uphills or run exceedingly slowly. Whenever possible, do your recovery runs on soft surfaces to help speed recovery that much more.

$\dot{V}O_2$max Intervals

The $\dot{V}O_2$max intervals in the schedules range from 600 meters to 1,600 meters in duration and are run at current 5K race pace. Though $\dot{V}O_2$max work is an important part of your marathon preparation, it's not as crucial in the marathon as it is in races such as the 5K and 10K. The $\dot{V}O_2$max sessions in these schedules, then, feature repeats that strike a balance between being long enough to provide a powerful training stimulus and short enough to leave you fresh for your other important workouts of the week.

The same reasoning applies for the prescribed pace in these $\dot{V}O_2$max workouts: Whereas runners focusing on shorter races need to do some of their intervals closer to 3K race pace, marathoners gain maximum benefit from sticking to 5K race pace. By sticking to the lower to middle end of the effective intensity range (i.e., about 93 to 95 percent of maximal heart rate or 91 to 94 percent of heart rate reserve), you'll provide a strong stimulus to improve your $\dot{V}O_2$max while recovering quickly for your other important workouts. For that reason, the training intensities for $\dot{V}O_2$max workouts in table 7.1 (see page 144) call for only the more conservative 5K-pace ranges.

The optimal amount of rest between intervals is debatable. One school of thought is to minimize rest so that your metabolic rate stays high during the entire workout. This strategy makes for very difficult workouts (which can be good), but you risk shortening your workouts. Another school of thought is to allow your heart rate to decrease to 70 percent of your maximal heart rate or 65 percent of your heart rate reserve during your recovery between intervals, which provides close to the optimal balance of effort and recovery.

For the lower-tech crowd, a useful rule of thumb is to allow 50 to 90 percent of the length of time it takes to do the interval for your recovery. For example, if you're running 1,000-meter repeats in 3:20, you would run slowly for 1:40 to 3:00 between intervals. We use this method of measuring recovery in the schedules.

Speed Training

Speed runs are repetitions of 50 to 150 meters that improve leg speed and running form. These workouts train your nervous system to allow you to maintain a faster rate of leg turnover during your races.

© Tom Hauck/Icon SMI

Speed runs train your nervous system to allow you to maintain a faster rate of leg turnover during your races.

These sessions are done after a thorough warm-up and often toward the end of a general aerobic run or a recovery run. Allow yourself plenty of rest between repetitions so that you can run each one with good technique.

A typical session is 10 repetitions of 100 meters in which you accelerate up to full speed over the first 70 meters and then float for the last 30 meters. It's critical to remain relaxed during these accelerations. Avoid clenching your fists, lifting your shoulders, tightening your neck muscles, and so on. Concentrate on running with good form, and focus on one aspect of good form, such as relaxed arms or complete hip extension, during each acceleration.

A typical rest is to jog and walk 100 to 200 meters between repetitions. The most important considerations are to maintain good running form and to concentrate on accelerating powerfully during each repetition.

The prescribed training intensities used in this chapter and in chapters 1 and 3 are summarized in table 7.1. These intensity ranges are appropriate for most experienced marathon runners. Less-experienced runners should generally train at the lower end of the recommended ranges, while elite runners will generally train at the high end of the ranges. (Heart rate isn't relevant during the short speed sessions, so we've left them out of this table.)

TABLE 7.1

Heart Rate Intensities for Marathon Training Workouts

	Maximal heart rate (%)	Heart rate reserve (%)
Long/Medium-long	74-84	65-78
Marathon pace	79-88	73-84
General aerobic	70-81	62-75
Recovery	<76	<70
Lactate threshold	82-91	77-88
$\dot{V}O_2$max (5K pace)	93-95	91-94

Doing Doubles

Marathoners have a tendency to start running twice a day before their weekly mileage warrants it. Doing doubles sounds like serious training, so runners often assume it must be better marathon preparation. The reality is quite different; as you increase your training mileage in preparation for a marathon, you should resist the urge to switch from single runs to doubles.

In chapter 1, we discussed the various training adaptations that are specific to improving your marathon performance. Marathon training focuses on endurance-based adaptations such as depleting your glycogen reserves to provide a stimulus for your body to store more glycogen and training your muscles to utilize more fat at a given speed. You'll provide a greater stimulus for these adaptations through a single 12-mile (19 km) run than by doing a 7-miler (11 km) and a 5-miler (8 km) at the same pace.

It might sound counterintuitive, but runners preparing for shorter races should run more doubles at a given level of weekly mileage than marathoners. Runners focusing on 5Ks, for example, should start adding doubles when their weekly mileage gets above 50. That's because the 5K specialists' main training emphasis is high-quality interval sessions, and more frequent, shorter runs will help keep their legs fresh for these workouts.

For marathoners, the basic guideline is to not do double workouts until you've maximized the amount you're running in single workouts. If you're preparing for a marathon and are running less than 75 miles (121 km) a week, then you shouldn't regularly be running doubles. If you're running less than 75 miles (121 km) a week, by the time you get in your long run and a midweek medium-long run, there's no reason to double more than once or twice a week to get in the remaining miles. It's better to get in longer runs and give your body 22 or 23 hours of recovery between runs.

Once you get above 75 miles (121 km) a week, however, double workouts have a definite role in your marathon program. As with any other aspect of training, doubles should be introduced gradually. Start by adding one double per week and then another, as you gradually increase your mileage. The schedules in chapters 8 through 12 reflect this approach to adding doubles, with double days called for only in the higher-mileage programs.

■ When Doubles Aren't Worth It

The minimum time for an added second run should be 25 minutes. If you run less than that, it's hardly worth the extra time and effort—both physiologically and in taking time from your busy life—to change, get yourself out the door, stretch, shower, and so on. That's especially the case if a too-short, not-crucial run means cutting into precious sleep time. In some situations, it's wiser to add cross-training to your program than to increase your risk of injury with more miles of running. Various options for cross-training are discussed in chapter 4.

How, then, should you introduce doubles into your program? The training schedules in this book add second runs to a day's training for specific reasons. One main category of second runs is on hard days. An easy run in the morning will loosen you up for an evening $\dot{V}O_2$max session or tempo run. Similarly, 30 minutes of easy running in the evening will help you recover from a morning tempo run.

A second main use of doubles in the schedules is on recovery days. When your mileage increases to where your recovery days call for more than 8 miles (13 km) of running, it's time to switch those days to easy doubles. It's easier on your body, and your recovery will be enhanced, if you do two runs of 5 miles (8 km) rather than a single 10-miler (16 km). Avoid the temptation to add mileage to your recovery days for the sole purpose of boosting your weekly mileage. Extra mileage on these days is counterproductive because your recovery will be less complete for your subsequent hard days.

The schedules may also call for an easy second run on the day of your medium-long run. These runs will provide an incremental training stimulus by depleting your carbohydrate stores and training your muscles to rely more on fat at a given speed. It's preferable to do the second, short run in the evening after a medium-long run in the morning. If your schedule is such that you'll be doing your medium-long run in the evening, be sure to run very easily in the morning. As we discuss earlier in this chapter and in chapter 1, medium-long runs bring you the most benefit if they're done at a good pace, so don't let a short morning run detract from the medium-long run's quality. A better-quality medium-long run is preferable to a double in which the medium-long run is a slog.

The schedules never call for a second run on the day of your weekly long run. This is a perfect example of mileage for mileage's sake because an evening run after your long run will only slow your recovery. As soon as you finish your long run, your objective switches to recovering as quickly as possible for your upcoming hard training days.

A Word About "Hard" Days

Looking at these schedules, you might be wondering, *Where are all the "speed" workouts*? After all, it's normal to think that anyone preparing for a marathon should be training as hard as possible, and what better way to be sure that you're doing so than by hitting the track at least once a week for lung-searing intervals, right?

In chapter 1, we explained at length the principles underlying these schedules. Briefly put, we designed the schedules to provide the optimal stimuli to the physiological systems that most determine marathoning success—endurance, lactate threshold, and $\dot{V}O_2max$, in that order of importance. In the long run, so to speak, it's your long runs and tempo runs that have the most relevance to your performance on marathon day, not how often you've churned out a sterling set of half-mile repeats.

During your long buildup, understanding the components of marathon success can provide confidence that you're training properly. Use the explanation of marathon physiology from chapter 1 not only to explain to your training buddies why you won't be joining them for quarters next week but also to remind yourself why you're doing yet another 15-miler (24 km) in the middle of the workweek. If your running friends continue to chide you that you're not training hard enough, invite them to follow the schedules with you for a few weeks, then report back. We suspect they'll have gotten the message by then.

What About Hill Workouts?

In the training schedules, we don't prescribe specific hill training sessions. That's because how much to focus on hill training depends on the topography of your marathon. For one of the pancake-flat courses designed to yield fast times, such as London, Chicago, or Berlin, you'll need to be prepared to run for more than 2 hours over unvarying terrain. If, however, you'll be racing on a hilly course, then the more closely you can simulate the terrain of the race in your training, both up and down, the better. (The classic course for which race simulation is essential is the Boston Marathon, which has sucked the lifeblood from many an unprepared runner.) By planning training runs to include hills of roughly the same length and steepness as your upcoming race, you'll give yourself the best chance for an optimal performance on race day.

Any of the workouts in the training schedules can be run on hills. Once or twice per week, your tempo runs, long runs, medium-long runs, and general aerobic runs should mimic the hill profile of your upcoming marathon. Simply adjust your pace to keep the effort at the correct intensity. (Allow your heart rate to increase by 5 to 8 beats per minute on the uphills, but be sure to ease up after the hills to get back into the appropriate range.) You can even do some of your $\dot{V}O_2$max sessions up and down hills, although it's easy to blow up by going too hard early in the workout.

If you live in the flatlands but are training for a hilly marathon, don't despair—with a bit of creativity you can gain the benefits of hill running. Runners in Miami have been known to run the ramps of a parking garage on Sunday mornings, and you can replicate almost any hill workout on a treadmill.

Correct uphill running technique is relatively simple. The most common error running uphill is leaning forward, which is counterproductive to maintaining speed. Looking ahead and not down will help you retain a more-upright posture. Let your stride shorten and your knees lift naturally so that you feel as efficient as possible. You will tend to use your arms more as you lift your knees, but try to keep your shoulders and arms relaxed. On downhills, try not to brake. Keep your center of gravity perpendicular to the hill so that gravity can help you get down it as quickly as possible.

Tweaking the Schedules

Part of the challenge of the marathon is that preparing for it takes so long and the training required is so demanding that roadblocks along the way to your goal are nearly inevitable. It's important not only to organize your training and life so that as few impediments as possible crop up but also to deal with the ones that nevertheless occur. The most common roadblocks are injuries and illnesses, bad weather, and outside commitments. Let's consider each of these intrusions into your marathon preparation to see how to adjust the schedules for them. Also, let's look at what, if any, adjustments older marathoners, who might need more recovery than younger runners, should make to the schedules.

Injuries and Illnesses

Injuries and illnesses are best caught early. Successful marathoners have the ability to recognize an injury or illness at an early stage before it becomes serious. Returning to training after an injury or illness requires careful analysis—too much too soon will result in additional time off. During this period, it's important to avoid the factors that caused the injury or illness in the first place, such as worn-out shoes, running on concrete, overtraining, or a lack of sleep. Be sure to carefully read chapter 3 to learn how to stay on top of your recovery so that your chances of getting hurt or sick are lessened.

If you're forced to miss more than a few days of training, then you need to decide whether to try to catch up or revise your marathon goal. This decision will be influenced by how much time you missed, how long you've been preparing, and how many weeks are left until your marathon. Missing 2 1/2 weeks of preparation when you have 16 weeks to go is no big deal, but missing that amount of time during the last 2 months of preparation will likely require you to modify your goal.

Table 7.2 provides guidelines for when you may need to revise your goals after an injury or illness. Typically, if you've lost less than 10 days of training, then you can safely start back where you should have been on the schedules. If you've missed $\dot{V}O_2$max workouts, however, you may need to slow your pace during your next few $\dot{V}O_2$max sessions to reflect the lost time. If you've lost 10 or more days of training in the 8 weeks before your marathon, be open to revising your goal. When you resume full training, gather information from your timed sessions to get a sense of how much fitness you've lost and whether your marathon goal pace needs to be slowed by at least a few seconds per mile (per 1.6 km).

TABLE 7.2

Making Up for Lost Time

Number of days missed	8 weeks or more until marathon	Less than 8 weeks until marathon
<10	Resume schedule	Resume schedule
10-20	Resume schedule	Revise goal
>20	Revise goal	Revise goal

Mother Nature

In general, you'll just have to deal with bad weather. Sometimes, however, Mother Nature dishes up a blizzard or blistering-hot weather that's counter-productive to continued healthy training. If you can, find a treadmill indoors or choose an appropriate cross-training activity for a couple of days until the weather becomes bearable.

As with other factors influencing your marathon preparation, weather might necessitate some not-minor changes in your life. For example, you might need to alter your normal schedule during oppressive summer heat so that you can get in reasonable training early in the morning. Or if your area has been snowed under for weeks, you'll probably need to find a few well-paved stretches where you can safely do multiple laps to get in your miles.

Try to anticipate weather when picking your marathon goal. If you don't run well in the heat and live in a sultry climate, it makes little sense to plan for a September marathon because your hardest training will need to occur during the least conducive weather of the year. Similarly, Boston in April can be a tough goal if you live in an area where winter running is a daily challenge.

The Real World

There's really no excuse for outside commitments to regularly interfere with your marathon preparation. Put more gently, don't set an ambitious marathon goal when you know the rest of your life will be busier than usual. Once you've picked your marathon and have decided how long you'll prepare for it, try to anticipate and eliminate factors that would significantly interfere with your training.

Of course, regardless of how focused you are on your training, you're going to have the occasional day when meeting your training goal is exceedingly difficult, if not impossible. A sick child, an unsympathetic boss, or a traffic accident all have a way of dashing plans for a high-quality tempo run. If necessary, juggle the days in the training schedule you're following so that you get in the most important workouts while still allowing for adequate recovery. A good rule of thumb is that if you can do 90 percent of the planned training schedule, then your preparation is going well.

Adjusting for Age

The training schedules in the following chapters are based on the classic stress/recovery principle of adaptation. That is, all runners need easy days after their key training sessions before they're ready to benefit from more hard work. Many older runners find that they need more of those easy days between long or fast workouts than their younger counterparts.

Because there's such great variance in how quickly masters runners recover, we're reluctant to offer hard-and-fast recommendations on how to adjust the schedules for age. After all, a runner in her early 50s who has been running for 5 years probably has fresher legs than a man in his 50s in his third decade of running. What we can say to our older readers is to pick which schedule to follow based on a sound assessment of your current capabilities rather than memories of how you could train in your glory days. That might mean aiming for a lower peak mileage, and it almost certainly means taking it very easy on your recovery days. You might find that you can better hit the key workouts—the long runs, the medium-long runs, the tempo and marathon-pace runs—by substituting cross-training for running on some recovery days. (See chapter 4 for more on this approach.)

If, after making these adjustments, you're still too tired to do the key sessions in the correct intensity range, then add in extra recovery days. You could, for example, convert the 12-week schedule into a 14-week schedule, thereby getting in the important workouts but spreading the stress over a longer buildup.

Older marathoners should pay special attention to the section in chapter 3 on accelerating recovery. We can well attest that less-than-ideal choices about training, stretching, diet, sleep, and so on take far more of a toll now than they did when we were in our late 20s. If you want to continue to aim high as a marathoner in middle age and beyond, we salute you. Maximize your chances of success by consistently doing the little nonrunning things that younger runners often ignore.

Now that we've looked at the principles behind successful marathon training and racing and how to implement those principles, let's get to what you probably care most about—the training schedules, which constitute the rest of this book.

Marathon Training on Up to 55 Miles (88 km) per Week

This chapter is for runners who typically train less than 40 miles (64 km) per week but who are willing to up their mileage to 55 miles (88 km) per week during marathon preparation. It includes two schedules: an 18-week schedule that starts at 33 miles (53 km) per week and a 12-week schedule that starts at 35 miles (56 km) per week. Each of these schedules increases weekly mileage progressively to a peak of 55 miles (88 km).

As discussed in chapter 1, it's useful to divide your overall training schedule into phases, called mesocycles. The training schedules consist of four mesocycles that focus on endurance, lactate threshold and endurance, race preparation, and tapering, respectively. A final schedule, which contains a 5-week postmarathon recovery program, can follow either of the training schedules.

Of the two training schedules presented in this chapter, we recommend the 18-week schedule for most situations. Eighteen weeks is plenty of time to stimulate the necessary adaptations to improve your marathon performance. At the same time, 18 weeks is short enough that you can focus your efforts without becoming bored with the process.

At times, however, you simply don't have 18 weeks to prepare for your marathon. The 12-week schedule includes the same mesocycles as the 18-week schedule, but because of the short time for preparation, each of these mesocycles is abbreviated. If you go into a marathon in a rush, you must realize that your preparation won't be as thorough as if you had longer to prepare. The 12-week schedule takes into account that sometimes circumstances don't allow you the optimal length of time for preparation and strives to provide a compact yet effective training program.

Before Starting the Schedules

These schedules are challenging right from the start and get harder as your marathon approaches. So that you can progress as the training increases in quantity and quality, and to minimize your chances of injury, you should be able to complete the first week of the schedule without too much effort.

Be realistic in assessing whether you're ready for the first week of the schedule. For example, if you've been running 20 miles (32 km) per week and your longest run in the last several weeks is 6 miles (10 km), now isn't the time to suddenly jump to a 33-mile (53 km) week containing a 12-mile (19 km) run and a 4-mile (6 km) tempo run, as the first week of the 18-week schedule calls for. The idea behind the schedules isn't to make you as tired as possible as soon as possible but to apply repeated training stress that you absorb and benefit from.

As a rule, you should be running at least 25 miles (40 km) a week before starting these schedules, and in the last month you should have comfortably completed a run close in length to the long run called for in the first week of the schedule.

Reading the Schedules

The schedules are presented in a day-by-day format. This is in response to requests from readers of our first book, *Road Racing for Serious Runners*, to provide schedules that specify what to do each day of the week.

The main limitation with this approach is that it's impossible to guess the myriad of outside factors that may influence your day-to-day nonrunning life. Work schedules, family life, relationships, school commitments, and Mother Nature all play a part in determining when you get to do your long runs and other aspects of marathon preparation. You'll no doubt require some flexibility in your training and will need to juggle days around from time to time. That's expected, and as long as you don't try to make up for lost time by doing several hard days in a row, you should be able to avoid injury and overtraining. By following the principles covered in the earlier chapters, you'll be able to safely fine-tune the training schedules to suit your circumstances.

The schedules express each day's training in miles and kilometers; use whichever you're accustomed to. The mile and kilometer figures for each day (and the weekly total) are rough equivalents of each other, not a conversion from one to the other accurate to the third decimal point.

Following the Schedules

Each column of the schedules represents a week's training. For example, in the 12-week schedule, the column for 11 weeks to goal indicates that at the end of that week you have 11 weeks until your marathon. The schedules continue week by week until race week.

We have included the specific workout for each day as well as the category of training for that day. For example, in the 18-week schedule, on the Friday of the 7-weeks-to-goal column, the specific workout is a 12-mile (19 km) run, and the category of training for that day is medium-long run. This aspect of the schedules allows you to quickly see the balance of training during each week and the progression of workouts from week to week. Look again at the 18-week schedule—it's easy to see that with 7 weeks to go until the marathon, there are four recovery days (two of running, two of rest or cross-training), along with a lactate-threshold session, a long run, and a medium-long run. Looking at the row for Sunday, it's easy to see how the long runs progress and then taper in the last few weeks before the marathon.

The workouts are divided into the following eight categories: long runs, medium-long runs, marathon-pace runs, general aerobic runs, lactate-threshold runs, recovery runs, VO_2max intervals, and speed training. Each of these categories is explained in depth in chapter 7, and the physiology behind the training is explained in chapter 1.

© Matthias B. Krause/Icon SMI

The 18-week schedule is recommended for most situations and is ideal for preparing for a marathon of great personal importance, like the New York City Marathon.

Racing Strategies

We discussed marathon race strategy at length in chapter 6. If you follow one of the schedules in this chapter, you're probably a midpack runner. Unlike the situation the runners at the front of the field often face, you'll probably have plenty of people around you to run with from start to finish. This can be good and bad.

On the plus side, obviously, you're less likely to face lonely stretches with nobody to run with. Use this probability to your advantage—soon after the start, try to find other runners who look capable of maintaining your goal pace through at least 20 miles (32 km), and encourage them to work with you. (If they fall apart at 21 miles, that's their problem, right?)

By following one of this chapter's schedules, you'll be better able to hold up past 20 miles (32 km) than most of the runners who begin the race at your pace. Your superior preparation will mean you'll have the pleasure of continually passing people until the finish. Look forward to this time. Pick a runner a few hundred yards or meters up the road, and set the short-term goal of catching him or her. Then go after your next victim, and keep doing so until the finish.

On the not-so-good side, you're more likely than those at the front of the field to feel crowded in the early miles. Try not to let this upset you. Tell yourself that the crowds are helping you not to go out too fast, and if need be, work up gradually to your goal pace.

Don't try to make up lost time suddenly if a break in the crowd appears. Instead, when you have clear running room, run no more than 10 seconds per mile (per 1.6 km) faster than goal pace until you're back on schedule; you will burn less glycogen and be less likely to accumulate lactate by catching up gradually. If the deficit you have to make up isn't too great, 5 seconds per mile (per 1.6 km) faster than goal pace is an even safer approach. Once you're back on track, ease back to goal pace.

After the Marathon

The final schedule in this chapter is a 5-week recovery schedule for after the marathon. This is the fifth mesocycle; it completes the training program and leaves you ready to prepare for future challenges.

The recovery schedule is purposely conservative. You have little to gain by rushing back into training, and your risk of injury is exceptionally high at this point, owing to the reduced resiliency of your muscles and connective tissue after the marathon.

The schedule starts with 2 days off from running, which is the bare minimum of time away from running you should allow yourself. If you still have acute soreness or tightness so severe that it will alter your form, or if you just don't feel like running, certainly feel free to take more than 2 days off. If ever there was a time to lose your marathoner's mind-set, the week after your goal race is it. Even most of the top runners in the world take days off after a marathon. They know that the nearly negligible benefits of a short run at this time are far outweighed by the risks. Not running now also increases your chances of being inspired to resume hard training when your body allows it.

Of course, some people don't consider themselves real runners unless they run pretty much every day of their lives. Plod through a few miles if you must, but be aware that you're prolonging your recovery.

What better aids recovery during this time is light cross-training, such as swimming or cycling. These activities increase blood flow through your muscles without subjecting them to pounding. Walking will also achieve this in the week after the marathon.

One way to ensure that you don't run too hard too soon after your marathon is to use a heart rate monitor. As discussed in chapter 3, a heart rate monitor can help prevent you from going too fast on recovery days. During the first few weeks after the marathon, keep your heart rate below 76 percent of your maximal heart rate or 70 percent of your heart rate reserve. Running at this intensity will help your body overcome the stress of the marathon as quickly as possible.

During this 5-week recovery schedule, the number of days of running per week increases from 3 to 5. At the end of the 5 weeks, you should be fully recovered from the marathon and, with a little luck, be injury free and mentally fresh.

Mesocycle 1—Endurance

	WEEKS TO GOAL					
	17	16	15	14	13	(Recovery) 12
Monday	Rest or cross-training	Rest or cross-training	Rest or cross-training	Rest or cross-training	Rest or cross-training	Rest or cross-training
Tuesday	Lactate threshold 8 mi (13 km) w/ 4 mi (6 km) @ 15K to half marathon race pace	General aerobic + speed 8 mi (13 km) w/ 10 × 100 m strides	General aerobic 10 mi (16 km)	General aerobic + speed 8 mi (13 km) w/ 10 × 100 m strides	Lactate threshold 9 mi (14 km) w/ 5 mi (8 km) @ 15K to half marathon race pace	General aerobic + speed 8 mi (13 km) w/ 10 × 100 m strides
Wednesday	Rest or cross-training	Rest or cross-training	Recovery 4 mi (6 km)	Recovery 5 mi (8 km)	Recovery 5 mi (8 km)	Recovery 5 mi (8 km)
Thursday	General aerobic 9 mi (14 km)	General aerobic 10 mi (16 km)	Lactate threshold 8 mi (13 km) w/ 4 mi (6 km) @ 15K to half marathon race pace	General aerobic 10 mi (16 km)	General aerobic 10 mi (16 km)	General aerobic 8 mi (13 km)
Friday	Rest or cross-training	Rest or cross-training	Rest or cross-training	Rest or cross-training	Rest or cross-training	Rest or cross-training
Saturday	Recovery 4 mi (6 km)	Recovery 5 mi (8 km)	Recovery 4 mi (6 km)	Recovery 4 mi (6 km)	Recovery 5 mi (8 km)	Recovery 4 mi (6 km)
Sunday	Medium-long run ·12 mi (19 km)	Marathon-pace run 13 mi (21 km) w/ 8 mi (13 km) @ marathon race pace	Medium-long run 14 mi (23 km)	Medium-long run 15 mi (24 km)	Marathon-pace run 16 mi (26 km) w/ 10 mi (16 km) @ marathon race pace	Medium-long run 12 mi (19 km)
Weekly volume	33 mi/53 km	36 mi/58 km	40 mi/64 km	42 mi/67 km	45 mi/72 km	37 mi/59 km

Mesocycle 2—Lactate Threshold + Endurance

	WEEKS TO GOAL				
				(Recovery)	
	11	**10**	**9**	**8**	**7**
Monday	Rest or cross-training	Rest or cross-training	Rest or cross-training	Rest or cross-training	Rest or cross-training
Tuesday	Lactate threshold 10 mi (16 km) w/ 5 mi (8 km) @ 15K to half marathon race pace	Recovery + speed 7 mi (11 km) w/ 6 × 100 m strides	Recovery 6 mi (10 km)	General aerobic 8 mi (13 km)	Recovery + speed 7 mi (11 km) w/ 6 × 100 m strides
Wednesday	Recovery 4 mi (6 km)	Medium-long run 12 mi (19 km)	Medium-long run 14 mi (23 km)	$\dot{V}O_2$max 8 mi (13 km) w/ 5 × 800 m @ 5K race pace; jog 50 to 90% interval time between	Lactate threshold 11 mi (18 km) w/ 7 mi (11 km) @ 15K to half marathon race pace
Thursday	Medium-long run 11 mi (18 km)	Rest or cross-training	Recovery 6 mi (10 km)	Recovery 5 mi (8 km)	Rest or cross-training
Friday	Rest or cross-training	Lactate threshold 10 mi (16 km) w/ 6 mi (10 km) @ 15K to half marathon race pace	Rest or cross-training	Rest or cross-training	Medium-long run 12 mi (19 km)
Saturday	General aerobic + speed 7 mi (11 km) w/ 8 × 100 m strides p.m.	Recovery 5 mi (8 km)	Recovery + speed 6 mi (10 km) w/ 6 × 100 m strides	General aerobic + speed 8 mi (13 km) w/ 8 × 100 m strides	Recovery 5 mi (8 km)
Sunday	Long run 18 mi (29 km)	Long run 20 mi (32 km)	Marathon-pace run 16 mi (26 km) w/ 12 mi (19 km) @ marathon race pace	Medium-long run 14 mi (23 km)	Long run 20 mi (32 km)
Weekly volume	50 mi/80 km	54 mi/86 km	48 mi/79 km	43 mi/70 km	55 mi/88 km

Mesocycle 3—Race Preparation

	WEEKS TO GOAL			
	6	5	4	3
Monday	Rest or cross-training	Rest or cross-training	Rest or cross-training	Rest or cross-training
Tuesday	$\dot{V}O_2$max 8 mi (13 km) w/ 5 × 600 m @ 5K race pace; jog 50 to 90% interval time between	General aerobic 8 mi (13 km)	$\dot{V}O_2$max 8 mi (13 km) w/ 5 × 600 m @ 5K race pace; jog 50 to 90% interval time between	Recovery + speed 7 mi (11 km) w/ 6 × 100 m strides
Wednesday	Medium-long run 12 mi (19 km)	$\dot{V}O_2$max 9 mi (14 km) w/ 5 × 1,000 m @ 5K race pace; jog 50 to 90% interval time between	Medium-long run 11 mi (18 km)	$\dot{V}O_2$max 10 mi (16 km) w/ 4 × 1,200 m @ 5K race pace; jog 50 to 90% interval time between
Thursday	Rest or cross-training	Rest or cross-training	Rest or cross-training	Rest or cross-training
Friday	Recovery + speed 5 mi (8 km) w/ 6 × 100 m strides	Medium-long run 12 mi (19 km)	Recovery + speed 4 mi (6 km) w/ 6 × 100 m strides	Medium-long run 11 mi (18 km)
Saturday	8K-15K tune-up race (total 9-13 mi/14-21 km)	Recovery 5 mi (8 km)	8K-15K tune-up race (total 9-13 mi/14-21 km)	Recovery 4 mi (6 km)
Sunday	Long run 17 mi (27 km)	Marathon-pace run 18 mi (29 km) w/ 14 mi (23 km) @ marathon race pace	Long run 17 mi (27 km)	Long run 20 mi (32 km)
Weekly volume	51-55 mi/81-88 km	52 mi/83 km	49-53 mi/78-85 km	52 mi/83 km

Mesocycle 4—Taper and Race

	WEEKS TO GOAL		
	2	**1**	**Race week**
Monday	Rest or cross-training	Rest or cross-training	Rest
Tuesday	$\dot{V}O_2$max 8 mi (13 km) w/ 5 × 600 m @ 5K race pace; jog 50 to 90% interval time between	General aerobic + speed 7 mi (11 km) w/ 8 × 100 m strides	Recovery 6 mi (10 km)
Wednesday	Recovery 6 mi (10 km)	$\dot{V}O_2$max 8 mi (13 km) w/ 3 × 1,600 m @ 5K race pace; jog 50 to 90% interval time between	Dress rehearsal 7 mi (11 km) w/ 2 mi (3 km) @ marathon race pace
Thursday	Rest or cross-training	Rest or cross-training	Rest
Friday	Recovery + speed 4 mi (6 km) w/ 6 × 100 m strides	Recovery + speed 5 mi (8 km) w/ 6 × 100 m strides	Recovery + speed 5 mi (8 km) w/ 6 × 100 m strides
Saturday	8K-10K tune-up race (total 9-11 mi/14-18 km)	Rest or cross-training	Recovery 4 mi (6 km)
Sunday	Long run 16 mi (26 km)	Medium-long run 12 mi (19 km)	Goal marathon
Weekly volume	43-45 mi/69-73 km	32 mi/51 km	22 mi/35 km (6 days prerace)

Mesocycle 1—Endurance

	WEEKS TO GOAL			
	11	**10**	**9**	**8**
Monday	Rest or cross-training	Rest or cross-training	Rest or cross-training	Rest or cross-training
Tuesday	General aerobic + speed 8 mi (13 km) w/ 10 × 100 m strides p.m.	Medium-long run 11 mi (18 km)	General aerobic + speed 8 mi (13 km) w/ 10 × 100 m strides	Recovery 5 mi (8 km)
Wednesday	Rest or cross-training	Rest or cross-training	Recovery 4 mi (6 km)	Lactate threshold 10 mi (16 km) w/ 5 mi (8 km) @ 15K to half marathon race pace
Thursday	General aerobic 9 mi (14 km)	Lactate threshold 8 mi (13 km) w/ 4 mi (6 km) @ 15K to half marathon race pace	Medium-long run 11 mi (18 km)	Medium-long run 11 mi (18 km)
Friday	Rest or cross-training	Rest or cross-training	Rest or cross-training	Rest or cross-training
Saturday	Recovery 5 mi (8 km)	Recovery 5 mi (8 km)	Recovery 4 mi (6 km)	Recovery 5 mi (8 km)
Sunday	Marathon-pace run 13 mi (21 km) w/ 8 mi (13 km) @ marathon race pace	Medium-long run 15 mi (24 km)	Marathon-pace run 16 mi (26 km) w/ 10 mi (16 km) @ marathon race pace	Long run 17 mi (27 km)
Weekly volume	35 mi/56 km	39 mi/63 km	43 mi/69 km	48 mi/77 km

Mesocycle 2—Lactate Threshold + Endurance

	WEEKS TO GOAL		
	(Recovery) 7	6	5
Monday	Rest or cross-training	Rest or cross-training	Rest or cross-training
Tuesday	Rest or cross-training	Recovery 5 mi (8 km)	Recovery + speed 6 mi (10 km) w/ 6 × 100 m strides p.m.
Wednesday	Medium-long run 12 mi (19 km)	V̇O₂max 10 mi (16 km) w/ 5 × 1,000 m @ 5K race pace; jog 50 to 90% interval time between	Medium-long run 12 mi (19 km)
Thursday	Rest or cross-training	Medium-long run 12 mi (19 km)	Rest or cross-training
Friday	Lactate threshold 9 mi (14 km) w/ 4 mi (6 km) @ 15K to half marathon race pace	Rest or cross-training	Lactate threshold 12 mi (19 km) w/ 7 mi (11 km) @ 15K to half marathon race pace
Saturday	Recovery 5 mi (8 km)	Recovery + speed 6 mi (10 km) w/ 6 × 100 m strides	Recovery 5 mi (8 km)
Sunday	Long run 16 mi (26 km)	Marathon-pace run 15 mi (24 km) w/ 12 mi (19 km) @ marathon race pace	Long run 20 mi (32 km)
Weekly volume	42 mi/67 km	48 mi/77 km	55 mi/88 km

Up to 55 Miles per Week
12-Week Schedule

Mesocycle 3—Race Preparation

	WEEKS TO GOAL		
	4	3	2
Monday	Rest or cross-training	Rest or cross-training	Rest or cross-training
Tuesday	$\dot{V}O_2$max 8 mi (13 km) w/ 5 × 600 m @ 5K race pace; jog 50 to 90% interval time between	Recovery + speed 7 mi (11 km) w/ 6 × 100 m strides	$\dot{V}O_2$max 8 mi (13 km) w/ 5 × 600 m @ 5K race pace; jog 50 to 90% interval time between
Wednesday	Medium-long run 11 mi (18 km)	$\dot{V}O_2$max 10 mi (16 km) w/ 4 × 1,200 m @ 5K race pace; jog 50 to 90% interval time between	Recovery 6 mi (10 km)
Thursday	Rest or cross-training	Rest or cross-training	Rest or cross-training
Friday	Recovery + speed 4 mi (6 km) w/ 6 × 100 m strides	Medium-long run 11 mi (18 km)	Recovery + speed 4 mi (6 km) w/ 6 × 100 m strides
Saturday	8K-15K tune-up race (total 9-13 mi/14-21 km)	Recovery 4 mi (6 km)	8K-10K tune-up race (total 9-11 mi/14-18 km)
Sunday	Long run 17 mi (27 km)	Long run 20 mi (32 km)	Long run 16 mi (26 km)
Weekly volume	49-53 mi/78-85 km	52 mi/84 km	43-45 mi/67-71 km

Mesocycle 4—Taper and Race

	WEEKS TO GOAL	
	1	**Race week**
Monday	Rest or cross-training	Rest
Tuesday	General aerobic + speed 7 mi (11 km) w/ 8 × 100 m strides	Recovery 6 mi (10 km)
Wednesday	$\dot{V}O_2$max 8 mi (13 km) w/ 3 × 1,600 m @ 5K race pace; jog 50 to 90% interval time between	Dress rehearsal 7 mi (11 km) w/ 2 mi (3 km) @ marathon race pace
Thursday	Rest or cross-training	Rest
Friday	Recovery + speed 5 mi (8 km) w/ 6 × 100 m strides	Recovery + speed 5 mi (8 km) w/ 6 × 100 m strides
Saturday	Rest or cross-training	Recovery 4 mi (6 km)
Sunday	Medium-long run 12 mi (19 km)	Goal marathon
Weekly volume	32 mi/51 km	22 mi/35 km (6 days prerace)

Mesocycle 5—Recovery

	WEEKS TO GOAL				
	1	2	3	4	5
Monday	Rest or cross-training	Rest or cross-training	Rest or cross-training	Rest or cross-training	Rest or cross-training
Tuesday	Rest or cross-training	Recovery 5 mi (8 km)	Recovery 5 mi (8 km)	General aerobic 7 mi (11 km)	General aerobic 7 mi (11 km)
Wednesday	Recovery 4 mi (6 km)	Recovery 5 mi (8 km)	Recovery 5 mi (8 km)	Recovery 5 mi (8 km)	Recovery 5 mi (8 km)
Thursday	Rest or cross-training	Rest or cross-training	Rest or cross-training	Rest or cross-training	Rest or cross-training
Friday	Recovery 4 mi (6 km)	Recovery 6 mi (10 km)	General aerobic + speed 7 mi (11 km) w/ 8 × 100 m strides	General aerobic + speed 8 mi (13 km) w/ 8 × 100 m strides	General aerobic + speed 8 mi (13 km) w/ 8 × 100 m strides
Saturday	Rest or cross-training	Rest or cross-training	Rest or cross-training	Rest or cross-training	Recovery 4 mi (6 km)
Sunday	Recovery 5 mi (8 km)	Recovery 7 mi (11 km)	General aerobic 9 mi (14 km)	General aerobic 10 mi (16 km)	Medium-long run 11 mi (18 km)
Weekly volume	13 mi/20 km	23 mi/37 km	26 mi/41 km	30 mi/48 km	35 mi/56 km

Up to 55 Miles per Week
Recovery

Marathon Training on 55 to 70 Miles (88 to 113 km) per Week

This chapter is for mid- to high-mileage marathoners who train 55 to 70 miles (88 to 113 km) per week. It includes two schedules: an 18-week schedule that starts at 54 miles (87 km) per week and a 12-week schedule that starts at 55 miles (88 km) per week. Each of these schedules increases weekly mileage progressively to a peak of 70 miles (113 km).

As discussed in chapter 1, it's useful to divide your overall training schedule into phases, called mesocycles. The training schedules consist of four mesocycles that focus on endurance, lactate threshold and endurance, race preparation, and tapering, respectively. A final schedule, which contains a 5-week postmarathon recovery program, can follow either of the training schedules.

Of the two training schedules presented in this chapter, we recommend the 18-week schedule for most situations. Eighteen weeks is plenty of time to stimulate the necessary adaptations to improve your marathon performance. At the same time, 18 weeks is short enough that you can focus your efforts without becoming bored with the process.

At times, however, you simply don't have 18 weeks to prepare for your marathon. The 12-week schedule includes the same mesocycles as the 18-week schedules, but because of the short time for preparation, each of these mesocycles is abbreviated. If you go into a marathon in a rush, you must realize that your preparation won't be as thorough as if you had longer to prepare. The 12-week schedule takes into account that sometimes circumstances don't allow you the optimal length of time for preparation and strives to provide a compact yet effective training program.

Before Starting the Schedules

These schedules are challenging right from the start and get harder as your marathon approaches. So that you can progress as the training increases in quantity and quality, and to minimize your chances of injury, you should be able to complete the first week of the schedule without too much effort.

Be realistic in assessing whether you're ready for the first week of the schedule. For example, if you've been running 30 miles (48 km) per week and your longest run in the last several weeks is 8 miles (13 km), now isn't the time to suddenly jump to a 54-mile (86 km) week containing a 15-mile (24 km) run and a 4-mile (6 km) tempo run, as the first week of the 18-week schedule calls for. The idea behind the schedules isn't to make you as tired as possible as soon as possible but to apply repeated training stress that you absorb and benefit from.

As a rule, you should be running at least 45 miles (72 km) a week before starting these schedules, and in the last month you should have comfortably completed a run close in length to the long run called for in the first week of the schedule.

Reading the Schedules

The schedules are presented in a day-by-day format. This is in response to requests from readers of our first book, *Road Racing for Serious Runners*, to provide schedules that specify what to do each day of the week.

The main limitation with this approach is that it's impossible to guess the myriad of outside factors that may influence your day-to-day nonrunning life. Work schedules, family life, relationships, school commitments, and Mother Nature all play a part in determining when you get to do your long runs and other aspects of marathon preparation. You'll no doubt require some flexibility in your training and will need to juggle days around from time to time. That's expected, and as long as you don't try to make up for lost time by doing several hard days in a row, you should be able to avoid injury and overtraining. By following the principles covered in the earlier chapters, you'll be able to safely fine-tune the training schedules to suit your circumstances.

The schedules express each day's training in miles and kilometers; use whichever you're accustomed to. The mile and kilometer figures for each day (and the weekly total) are rough equivalents of each other, not a conversion from one to the other accurate to the third decimal point.

Following the Schedules

Each column of the schedules represents a week's training. For example, in the 12-week schedule, the column for 11 weeks to goal indicates that at the end of that week you have 11 weeks until your marathon. The schedules continue week by week until race week.

We have included the specific workout for each day as well as the category of training for that day. For example, in the 18-week schedule, on the Tuesday of the 7-weeks-to-go column, the specific workouts are a 6-mile (10 km) run and a 4-mile (6 km) run, and the category of training for that day is recovery. This aspect of the schedules allows you to quickly see the balance of training during each week and the progression of workouts from week to week. Look again at the 18-week schedule—it's easy to see that with 7 weeks to go until the marathon, there are four recovery days that week, along with a lactate-threshold session, a long run, and a medium-long run. Looking at the row for Sunday, it's easy to see how the long runs progress and then taper in the last few weeks before the marathon.

The workouts are divided into the following eight categories: long runs, medium-long runs, marathon-pace runs, general aerobic runs, lactate-threshold runs, recovery runs, VO_2max intervals, and speed training. Each of these categories is explained in depth in chapter 7, and the physiology behind the training is explained in chapter 1.

As discussed in chapter 4, sometimes marathoners benefit from running twice a day. This is obviously the case for elites cranking out 130-mile (209 km) weeks, but it isn't necessary on a regular basis if you're running 50 to 70 miles (80 to 113 km) per week. In these schedules, doubles are called for only on the occasional recovery day, with a total of 10 miles (16 km) for the day. On these days, your recovery will be enhanced by doing a 6-miler (10 km) and a 4-miler (6 km) rather than putting in one 10-mile (16 km) run. Instead of making you more tired, splitting your mileage like this on easy days will speed your recovery because each run will increase blood flow to your muscles yet take little out of you.

Racing Strategies

We discussed marathon race strategy at length in chapter 6. Part of that discussion centered on running with a group when possible. If you follow one of the schedules in this chapter, you might well be finishing within the top quarter or third of the field in your marathon. That means you're likely to have runners around you throughout the marathon, especially in a big-city race, but there won't be so many people in front of you at the start that you'll spend the first few miles navigating around crowds. Make use of this probable position within the field; once you feel as if you're running

During the race, try to find others who appear to be able to sustain your pace until the end and run with them.

comfortably at your goal pace, look around for other runners who appear able to sustain the pace until the end. Talk to them, ask what their goals are, and try to find others to run with.

In chapter 6, we also discuss the importance of a conservative early pace. Although you'll be well trained if you follow one of these schedules, you won't have as large a margin of error as those who have regularly put in 85 miles (137 km) a week or more. If you run intelligently in the early part of the race, then you'll have runners to pick off regularly in the last 10 miles (16 km) or so because others who are either less prepared or more foolhardy will come back to you.

After the Marathon

The final schedule in this chapter is a 5-week recovery schedule for after the marathon. This is the fifth mesocycle; it completes the training program and leaves you ready to prepare for future challenges.

The recovery schedule is purposely conservative. You have little to gain by rushing back into training, and your risk of injury is exceptionally high at this point, owing to the reduced resiliency of your muscles and connective tissue after the marathon.

The schedule starts with 2 days off from running, which is the bare minimum of time away from running you should allow yourself. If you still have acute soreness or tightness so severe that it will alter your form, or if you just don't feel like running, certainly feel free to take more than 2 days off. If ever there was a time to lose your marathoner's mind-set, the week after your goal race is it. Even most of the top runners in the world take days off after a marathon. They know that the nearly negligible benefits of a short run at this time are far outweighed by the risks. Not running now will also increase your chances of being inspired to resume hard training when your body allows it.

Of course, some people don't consider themselves real runners unless they run pretty much every day of their lives. Plod through a few miles if you must, but be aware that you're prolonging your recovery.

What better aids recovery during this time is light cross-training, such as swimming or cycling. These activities increase blood flow through your muscles without subjecting them to pounding. Walking will also achieve this in the week after the marathon.

One way to ensure that you don't run too hard too soon after your marathon is to use a heart rate monitor. As discussed in chapter 3, a heart rate monitor can help prevent you from going too fast on recovery days. During the first few weeks after the marathon, keep your heart rate below 76 percent of your maximal heart rate or 70 percent of your heart rate reserve. Running at this intensity will help your body overcome the stress of the marathon as quickly as possible.

During this 5-week recovery schedule, the number of days of running per week increases from 3 to 5. At the end of the 5 weeks, you should be fully recovered from the marathon and, with a little luck, injury free and mentally fresh.

Mesocycle 1—Endurance

	WEEKS TO GOAL					
	17	16	15	14	13	(Recovery) 12
Monday	Rest or cross-training	Rest or cross-training	Rest or cross-training	Rest or cross-training	Rest or cross-training	Rest or cross-training
Tuesday	Lactate threshold 9 mi (14 km) w/ 4 mi (6 km) @ 15K to half marathon race pace	General aerobic + speed 8 mi (13 km) w/ 10 × 100 m strides	Medium-long run 11 mi (18 km)	General aerobic + speed 9 mi (14 km) w/ 10 × 100 m strides	Lactate threshold 9 mi (14 km) w/ 5 mi (8 km) @ 15K to half marathon race pace	General aerobic + speed 8 mi (13 km) w/ 10 × 100 m strides
Wednesday	Medium-long run 11 mi (18 km)	Medium-long run 12 mi (19 km)	Medium-long run 13 mi (21 km)	Medium-long run 14 mi (23 km)	Medium-long run 14 mi (23 km)	Medium-long run 12 mi (19 km)
Thursday	Recovery 5 mi (8 km)	Recovery 5 mi (8 km)	Recovery 5 mi (8 km)	Recovery 5 mi (8 km)	Recovery 5 mi (8 km)	Recovery 5 mi (8 km)
Friday	General aerobic 9 mi (14 km)	General aerobic 9 mi (14 km)	Lactate threshold 9 mi (14 km) w/ 4 mi (6 km) @ 15K to half marathon race pace	Medium-long run 11 mi (18 km)	Medium-long run 12 mi (19 km)	General aerobic 10 mi (16 km)
Saturday	Recovery 5 mi (8 km)	Recovery 5 mi (8 km)	Recovery 5 mi (8 km)	Recovery 5 mi (8 km)	Recovery 5 mi (8 km)	Recovery 5 mi (8 km)
Sunday	Medium-long run 15 mi (24 km)	Marathon-pace run 16 mi (26 km) w/ 8 mi (13 km) @ marathon race pace	Medium-long run 15 mi (24 km)	Long run 18 mi (29 km)	Marathon-pace run 18 mi (29 km) w/ 10 mi (16 km) @ marathon race pace	Medium-long run 15 mi (24 km)
Weekly volume	54 mi/86 km	55 mi/88 km	58 mi/93 km	62 mi/100 km	63 mi/101 km	55 mi/88 km

Mesocycle 2—Lactate Threshold + Endurance

	WEEKS TO GOAL				
	11	10	9	(Recovery) 8	7
Monday	Rest or cross-training	Rest or cross-training	Rest or cross-training	Rest or cross-training	Rest or cross-training
Tuesday	Lactate threshold 10 mi (16 km) w/ 5 mi (8 km) @ 15K to half marathon race pace	Recovery 6 mi (10 km) a.m. 4 mi (6 km) p.m.	Recovery 6 mi (10 km) a.m. 4 mi (6 km) p.m.	General aerobic 9 mi (14 km)	Recovery 6 mi (10 km) a.m. 4 mi (6 km) p.m.
Wednesday	Medium-long run 14 mi (23 km)	Medium-long run 14 mi (23 km)	Medium-long run 15 mi (24 km)	$\dot{V}O_2$max 9 mi (14 km) w/ 6 × 800 m @ 5K race pace; jog 50 to 90% interval time between	Medium-long run 15 mi (24 km)
Thursday	Recovery 5 mi (8 km)	Recovery 5 mi (8 km)	Recovery 6 mi (10 km)	Recovery 6 mi (10 km)	Recovery 6 mi (10 km)
Friday	Medium-long run 11 mi (18 km)	Lactate threshold 11 mi (18 km) w/ 6 mi (10 km) @ 15K to half marathon race pace	Medium-long run 13 mi (21 km)	Medium-long run 11 mi (18 km)	Lactate threshold 12 mi (19 km) w/ 7 mi (11 km) @ 15K to half marathon race pace
Saturday	General aerobic + speed 7 mi (11 km) w/ 10 × 100 m strides	Recovery 6 mi (10 km)	Recovery + speed 7 mi (11 km) w/ 6 × 100 m strides	General aerobic + speed 8 mi (13 km) w/ 10 × 100 m strides	Recovery 5 mi (8 km)
Sunday	Long run 21 mi (34 km)	Long run 20 mi (32 km)	Marathon-pace run 16 mi (26 km) w/ 12 mi (19 km) @ marathon race pace	Medium-long run 15 mi (24 km)	Long run 22 mi (35 km)
Weekly volume	68 mi/110 km	66 mi/107 km	67 mi/108 km	58 mi/93 km	70 mi/113 km

Mesocycle 3—Race Preparation

	WEEKS TO GOAL			
	6	**5**	**4**	**3**
Monday	Rest or cross-training	Rest or cross-training	Rest or cross-training	Rest or cross-training
Tuesday	$\dot{V}O_2$max 9 mi (14 km) w/ 5 × 600 m @ 5K race pace; jog 50 to 90% interval time between	$\dot{V}O_2$max 10 mi (16 km) w/ 6 × 1,000 m @ 5K race pace; jog 50 to 90% interval time between	$\dot{V}O_2$max 9 mi (14 km) w/ 5 × 600 m @ 5K race pace; jog 50 to 90% interval time between	Recovery 6 mi (10 km) a.m. 4 mi (6 km) p.m.
Wednesday	Medium-long run 14 mi (23 km)	Medium-long run 15 mi (24 km)	Medium-long run 14 mi (23 km)	$\dot{V}O_2$max 11 mi (18 km) w/ 5 × 1,200 m @ 5K race pace; jog 50 to 90% interval time between
Thursday	Recovery + speed 6 mi (10 km) w/ 6 × 100 m strides a.m. 4 mi (6 km) p.m.	Recovery 6 mi (10 km) a.m. 4 mi (6 km) p.m.	Recovery + speed 6 mi (10 km) w/ 6 × 100 m strides	Medium-long run 14 mi (23 km)
Friday	Recovery 5 mi (8 km)	Medium-long run 12 mi (19 km)	Recovery 5 mi (8 km)	General aerobic + speed 8 mi (13 km) w/ 8 × 100 m strides
Saturday	8K-15K tune-up race (total 9-13 mi/14-21 km)	Recovery 5 mi (8 km)	8K-15K tune-up race (total 9-13 mi/14-21 km)	Recovery 5 mi (8 km)
Sunday	Long run 18 mi (29 km)	Marathon-pace run 18 mi (29 km) w/ 14 mi (23 km) @ marathon race pace	Long run 17 mi (27 km)	Long run 20 mi (32 km)
Weekly volume	65-69 mi/104-111 km	70 mi/112 km	60-64 mi/96-103 km	68 mi/110 km

Mesocycle 4—Taper and Race

	WEEKS TO GOAL		
	2	1	Race week
Monday	Rest or cross-training	Rest	Rest
Tuesday	Recovery + speed 7 mi (11 km) w/ 8 × 100 m strides	General aerobic + speed 7 mi (11 km) w/ 8 × 100 m strides	Recovery 7 mi (11 km)
Wednesday	Medium-long run 12 mi (19 km)	Recovery 4 mi (6 km)	Dress rehearsal 7 mi (11 km) w/ 2 mi (3 km) @ marathon race pace
Thursday	Recovery + speed 5 mi (8 km) w/ 6 × 100 m strides	$\dot{V}O_2$max 8 mi (13 km) w/ 3 × 1,600 m @ 5K race pace; jog 50 to 90% interval time between	Recovery 5 mi (8 km)
Friday	Recovery 5 mi (8 km)	Recovery 5 mi (8 km)	Recovery + speed 5 mi (8 km) w/ 6 × 100 m strides
Saturday	8K-10K tune-up race (total 9-11 mi/14-18 km)	Recovery + speed 6 mi (10 km) w/ 8 × 100 m strides	Recovery 4 mi (6 km)
Sunday	Long run 17 mi (27 km)	Medium-long run 13 mi (21 km)	Goal marathon
Weekly volume	55-57 mi/88-92 km	43 mi/69 km	28 mi/44 km (6 days prerace)

Mesocycle 1—Endurance

	WEEKS TO GOAL			
	11	**10**	**9**	**8**
Monday	Rest or cross-training	Rest or cross-training	Rest or cross-training	Rest or cross-training
Tuesday	General aerobic + speed 8 mi (13 km) w/ 10 × 100 m strides	Medium-long run 12 mi (19 km)	General aerobic + speed 9 mi (14 km) w/ 10 × 100 m strides	Medium-long run 13 mi (21 km)
Wednesday	Medium-long run 11 mi (18 km)	Medium-long run 11 mi (18 km)	Medium-long run 14 mi (22 km)	Medium-long run 15 mi (24 km)
Thursday	Recovery 5 mi (8 km)	Recovery 5 mi (8 km)	Recovery 5 mi (8 km)	Recovery 5 mi (8 km)
Friday	Medium-long run 11 mi (18 km)	Lactate threshold 9 mi (14 km) w/ 4 mi (6 km) @ 15K to half marathon race pace	Medium-long run 12 mi (19 km)	Lactate threshold 10 mi (16 km) w/ 5 mi (8 km) @ 15K to half marathon race pace
Saturday	Recovery 5 mi (8 km)	Recovery 5 mi (8 km)	Recovery 5 mi (8 km)	Recovery 5 mi (8 km)
Sunday	Marathon-pace run 15 mi (24 km) w/ 8 mi (13 km) @ marathon race pace	Long run 17 mi (27 km)	Marathon-pace run 17 mi (27 km) w/ 10 mi (16 km) @ marathon race pace	Long run 18 mi (29 km)
Weekly volume	55 mi/89 km	59 mi/94 km	62 mi/99 km	66 mi/106 km

Mesocycle 2—Lactate Threshold + Endurance

	WEEKS TO GOAL		
	(Recovery) 7	**6**	**5**
Monday	Rest or cross-training	Rest or cross-training	Rest or cross-training
Tuesday	General aerobic + speed 8 mi (13 km) w/ 10 × 100 m strides	Recovery 6 mi (10 km) a.m. 4 mi (6 km) p.m.	General aerobic + speed 9 mi (14 km) w/ 10 × 100 m strides
Wednesday	Medium-long run 15 mi (24 km)	$\dot{V}O_2$max 11 mi (18 km) w/ 5 × 1,200 m @ 5K race pace; jog 50 to 90% interval time between	Medium-long run 15 mi (24 km)
Thursday	Recovery 5 mi (8 km)	Medium-long run 15 mi (24 km)	Recovery 7 mi (11 km)
Friday	Lactate threshold 10 mi (16 km) w/ 4 mi (6 km) @ 15K to half marathon race pace	General aerobic 10 mi (16 km)	Lactate threshold 12 mi (19 km) w/ 7 mi (11 km) @ 15K to half marathon race pace
Saturday	General aerobic 7 mi (11 km)	Recovery 6 mi (10 km)	Recovery 6 mi (10 km)
Sunday	Long run 17 mi (27 km)	Marathon-pace run 18 mi (29 km) w/ 12 mi (19 km) @ marathon race pace	Long run 21 mi (34 km)
Weekly volume	59 mi/94 km	70 mi/113 km	70 mi/113 km

55 to 70 Miles per Week
12-Week Schedule

Mesocycle 3—Race Preparation

	WEEKS TO GOAL		
	4	3	2
Monday	Rest or cross-training	Rest or cross-training	Rest or cross-training
Tuesday	$\dot{V}O_2$max 9 mi (14 km) w/ 5 × 600 m @ 5K race pace; jog 50 to 90% interval time between	Recovery 6 mi (10 km) a.m. 4 mi (6 km) p.m.	$\dot{V}O_2$max 8 mi (13 km) w/ 5 × 600 m @ 5K race pace; jog 50 to 90% interval time between
Wednesday	Medium-long run 15 mi (24 km)	$\dot{V}O_2$max 11 mi (18 km) w/ 6 × 1,000 m @ 5K race pace; jog 50 to 90% interval time between	Medium-long run 12 mi (19 km)
Thursday	Recovery + speed 7 mi (11 km) w/ 6 × 100 m strides	Medium-long run 15 mi (24 km)	Recovery 6 mi (10 km) w/ 6 × 100 m strides
Friday	Recovery 6 mi (10 km)	General aerobic 8 mi (13 km)	Recovery 5 mi (8 km)
Saturday	8K-15K tune-up race (total 9-13 mi/14-21 km)	Recovery 6 mi (10 km)	8K-10K tune-up race (total 9-11 mi/14-21 km)
Sunday	Long run 18 mi (29 km)	Long run 20 mi (32 km)	Long run 17 mi (27 km)
Weekly volume	64-68 mi/102-109 km	70 mi/113 km	57-59 mi/92-95 km

Mesocycle 4—Taper and Race

	WEEKS TO GOAL	
	1	Race week
Monday	Rest or cross-training	Rest
Tuesday	General aerobic + speed 8 mi (13 km) w/ 10 × 100 m strides	Recovery 7 mi (11 km)
Wednesday	Recovery 4 mi (6 km)	Dress rehearsal 7 mi (11 km) w/ 2 mi (3 km) @ marathon race pace
Thursday	$\dot{V}O_2$max 8 mi (13 km) w/ 3 × 1,600 m @ 5K race pace; jog 50 to 90% interval time between	Recovery 5 mi (8 km)
Friday	Recovery 5 mi (8 km)	Recovery + speed 5 mi (8 km) w/ 6 × 100 m strides
Saturday	Recovery + speed 6 mi (10 km) w/ 10 × 100 m strides	Recovery 4 mi (6 km)
Sunday	Medium-long run 13 mi (21 km)	Goal marathon
Weekly volume	44 mi/71 km	28 mi/44 km (6 days prerace)

Mesocycle 5—Recovery

	WEEKS TO GOAL				
	1	**2**	**3**	**4**	**5**
Monday	Rest or cross-training	Rest or cross-training	Rest or cross-training	Rest or cross-training	Rest or cross-training
Tuesday	Rest or cross-training	Recovery 5 mi (8 km)	Recovery 5 mi (8 km)	Recovery 5 mi (8 km)	Recovery 6 mi (10 km)
Wednesday	Recovery 4 mi (6 km)	Recovery 5 mi (8 km)	Recovery 5 mi (8 km)	General aerobic 7 mi (11 km)	General aerobic 8 mi (13 km)
Thursday	Rest or cross-training	Rest or cross-training	Rest or cross-training	Rest or cross-training	Rest or cross-training
Friday	Recovery 5 mi (8 km)	Recovery 6 mi (10 km)	General aerobic + speed 7 mi (11 km) w/ 8 × 100 m strides	General aerobic + speed 8 mi (13 km) w/ 8 × 100 m strides	General aerobic + speed 9 mi (14 km) w/ 8 × 100 m strides
Saturday	Rest or cross-training	Rest or cross-training	Recovery 5 mi (8 km)	Recovery 5 mi (8 km)	Recovery 6 mi (10 km)
Sunday	Recovery 6 mi (10 km)	Recovery 8 mi (13 km)	General aerobic 9 mi (14 km)	Medium-long run 11 mi (18 km)	Medium-long run 12 mi (19 km)
Weekly volume	15 mi/24 km	24 mi/39 km	31 mi/49 km	36 mi/58 km	41 mi/66 km

55 to 70 Miles per Week
Recovery

178

10

Marathon Training on 70 to 85 Miles (113 to 137 km) per Week

This chapter is for high-mileage marathoners. It includes two schedules: an 18-week schedule that starts at 65 miles (105 km) per week and a 12-week schedule that starts at 67 miles (108 km) per week. Each of these schedules increases weekly mileage progressively and builds to a peak of 87 miles (140 km).

As discussed in chapter 1, it's useful to divide your overall training schedule into phases, called mesocycles. The training schedules consist of four mesocycles that focus on endurance, lactate threshold and endurance, race preparation, and tapering, respectively. A final schedule, which contains a 5-week postmarathon recovery program, can follow either of the training schedules.

Of the two training schedules presented in this chapter, we recommend the 18-week schedule for most situations. Eighteen weeks is plenty of time to stimulate the necessary adaptations to improve your marathon performance. At the same time, 18 weeks is short enough that you can focus your efforts without becoming bored with the process.

At times, however, you simply don't have 18 weeks to prepare for your marathon. The 12-week schedule includes the same mesocycles as the 18-week schedule, but because of the short time for preparation, each of these mesocycles is abbreviated. If you go into a marathon in a rush, you must realize that your preparation won't be as thorough as if you had longer to prepare. The 12-week schedule takes into account that sometimes circumstances don't allow you the optimal length of time for preparation and strives to provide a compact yet effective training program.

Before Starting the Schedules

These schedules are challenging right from the start and get harder as your marathon approaches. So that you can progress as the training increases in quantity and quality and to minimize your chances of injury, you should be able to complete the first week of the schedule without too much effort.

Be realistic in assessing whether you're ready for the first week of the schedule. For example, if you've been running 40 miles (64 km) per week and your longest run in the last several weeks is 12 miles (19 km), now isn't the time to suddenly jump to a 65-mile (105 km) week containing a 17-mile (27 km) run, as the first week of the 18-week schedule calls for. The idea behind the schedules isn't to make you as tired as possible as soon as possible but to apply repeated training stress that you absorb and benefit from.

As a rule, you should be running at least 55 miles (88 km) a week before starting these schedules, and in the last month, you should have comfortably completed a run close in length to the long run called for in the first week of the schedule.

Reading the Schedules

The schedules are presented in a day-by-day format. This is in response to requests from readers of our first book, *Road Racing for Serious Runners*, to provide schedules that specify what to do each day of the week.

The main limitation with this approach is that it's impossible to guess the myriad of outside factors that may influence your day-to-day nonrunning life (assuming you still have one at this level of volume). Work schedules, family life, relationships, school commitments, and Mother Nature all play a part in determining when you get to do your long runs and other aspects of marathon preparation. You'll no doubt require some flexibility in your training and will need to juggle days around from time to time. That's expected, and as long as you don't try to make up for lost time by doing several hard days in a row, you should be able to avoid injury and overtraining. By following the principles covered in the earlier chapters, you will be able to safely fine-tune the training schedules to suit your circumstances.

The schedules express each day's training in miles and kilometers; use whichever you're accustomed to. The mile and kilometer figures for each day (and the weekly total) are rough equivalents of each other, not a conversion from one to the other accurate to the third decimal point.

Following the Schedules

Each column of the schedules represents a week's training. For example, in the 12-week schedule, the column for 11 weeks to goal indicates that at the end of that week you have 11 weeks until your marathon. The schedules continue week by week until race week.

We have included the specific workout for each day as well as the category of training for that day. For example, in the 18-week schedule, on the Monday of the 7-weeks-to-go column, the specific workouts are a 6-mile (10 km) run and a 4-mile (6 km) run, and the category of training for that day is recovery. This aspect of the schedules allows you to quickly see the balance of training during each week and the progression of workouts from week to week. Look again at the 18-week schedule—it's easy to see that with 7 weeks to go until the marathon, there are two recovery days that week, plus two general aerobic runs, a lactate-threshold session, a long run, and a medium-long run. Looking at the row for Sunday, it's easy to see how the long runs progress and then taper in the last few weeks before the marathon.

The workouts are divided into the following eight categories: long runs, medium-long runs, marathon-pace runs, general aerobic runs, lactate-threshold runs, recovery runs, VO_2max intervals, and speed training. Each of these categories is explained in depth in chapter 7, and the physiology behind the training is explained in chapter 1.

Doing Doubles

As discussed in chapter 4, sometimes marathoners benefit from running twice a day. This is obviously the case for elites cranking out 130-mile (209 km) weeks, but it can also be true for anyone running more than 70 miles (113 km) a week. In these schedules, for example, recovery days of 10 miles (16 km) are often broken into two short runs. Rather than making you more tired, splitting your mileage like this on easy days will speed your recovery because each run will increase blood flow to your muscles yet take little out of you.

As we mention at the beginning of this chapter, we know that not everyone will be able to follow these schedules exactly as they appear. That applies on the days that call for a lactate-threshold workout in the morning and an easy recovery run in the evening. If your schedule makes it more likely that you'll do a high-quality tempo run in the evening rather than the morning, then simply flip the workouts prescribed for these days. Just be sure to make the short morning run a true recovery run.

When a second run is called for on the day of a medium-long run, however, try to stick to the schedule as written. As explained in chapter 4, a short evening run on these days provides an additional endurance boost, whereas doing a short morning run and a medium-long run in the evening will likely detract from the quality of the medium-long run. Again, though, use your best judgment. If your schedule means that you'll have to do a midweek medium-long run at 4:30 a.m., you're probably better off making time for it in the evening.

Racing Strategies

We discussed marathon race strategy at length in chapter 6. If you follow one of the schedules in this chapter, you'll probably find yourself near the front part of the field once everyone settles into their paces. Still, you might be running with people who aren't as well prepared as you (e.g., a fit-looking man in his late 20s whose goal is to break 3:00, more because it's a nice round number than because that's what his training has prepared him for). If you wind up in a group early on, talk to the others to get a sense of whom you can count on still being there with 10 miles (16 km) to go.

Because of your strong preparation followed by an effective taper, you'll probably find your goal pace in the early miles quite easy. After all, you were doing long runs with lengthy sections at goal pace in the midst of your heaviest training. Now that you're rested and are filled with race-day excitement, goal pace should feel eminently doable. You'll need to be disciplined and resist the temptation to go too fast so that you can use your fitness in the second half of the race and run even splits. Although your outstanding preparation makes you less likely than most to blow up late in the race from a too-hasty start, there's still no point in squandering months of hard work with an overly ambitious early pace.

After the Marathon

The final schedule in this chapter is a 5-week recovery schedule for after the marathon. This is the fifth mesocycle; it completes the training program and leaves you ready to prepare for future challenges.

The recovery schedule is purposely conservative. You have little to gain by rushing back into training, and your risk of injury is exceptionally high at this point, owing to the reduced resiliency of your muscles and connective tissue after the marathon.

The schedule starts with 2 days off from running, which is the bare minimum of time away from running you should allow yourself. If you still have acute soreness or tightness so severe that it will alter your form, or if you just don't feel like running, certainly feel free to take more than 2 days off. If ever there was a time to lose your marathoner's mind-set, the week after your goal race is it. Even most of the top runners in the world take days off after a marathon. They know that the nearly negligible benefits of a short

After the big race, you have little to gain and may risk injury by rushing back into training.

run at this time are far outweighed by the risks. Not running now will also increase your chances of being inspired to resume hard training when your body allows it.

Of course, some people don't consider themselves real runners unless they run pretty much every day of their lives. Plod through a few miles if you must, but be aware that you're prolonging your recovery.

What better aids recovery during this time is light cross-training, such as swimming or cycling. These activities increase blood flow through your muscles without subjecting them to pounding. Walking will also achieve this in the week after the marathon.

One way to ensure that you don't run too hard too soon after your marathon is to use a heart rate monitor. As discussed in chapter 3, a heart rate monitor can help prevent you from going too fast on recovery days. During the first few weeks after the marathon, keep your heart rate below 76 percent of your maximal heart rate or 70 percent of your heart rate reserve. Running at this intensity will help your body overcome the stress of the marathon as quickly as possible.

During this 5-week recovery schedule, the number of days of running per week increases from 3 to 6. At the end of the 5 weeks, you should be fully recovered from the marathon and, with a little luck, injury free and mentally fresh.

Mesocycle 1—Endurance

	WEEKS TO GOAL					
	17	16	15	14	13	(Recovery) 12
Monday	Recovery 5 mi (8 km)	Recovery 6 mi (10 km)	Recovery 6 mi (10 km)	Recovery 6 mi (10 km)	Recovery 6 mi (10 km) a.m. 4 mi (6 km) p.m.	Recovery 7 mi (11 km)
Tuesday	Lactate threshold 9 mi (14 km) w/ 4 mi (6 km) @ 15K to half marathon race pace	General aerobic + speed 8 mi (13 km) w/ 10 × 100 m strides	Lactate threshold 10 mi (16 km) w/ 5 mi (8 km) @ 15K to half marathon race pace	General aerobic + speed 10 mi (16 km) w/ 10 × 100 m strides	Lactate threshold 10 mi (16 km) w/ 4 mi (6 km) @ 15K to half marathon race pace	General aerobic + speed 10 mi (16 km) w/ 10 × 100 m strides
Wednesday	Medium-long run 12 mi (19 km)	Medium-long run 13 mi (21 km)	Medium-long run 14 mi (23 km)	Medium-long run 14 mi (23 km)	Medium-long run 15 mi (24 km)	Medium-long run 13 miles (21 km)
Thursday	Recovery 6 mi (10 km)	Recovery 6 mi (10 km)	Recovery 6 mi (10 km)	Recovery 6 mi (10 km)	Recovery 6 mi (10 km)	Recovery 6 mi (10 km)
Friday	General aerobic 10 mi (16 km)	Medium-long run 11 miles (18 km)	Medium-long run 12 mi (19 km)	Medium-long run 12 miles (19 km)	Medium-long run 13 mi (21 km)	General aerobic 10 mi (16 km)
Saturday	Recovery 6 mi (10 km)	Recovery 6 mi (10 km)	Recovery 6 mi (10 km)	Recovery 6 mi (10 km)	Recovery 6 mi (10 km)	Recovery 6 mi (10 km)
Sunday	Long run 17 mi (27 km)	Marathon-pace run 17 mi (27 km) w/ 8 mi (13 km) @ marathon race pace	Medium-long run 16 mi (26 km)	Long run 20 mi (32 km)	Marathon-pace run 18 mi (29 km) w/ 10 mi (16 km) @ marathon race pace	Long run 16 mi (26 km)
Weekly volume	65 mi (104 km)	67 mi (109 km)	70 mi (114 km)	74 mi (120 km)	78 mi (126 km)	68 mi (110 km)

Mesocycle 2—Lactate Threshold + Endurance

	WEEKS TO GOAL				
	11	10	9	8	(Recovery) 7
Monday	Recovery 6 mi (10 km) a.m. 4 mi (6 km) p.m.	Recovery 6 mi (10 km) a.m. 4 mi (6 km) p.m.	Recovery 6 mi (10 km) a.m. 4 mi (6 km) p.m.	Recovery 6 mi (10 km) a.m. 4 mi (6 km) p.m.	Recovery 6 mi (10 km) a.m. 4 mi (6 km) p.m.
Tuesday	Lactate threshold 11 mi (18 km) w/5 mi (8 km) @ 15K to half marathon race pace	General aerobic 9 mi (14 km)	General aerobic 9 mi (14 km)	General aerobic 9 mi (14 km)	General aerobic 8 mi (13 km)
Wednesday	Medium-long run 15 mi (24 km)	Medium-long run 15 mi (24 km)	Medium-long run 15 mi (24 km)	$\dot{V}O_2max$ 9 mi (14 km) w/ 6 × 800 m @ 5K race pace; jog 50 to 90% interval time between	Medium-long run 15 mi (24 km)
Thursday	Recovery 7 mi (11 km)	Recovery 7 mi (11 km)	Recovery 8 mi (13 km)	Recovery 7 mi (11 km)	Recovery 6 mi (10 km) a.m. 4 mi (6 km) p.m.
Friday	Medium-long run 13 mi (21 km)	Lactate threshold 12 mi (19 km) w/ 6 mi (10 km) @ 15K to half marathon race pace	Medium-long run 13 mi (21 km)	Medium-long run 11 mi (18 km) a.m. Recovery 4 mi (6 km) p.m.	Lactate threshold 12 mi (19K) w/ 7 mi (11 km) @ 15K to half marathon race pace
Saturday	General aerobic + speed 8 mi (13 km) w/ 10 × 100 m strides	Recovery 7 mi (11 km)	Recovery + speed 7 mi (11 km) w/ 6 × 100 m strides	General aerobic + speed 8 mi (13 km) w/ 10 × 100 m strides	General aerobic 8 mi (13 km)
Sunday	Long run 20 mi (32 km)	Long run 22 mi (35 km)	Marathon-pace run 18 mi (29 km) w/ 12 mi (19 km) @ marathon race pace	Long run 16 mi (26 km)	Long run 24 mi (39 km)
Weekly volume	84 mi (135 km)	82 mi (130km)	80 mi (128 km)	74 mi (118 km)	87 mi (140 km)

185

Mesocycle 3—Race Preparation

	WEEKS TO GOAL			
	6	**5**	**4**	**3**
Monday	Recovery 6 mi (10 km) a.m. 4 mi (6 km) p.m.	Recovery 6 mi (10 km) a.m. 4 mi (6 km) p.m.	Recovery 6 mi (10 km) a.m. 4 mi (6 km) p.m.	Recovery 6 mi (10 km) a.m. 4 mi (6 km) p.m.
Tuesday	$\dot{V}O_2$max 9 mi (14 km) w/ 5 × 600 m @ 5K race pace; jog 50 to 90% interval time between	$\dot{V}O_2$max 12 mi (19 km) w/ 6 × 1,000 m @ 5K race pace; jog 50 to 90% interval time between	$\dot{V}O_2$max 9 mi (14 km) w/ 5 × 600 m @ 5K race pace; jog 50 to 90% interval time between	General aerobic 8 mi (13 km)
Wednesday	Medium-long run 15 mi (24 km)	Medium-long run 15 mi (24 km)	Medium-long run 14 mi (22 km)	$\dot{V}O_2$max 12 mi (19 km) w/ 6 × 1,200 m @ 5K race pace; jog 50 to 90% interval time between
Thursday	Recovery + speed 7 mi (11 km) w/ 6 × 100 m strides	Recovery 6 mi (10 km) a.m. 4 mi (6 km) p.m.	Recovery + speed 7 mi (11 km) w/ 6 × 100 m strides	Medium-long run 15 mi (24 km) a.m. Recovery 4 mi (6 km) p.m.
Friday	Recovery 6 mi (10 km)	Medium-long run 12 mi (19 km)	Recovery 6 mi (10 km)	General aerobic + speed 8 mi (13 km) w/ 8 × 100 m strides
Saturday	8K-15K tune-up race (total 9-13 mi/14-21 km)	Recovery 7 mi (11 km)	8K-15K tune-up race (total 9-13 mi/14-21 km)	Recovery 6 mi (10 km)
Sunday	Long run 18 mi (29 km)	Marathon-pace run 20 mi (32 km) w/ 14 mi (23 km) @ marathon race pace	Long run 18 mi (29 km)	Long run 22 mi (35 km)
Weekly volume	74-78 mi (108-115 km)	86 mi (137 km)	73-77 mi (117-124 km)	85 mi (130 km)

Mesocycle 4—Taper and Race

	WEEKS TO GOAL		
	2	**1**	**Race week**
Monday	Recovery 6 mi (10 km)	Recovery 6 mi (10 km)	Recovery 6 mi (10 km)
Tuesday	$\dot{V}O_2$max 9 mi (14 km) w/ 5 × 600 m @ 5K race pace; jog 50 to 90% interval time between	General aerobic + speed 8 mi (13 km) w/ 8 × 100 m strides	General aerobic 7 mi (11 km)
Wednesday	Medium-long run 14 mi (23 km)	Recovery 6 mi (10 km)	Dress rehearsal 8 mi (13 km) w/ 2 mi (3 km) @ marathon race pace
Thursday	Recovery + speed 7 mi (11 km) w/ 6 × 100 m strides	$\dot{V}O_2$max 9 mi (14 km) w/ 3 × 1,600 m @ 5K race pace; jog 50 to 90% interval time between	Recovery 6 mi (10 km)
Friday	Recovery 6 mi (10 km)	Recovery 5 mi (8 km)	Recovery + speed 5 mi (8 km) w/ 6 × 100 m strides
Saturday	8K-10K tune-up race (total 9-11 mi/14-18 km)	General aerobic + speed 7 mi (11 km) w/ 8 × 100 m strides	Recovery 4 mi (6 km)
Sunday	Long run 17 mi (27 km)	Medium-long run 13 mi (21 km)	Goal marathon
Weekly volume	68-70 mi (109-113 km)	54 mi (87 km)	36 mi (58 km) (6 days prerace)

Mesocycle 1—Endurance

	WEEKS TO GOAL			
	11	**10**	**9**	**8**
Monday	Recovery 6 mi (10 km)	Recovery 6 mi (10 km) a.m. 4 mi (6 km) p.m.	Recovery 6 mi (10 km) a.m. 4 mi (6 km) p.m.	Recovery 6 mi (10 km) a.m. 4 mi (6 km) p.m.
Tuesday	General aerobic + speed 8 mi (13 km) w/ 10 × 100 m strides	Lactate threshold 10 mi (16 km) w/ 4 mi (6 km) @ 15K to half marathon race pace	General aerobic + speed 8 mi (13 km) w/ 10 × 100 m strides	Lactate threshold 10 mi (16 km) w/ 5 mi (8 km) @ 15K to half marathon race pace
Wednesday	Medium-long run 12 mi (19 km)	General aerobic 10 mi (16 km)	Medium-long run 13 mi (21 km)	Medium-long run 15 mi (24 km)
Thursday	Recovery 6 mi (10 km)	Recovery 6 mi (10 km)	Recovery 6 mi (10 km)	Recovery 6 mi (10 km)
Friday	Medium-long run 11 mi (18 km)	Medium-long run 12 mi (19 km)	Medium-long run 13 mi (21 km)	Medium-long run 13 mi (21 km)
Saturday	Recovery 6 mi (10 km)	Recovery 6 mi (10 km)	Recovery 6 mi (10 km)	Recovery 6 mi (10 km)
Sunday	Marathon-pace run 17 mi (27 km) w/ 8 mi (13 km) @ marathon race pace	Long run 18 mi (29 km)	Marathon-pace run 19 mi (31 km) w/ 10 mi (16 km) @ marathon race pace	Long run 17 mi (27 km)
Weekly volume	66 mi (107 km)	72 mi (116 km)	75 mi (122 km)	77 mi (124 km)

Mesocycle 2—Lactate Threshold + Endurance

	WEEKS TO GOAL		
	(Recovery) 7	**6**	**5**
Monday	Recovery 6 mi (10 km)	Recovery 6 mi (10 km) a.m. 4 mi (6 km) p.m.	Recovery 6 mi (10 km) a.m. 4 mi (6 km) p.m.
Tuesday	General aerobic + speed 8 mi (13 km) w/ 10 × 100 m strides	General aerobic 9 mi (14 km)	General aerobic + speed 10 mi (16 km) w/ 10 × 100 m strides
Wednesday	Medium-long run 15 mi (24 km)	$\dot{V}O_2$max 12 mi (19 km) w/ 5 × 1,200 m @ 5K race pace; jog 50 to 90% interval time between	Medium-long run 15 mi (24 km)
Thursday	Recovery 6 mi (10 km) a.m. 4 mi (6 km) p.m.	Medium-long run 15 mi (24 km) a.m. Recovery 4 mi (6 km) p.m.	Recovery 6 mi (10 km) a.m. 4 mi (6 km) p.m.
Friday	Lactate threshold 10 mi (16 km) w/ 4 mi (6 km) @ 15K to half marathon race pace	General aerobic 10 mi (16 km)	Lactate threshold 12 mi (19 km) w/ 7 mi (11 km) @ 15K to half marathon race pace
Saturday	General aerobic + speed 7 mi (11 km) w/ 6 × 100 m strides	Recovery + speed 7 mi (11 km) w/ 6 × 100 m strides	General aerobic + speed 8 mi (13 km) w/ 6 × 100 m strides
Sunday	Long run 18 mi (29 km)	Marathon-pace run 17 mi (27 km) w/ 12 mi (19 km) @ marathon race pace	Long run 22 mi (35 km)
Weekly volume	70 mi (113 km)	84 mi (135 km)	87 mi (139 km)

70 to 85 Miles per Week
12-Week Schedule

Mesocycle 3—Race Preparation

	WEEKS TO GOAL		
	4	3	2
Monday	Recovery 6 mi (10 km) a.m. 4 mi (6 km) p.m.	Recovery 6 mi (10 km) a.m. 4 mi (6 km) p.m.	Recovery 6 mi (10 km) a.m. 4 mi (6 km) p.m.
Tuesday	$\dot{V}O_2$max 9 mi (14 km) w/ 5 × 600 m @ 5K race pace; jog 50 to 90% interval time between	General aerobic 9 mi (14 km)	$\dot{V}O_2$max 9 mi (14 km) w/ 5 × 600 m @ 5K race pace; jog 50 to 90% interval time between
Wednesday	Medium-long run 15 mi (24 km) Recovery 4 mi (6 km) p.m.	$\dot{V}O_2$max 11 mi (18 km) w/ 6 × 1,000 m @ 5K race pace; jog 50 to 90% interval time between	Medium-long run 12 mi (19 km)
Thursday	Recovery + speed 7 mi (11 km) w/ 6 × 100 m strides	Medium-long run 15 mi (24 km)	Recovery + speed 6 mi (10 km) w/ 6 × 100 m strides
Friday	Recovery 6 mi (10 km)	General aerobic 10 mi (16 km)	Recovery 6 mi (10 km)
Saturday	8K-15K tune-up race (total 9-13 mi/14-21 km)	General aerobic + speed 8 mi (13 km) w/ 6 × 100 m strides	8K-10K tune-up race (total 9-11 mi/14-18 km)
Sunday	Long run 18 mi (29 km)	Long run 20 mi (32 km)	Long run 17 mi (27 km)
Weekly volume	78-82 mi (124-131 km)	83 mi (133 km)	69-71 mi (110-114 km)

Mesocycle 4—Taper and Race

	WEEKS TO GOAL	
	1	**Race week**
Monday	Recovery 6 mi (10 km)	Recovery 6 mi (10 km)
Tuesday	General aerobic + speed 8 mi (13 km) w/ 8 × 100 m strides	General aerobic 7 mi (11 km)
Wednesday	Recovery 6 mi (10 km)	Dress rehearsal 8 mi (13 km) w/ 2 mi (3 km) @ marathon race pace
Thursday	$\dot{V}O_2$max 9 mi (14 km) w/ 3 × 1,600 m @ 5K race pace; jog 50 to 90% interval time between	Recovery 6 mi (10 km)
Friday	Recovery 5 mi (8 km)	Recovery + speed 5 mi (8 km) w/ 6 × 100 m strides
Saturday	General aerobic + speed 7 mi (11 km) w/ 10 × 100 m strides	Recovery 4 mi (6 km)
Sunday	Medium-long run 13 mi (21 km)	Goal marathon
Weekly volume	54 mi (87 km)	36 mi (58 km) (6 days prerace)

70 to 85 Miles per Week
12-Week Schedule

Mesocycle 5—Recovery

	WEEKS TO GOAL				
	1	2	3	4	5
Monday	Rest or cross-training	Rest or cross-training	Rest or cross-training	Rest or cross-training	Rest or cross-training
Tuesday	Rest or cross-training	Recovery 5 mi (8 km)	Recovery 6 mi (10 km)	Recovery 6 mi (10 km)	Recovery 6 mi (10 km)
Wednesday	Recovery 4 mi (6 km)	Recovery 5 mi (8 km)	Recovery 6 mi (10 km)	General aerobic 9 mi (14 km)	General aerobic 9 mi (14 km)
Thursday	Rest or cross-training	Rest or cross-training	Rest or cross-training	Rest or cross-training	Recovery 6 mi (10 km)
Friday	Recovery 5 mi (8 km)	Recovery 6 mi (10 km)	General aerobic + speed 8 mi (13 km) w/ 8 × 100 m strides	General aerobic + speed 9 mi (14 km) w/ 8 × 100 m strides	General aerobic + speed 10 mi (16 km) w/ 8 × 100 m strides
Saturday	Rest or cross-training	Recovery 5 mi (8 km)	Recovery 6 mi (10 km)	Recovery 6 mi (10 km)	Recovery 6 mi (10 km)
Sunday	Recovery 7 mi (11 km)	General aerobic 10 mi (16 km)	General aerobic 10 mi (16 km)	Medium-long run 12 mi (19 km)	Medium-long run 13 mi (21 km)
Weekly volume	16 mi (26 km)	31 mi (50 km)	36 mi (59 km)	42 mi (67 km)	50 mi (80 km)

11

Marathon Training on More Than 85 Miles (137 km) per Week

This chapter is for true high-volume marathoners who can devote their full energy to training. It includes two schedules: an 18-week schedule that starts at 80 miles (129 km) per week and a 12-week schedule that starts at 82 miles (132 km) per week. Each of these schedules increases weekly volume progressively, building to a peak of at least 105 miles (170 km).

As discussed in chapter 1, it's useful to divide your overall training schedule into phases, called mesocycles. The training schedules consist of four mesocycles that focus on endurance, lactate threshold and endurance, race preparation, and tapering, respectively. A final schedule, which contains a 5-week postmarathon recovery program, can follow either of the training schedules.

Of the two training schedules presented in this chapter, we recommend the 18-week schedule for most situations. Eighteen weeks is plenty of time to stimulate the necessary adaptations to improve your marathon performance. At the same time, 18 weeks is short enough that you can focus your efforts without becoming bored with the process.

At times, however, you simply don't have 18 weeks to prepare for your marathon. The 12-week schedule includes the same mesocycles as the 18-week schedules, but because of the short time for preparation, each of these mesocycles is abbreviated. If you go into a marathon in a rush, you must realize that your preparation won't be as thorough as if you had longer to prepare. The 12-week schedule takes into account that sometimes circumstances don't allow you the optimal length of time for preparation and strives to provide a compact yet effective training program.

Before Starting the Schedules

These schedules are challenging right from the start and get harder as your marathon approaches. So that you can progress as the training increases in quantity and quality and to minimize your chances of injury, you should be able to complete the first week of the schedule without too much effort.

Be realistic in assessing whether you're ready for the first week of the schedule. For example, if you've been running 60 miles (97 km) per week and your longest run in the last several weeks is 12 miles (19 km), now isn't the time to suddenly jump to an 82-mile (132 km) week containing a 17-mile (27 km) run, as the first week of the 12-week schedule calls for. The idea behind the schedules isn't to make you as tired as possible as soon as possible but to apply repeated training stress that you absorb and benefit from.

As a rule, you should be running at least 70 to 75 miles (113 to 121 km) a week before starting these schedules, and in the last month, you should have comfortably completed a run of at least 15 miles (24 km).

Reading the Schedules

The schedules are presented in a day-by-day format. This is in response to requests from readers of our first book, *Road Racing for Serious Runners*, to provide schedules that specify what to do each day of the week.

The main limitation with this approach is that it's impossible to guess the myriad of outside factors that may influence your day-to-day nonrunning life (assuming you still have one at this level of volume). Work schedules, family life, relationships, school commitments, and Mother Nature all play a part in determining when you get to do your long runs and other aspects of marathon preparation. You'll no doubt require some flexibility in your training and will need to juggle days around from time to time. That's expected, and as long as you don't try to make up for lost time by doing several hard days in a row, you should be able to avoid injury and overtraining. By following the principles covered in the earlier chapters, you will be able to safely fine-tune the training schedules to suit your circumstances.

The schedules express each day's training in miles and kilometers; use whichever you're accustomed to. The mile and kilometer figures for each day (and the weekly total) are rough equivalents of each other, not a conversion from one to the other accurate to the third decimal point.

Following the Schedules

Each column of the schedules represents a week's training. For example, in the 12-week schedule, the column for 11 weeks to goal indicates that at the end of that week you have 11 weeks until your marathon. The schedules continue week by week until race week.

We have included the specific workout for each day as well as the category of training for that day. For example, in the 18-week schedule, on the Monday of the 5-weeks-to-go column, the specific workouts are two 6-mile (10 km) runs and the category of training for that day is recovery. This aspect of the schedules allows you to quickly see the balance of training during each week and the progression of workouts from week to week. Look again at the 18-week schedule—it's easy to see that with 5 weeks to go until the marathon, there are two recovery days that week with a lactate-threshold session, a long run, a medium-long run, and two general aerobic runs. Looking at the row for Sunday, it's easy to see how the long runs progress and then taper in the last few weeks before the marathon.

The workouts are divided into the following eight categories: long runs, medium-long runs, marathon-pace runs, general aerobic runs, lactate-threshold runs, recovery runs, $\dot{V}O_2$max intervals, and speed training. Each of these categories is explained in depth in chapter 7, and the physiology behind the training is explained in chapter 1.

Doing Doubles

As discussed in chapter 7, sometimes marathoners benefit from running twice a day. This is obviously the case for anyone cranking out 100-mile (161 km) weeks. In these schedules, for example, recovery days of 10 to 12 miles (16 to 19 km) are often broken into two short runs. Rather than making you

For high-mileage weekly training, sometimes splitting your runs on easy days is a good idea. Rather than making you more tired, this can speed recovery because each run will increase blood flow to your muscles yet take little out of you.

more tired, splitting your volume like this on easy days will speed your recovery because each run will increase blood flow to your muscles yet take so little out of you.

As we mention at the beginning of this chapter, we know that not everyone will be able to follow these schedules exactly as they appear. That applies on the days that call for a recovery run in the morning and a lactate-threshold workout in the evening. If your schedule makes it more likely that you'll do a high-quality tempo run in the morning rather than the evening, then simply flip the workouts prescribed for these days.

When 105 Miles per Week Just Isn't Enough

The hardy few among you might want to do more volume than what's prescribed in the schedules. If you're in this group, be sure to follow the spirit of the schedules when adding miles—that is, your volume should build gradually during mesocycle 1, peak at the end of mesocycle 2, come down slightly during mesocycle 3, and fall dramatically during mesocycle 4.

Where should you add miles to the schedules? Try adding a bit of volume to the general aerobic runs and medium-long runs if you sense that doing so doesn't detract from your week's most important sessions. (Remember, volume is a means to a goal, not a primary goal in itself. At your volume level, the risk of injury increases rapidly if additional distance is added haphazardly.) You could also add miles to your warm-ups and cool-downs on $\dot{V}O_2$max and lactate-threshold workout days. If you're going to do more doubles than the schedules stipulate, refer to the section on two-a-day runs in chapter 7.

Racing Strategies

We discussed marathon race strategy at length in chapter 6. If you follow one of the schedules in this chapter, you will be more thoroughly prepared for your marathon than most of the other runners in the race. Few others in the field will have done the combination of volume and targeted quality that you have.

Despite your commitment and eagerness, though, you'll need to not get carried away in the early miles, even if your goal pace in the first half feels quite easy. The temptation to try to capitalize on that good feeling will be strong. Perhaps more than any other readers of this book, you will need to be disciplined in the early miles to stick to your goal pace so that you can use your fitness in the second half of the race and run even splits. Although your outstanding preparation makes you less likely than most to blow up late in the race from a too-hasty start, there's still no point in squandering months of hard work with an overly ambitious early pace.

At the same time, it's likely that among readers of this book you'll be attempting to race the marathon at the greatest differential from your normal training pace. For that reason, in the days before your marathon, your goal pace might seem especially daunting. Draw confidence from your long runs, tempo runs, and marathon-pace runs that you can sustain your ambitious goal pace for 26.2 miles (42.2 km). Also, focus on your goal-pace splits to increase your chances of running the first half of the race intelligently and thereby vastly increasing your chances of being able to hold goal pace past 20 miles (32 km) all the way to the finish line.

After the Marathon

The final schedule in this chapter is a 5-week recovery schedule for after the marathon. This is the fifth mesocycle; it completes the training program and leaves you ready to prepare for future challenges.

The recovery schedule is purposely conservative. You have little to gain by rushing back into training, and your risk of injury is exceptionally high at this point, owing to the reduced resiliency of your muscles and connective tissue after the marathon.

The schedule starts with 2 days off from running, which is the bare minimum of time away from running you should allow yourself. If you still have acute soreness or tightness so severe that it will alter your form, or if you just don't feel like running, certainly feel free to take more than 2 days off. If ever there was a time to lose your marathoner's mind-set, the week after your goal race is it. Even most of the top runners in the world take days off after a marathon. They know that the nearly negligible benefits of a short run at this time are far outweighed by the risks. Not running now will also increase your chances of being inspired to resume hard training when your body allows it.

Of course, some people don't consider themselves real runners unless they run pretty much every day of their lives. Plod through a few miles if you must, but be aware that you're prolonging your recovery.

What better aids recovery during this time is light cross-training, such as swimming or cycling. These activities increase blood flow through your muscles without subjecting them to pounding. Walking will also achieve this in the week after the marathon.

One way to ensure that you don't run too hard too soon after your marathon is to use a heart rate monitor. As discussed in chapter 3, a heart rate monitor can help prevent you from going too fast on recovery days. During the first few weeks after the marathon, keep your heart rate below 76 percent of your maximal heart rate or 70 percent of your heart rate reserve. Running at this intensity will help your body overcome the stress of the marathon as quickly as possible.

During this 5-week recovery schedule, the number of days of running per week increases from 3 to 6. At the end of the 5 weeks, you should be fully recovered from the marathon and, with a little luck, injury free and mentally fresh.

Mesocycle 1—Endurance

	WEEKS TO GOAL					
	17	16	15	14	13	(Recovery) 12
Monday	Recovery 6 mi (10 km) a.m. 5 mi (8 km) p.m.	Recovery 6 mi (10 km) a.m. 5 mi (8 km) p.m.	Recovery 5 mi (8 km) a.m. 5 mi (8 km) p.m.	Recovery 6 mi (10 km) a.m. 6 mi (10 km) p.m.	Recovery 6 mi (10 km) a.m. 6 mi (10 km) p.m.	Recovery 6 mi (10 km) a.m. 6 mi (10 km) p.m.
Tuesday	Recovery 4 mi (6 km) a.m. Lactate threshold 10 mi (16 km) w/ 4 mi (6 km) @ 15K to half marathon race pace p.m.	Recovery 4 mi (6 km) a.m. General aerobic + speed 10 mi (16 km) w/ 10 × 100 m strides p.m.	Recovery 4 mi (6 km) a.m. Lactate threshold 10 mi (16 km) w/ 5 mi (8 km) @ 15K to half marathon race pace p.m.	Recovery 4 mi (6 km) a.m. General aerobic + speed 10 mi (16 km) w/ 10 × 100 m strides p.m.	Recovery 5 mi (8 km) a.m. Lactate threshold 10 mi (16 km) w/ 5 mi (8 km) @ 15K to half marathon race pace p.m.	General aerobic + speed 10 mi (16 km) w/ 10 × 100 m strides
Wednesday	Medium-long run 12 miles (19 km)	Medium-long run 13 miles (21 km)	Medium-long run 14 miles (22 km)	Medium-long run 15 miles (24 km)	Medium-long run 15 miles (24 km)	Medium-long run 13 miles (21 km)
Thursday	Recovery 6 mi (10 km) a.m. 5 mi (8 km) p.m.	Recovery 6 mi (10 km) a.m. 5 mi (8 km) p.m.	Recovery 6 mi (10 km) a.m. 5 mi (8 km) p.m.	Recovery 6 mi (10 km) a.m. 5 mi (8 km) p.m.	Recovery 6 mi (10 km) a.m. 5 mi (8 km) p.m.	Recovery 6 mi (10 km) a.m. 5 mi (8 km) p.m.
Friday	General aerobic + speed 10 mi (16 km) w/ 10 × 100 m strides	Medium-long run 12 miles (19 km)	Medium-long run 12 mi (19 km)	Medium-long run 13 miles (21 km)	Medium-long run 14 mi (22 km)	Medium-long run 12 mi (19 km)
Saturday	Recovery 6 mi (10 km)	Recovery 6 mi (10 km)	General aerobic 9 mi (14 km)	Recovery 7 mi (11 km)	General aerobic 8 mi (13 km)	General aerobic 8 mi (13 km)
Sunday	Long run 16 mi (26 km)	Marathon-pace run 17 mi (27 km) w/ 8 mi (13 km) @ marathon race pace	Long run 18 mi (29 km)	Long run 20 mi (32 km)	Marathon-pace run 20 mi (32 km) w/ 10 mi (16 km) @ marathon race pace	Long run 16 mi (26 km)
Weekly volume	80 mi/129 km	84 mi/135 km	88 mi/141 km	92 mi/148 km	95 mi/153 km	82 mi/133 km

Mesocycle 2—Lactate Threshold + Endurance

	WEEKS TO GOAL			(Recovery)	
	11	**10**	**9**	**8**	**7**
Monday	Recovery 6 mi (10 km) a.m. 5 mi (8 km) p.m.	Recovery 6 mi (10 km) a.m. 5 mi (8 km) p.m.	Recovery 6 mi (10 km) a.m. 5 mi (8 km) p.m.	Recovery 6 mi (10 km) a.m. 5 mi (8 km) p.m.	Recovery 6 mi (10 km) a.m. 6 mi (10 km) p.m.
Tuesday	Recovery 5 mi (8 km) a.m. Lactate threshold 10 mi (16 km) w/ 5 mi (8 km) @ 15K to half marathon race pace p.m.	Recovery 6 mi (10 km) a.m. General aerobic + speed 10 mi (16 km) w/ 10 × 100 m strides p.m.	General aerobic 10 mi (16 km)	General aerobic + speed 10 mi (16 km) w/ 10 × 100 m strides	Recovery 6 mi (10 km) a.m. General aerobic + speed 10 mi (16 km) w/ 10 × 100 m strides p.m.
Wednesday	Recovery 5 mi (8 km) a.m. Medium-long run 15 mi (24 km) p.m.	Medium-long run 15 mi (24 km)	Recovery 6 mi (10 km) a.m. Medium-long run 15 mi (24 km) p.m.	VO$_2$max 10 mi (16 km) w/ 5 × 800 m @ 5K race pace; jog 50 to 90% interval time between	Medium-long run 15 mi (24 km)
Thursday	Recovery 6 mi (10 km) a.m. 5 mi (8 km) p.m.	Recovery 6 mi (10 km) a.m. 5 mi (8 km) p.m.	Recovery 6 mi (10 km) a.m. 5 mi (8 km) p.m.	Recovery 6 mi (10 km) a.m. 5 mi (8 km) p.m.	Recovery 6 mi (10 km) a.m. 6 mi (10 km) p.m.
Friday	Medium-long run 13 mi (21 km)	Recovery 6 mi (10 km) a.m. Lactate threshold 11 mi (18 km) w/ 6 mi (10 km) @ 15K to half marathon race pace	Recovery 6 mi (10 km) a.m. Medium-long run 14 mi (22 km) p.m.	Recovery 5 mi (8 km) a.m. Medium-long run 13 mi (21 km) p.m.	Recovery 6 mi (10 km) a.m. Lactate threshold 12 mi (19 km) w/ 7 mi (11 km) @ 15K to half marathon race pace
Saturday	General aerobic + speed 10 mi (16 km) w/ 10 × 100 m strides	General aerobic 10 mi (16 km)	General aerobic + speed 10 mi (16 km) w/ 10 × 100 m strides	General aerobic 10 mi (16 km)	General aerobic 10 mi (16 km)
Sunday	Long run 20 mi (32 km)	Long run 22 mi (35 km)	Marathon-pace run 20 mi (32 km) w/ 12 mi (19 km) @ marathon race pace	Long run 16 mi (26 km)	Long run 24 mi (39 km)
Weekly volume	100 mi/161 km	102 mi/165 km	103 mi/167 km	86 mi/139 km	107 mi/174 km

Mesocycle 3—Race Preparation

	WEEKS TO GOAL			
	6	5	4	3
Monday	Recovery 6 mi (10 km) a.m. 6 mi (10 km) p.m.	Recovery 6 mi (10 km) a.m. 6 mi (10 km) p.m.	Recovery 6 mi (10 km) a.m. 5 mi (8 km) p.m.	Recovery 6 mi (10 km) a.m. 5 mi (8 km) p.m.
Tuesday	Recovery 5 mi (8 km) a.m. $\dot{V}O_2$max 10 mi (16 km) w/ 5 × 800 m @ 5K race pace p.m.; jog 50 to 90% interval time between	Recovery 5 mi (8 km) a.m. General aerobic + speed 10 mi (16 km) w/ 8 × 100 m strides p.m.	Recovery 5 mi (8 km) a.m. $\dot{V}O_2$max 10 mi (16 km) w/ 5 × 800 m @ 5K race pace p.m.; jog 50 to 90% interval time between	General aerobic 10 mi (16 km)
Wednesday	Recovery 5 mi (8 km) a.m. Medium-long run 15 mi (24 km) p.m.	Recovery 5 mi (8 km) a.m. Medium-long run 15 mi (24 km) p.m.	Recovery 5 mi (8 km) a.m. Medium-long run 15 mi (24 km) p.m.	Recovery 4 mi (6 km) a.m. $\dot{V}O_2$max 10 mi (16 km) w/ 6 × 1,200 m @ 5K race pace p.m.; jog 50 to 90% interval time between
Thursday	Recovery 5 mi (8 km) a.m. Recovery + speed 6 mi (10 km) w/ 8 × 100 m strides p.m.	Recovery 6 mi (10 km) a.m. 5 mi (8 km) p.m.	Recovery 5 mi (8 km) a.m. Recovery + speed 8 mi (13 km) w/ 8 × 100 m strides p.m.	Recovery 5 mi (8 km) a.m. Medium-long run 15 mi (24 km) p.m.
Friday	Recovery 6 mi (10 km)	Lactate threshold 12 mi (19 km) w/ 7 mi (11 km) @ 15K to half marathon race pace	Recovery 6 mi (10 km)	Recovery 4 mi (6 km) a.m. General aerobic 10 mi (16 km) p.m.
Saturday	15K to half marathon tune-up race (total 13-17 mi/21-27 km)	General aerobic + speed 10 mi (16 km) w/ 8 × 100 m strides	8K-15K tune-up race (total 9-13 mi/14-21 km)	Recovery 4 mi (5 km) a.m. General aerobic + speed 8 mi (13 km) w/ 8 × 100 m strides p.m.
Sunday	General aerobic 8 mi (13 km)	Long run 22 mi (35 km)	Long run 18 mi (29 km)	Long run 21 mi (34 km)
Weekly volume	85-89 mi/138-144 km	102 mi/164 km	92-96 mi/148-155 km	102 mi/162 km

Mesocycle 4—Taper and Race

	WEEKS TO GOAL		
	2	**1**	**Race week**
Monday	Recovery 6 mi (10 km) a.m. 5 mi (8 km) p.m.	Recovery 6 mi (10 km)	Recovery 6 mi (10 km)
Tuesday	$\dot{V}O_2$max 10 mi (16 km) w/ 5 × 800 m @ 5K race pace; jog 50 to 90% interval time between	General aerobic + speed 10 mi (16 km) w/ 10 × 100 m strides	Recovery 6 mi (10 km) a.m. 4 mi (6 km) p.m.
Wednesday	Medium-long run 13 mi (21 km)	Recovery 6 mi (10 km) a.m. 4 mi (6 km) p.m.	Dress rehearsal 9 mi (14 km) w/ 2.5 mi (4 km) @ marathon race pace
Thursday	Recovery 4 mi (6 km) a.m. General aerobic + speed 8 mi (13 km) w/ 8 × 100 m strides p.m.	$\dot{V}O_2$max 9 mi (14 km) w/ 3 × 1,600 m @ 5K race pace; jog 50 to 90% interval time between	Recovery 6 mi (10 km)
Friday	Recovery 6 mi (10 km)	Recovery 6 mi (10 km)	Recovery + speed 5 mi (8 km) w/ 6 × 100 m strides
Saturday	8K-10K tune-up race (total 9-11 mi/14-18 km)	General aerobic + speed 8 mi (13 km) w/ 8 × 100 m strides	Recovery 4 mi (6 km)
Sunday	Long run 17 mi (27 km)	Medium-long run 13 mi (21 km)	Goal marathon
Weekly volume	78-80 mi/125-129 km	62 mi/100 km	40 mi/64 km (6 days prerace)

Mesocycle 1—Endurance

	WEEKS TO GOAL			
	11	**10**	**9**	**8**
Monday	Recovery 6 mi (10 km) a.m. 5 mi (8 km) p.m.	Recovery 6 mi (10 km) a.m. 5 mi (8 km) p.m.	Recovery 6 mi (10 km) a.m. 5 mi (8 km) p.m.	Recovery 6 mi (10 km) a.m. 5 mi (8 km) p.m.
Tuesday	General aerobic + speed 10 mi (16 km) w/ 10 × 100 m strides	Recovery 4 mi (6 km) a.m. Lactate threshold 10 mi (16 km) w/ 5 mi (8 km) @ 15K to half marathon race pace	Recovery 4 mi (6 km) a.m. General aerobic + speed 10 mi (16 km) w/ 10 × 100 m strides p.m.	Recovery 4 mi (6 km) a.m. Lactate threshold 11 mi (18 km) w/ 5 mi (8 km) @ 15K to half marathon race pace
Wednesday	Medium-long run 14 mi (23 km)	Medium-long run 15 mi (24 km)	Medium-long run 15 mi (24 km)	Recovery 5 mi (8 km) a.m. Medium-long run 15 mi (24 km) p.m.
Thursday	Recovery 6 mi (10 km) a.m. 4 mi (6 km) p.m.	Recovery 6 mi (10 km) a.m. 4 mi (6 km) p.m.	Recovery 6 mi (10 km) a.m. 4 mi (6 km) p.m.	Recovery 6 mi (10 km) a.m. 6 mi (10 km) p.m.
Friday	Medium-long run 12 mi (19 km)	Medium-long run 12 mi (19 km)	Medium-long run 14 mi (23 km)	Medium-long run 14 mi (23km)
Saturday	General aerobic + speed 8 mi (13 km) w/ 8 × 100 m strides	General aerobic + speed 8 mi (13 km) w/ 8 × 100 m strides	General aerobic + speed 10 mi (16 km) w/ 8 × 100 m strides	General aerobic + speed 10 mi (16 km) w/ 8 × 100 m strides
Sunday	Marathon-pace run 17 mi (27 km) w/ 8 mi (13 km) @ marathon race pace	Long run 18 mi (29 km)	Long run 20 mi (32 km)	Marathon-pace run 18 mi (29 km) w/ 10 mi (16 km) @ marathon race pace
Weekly volume	82 mi/132 km	88 mi/141 km	94 mi/151 km	100 mi/162 km

Mesocycle 2—Lactate Threshold + Endurance

	WEEKS TO GOAL		
	7	6	5
Monday	Recovery 6 mi (10 km) a.m. 5 mi (8 km) p.m.	Recovery 6 mi (10 km) a.m. 6 mi (10 km) p.m.	Recovery 6 mi (10 km) a.m. 6 mi (10 km) p.m.
Tuesday	Recovery 6 mi (10 km) a.m. General aerobic + speed 10 mi (16 km) w/ 10 × 100 m strides p.m.	Recovery 6 mi (10 km) a.m. General aerobic 10 mi (16 km) p.m.	Recovery 6 mi (10 km) a.m. General aerobic + speed 10 mi (16 km) w/ 8 × 100 m strides p.m.
Wednesday	Medium-long run 15 mi (24 km)	V̇O₂max 10 mi (16 km) w/ 6 × 1,200 m @ 5K race pace; jog 50 to 90% interval time between	Recovery 6 mi (10 km) a.m. Medium-long run 15 mi (24 km) p.m.
Thursday	Recovery 6 mi (10 km) a.m. 6 mi (10 km) p.m.	Recovery 6 mi (10 km) a.m. Medium-long run 15 mi (24 km) p.m.	Recovery 6 mi (10 km) a.m. 6 mi (10 km) p.m.
Friday	Lactate threshold 10 mi (16 km) w/ 4 mi (6 km) @ 15K to half marathon race pace	Recovery 6 mi (10 km) a.m. General aerobic 10 mi (16 km) p.m.	Lactate threshold 12 mi (19 km) w/ 7 mi (11 km) @ 15K to half marathon race pace
Saturday	General aerobic + speed 10 mi (16 km) w/ 8 × 100 m strides	General aerobic + speed 10 mi (16 km) w/ 8 × 100 m strides	General aerobic + speed 10 mi (16 km) w/ 8 × 100 m strides
Sunday	Long run 18 mi (29 km)	Marathon-pace run 18 mi (29 km) w/ 12 mi (19 km) @ marathon race pace	Long run 22 mi (35 km)
Weekly volume	86 mi/139 km	103 mi/167 km	105 mi/170 km

Mesocycle 3—Race Preparation

	WEEKS TO GOAL		
	4	3	2
Monday	Recovery 6 mi (10 km) a.m. 5 mi (8 km) p.m.	Recovery 6 mi (10 km) a.m. 5 mi (8 km) p.m.	Recovery 6 mi (10 km) a.m. 5 mi (8 km) p.m.
Tuesday	Recovery 5 mi (8 km) a.m. $\dot{V}O_2$max 10 mi (16 km) w/ 5 × 800 m @ 5K race pace p.m.; jog 50 to 90% interval time between	General aerobic 10 mi (16 km)	$\dot{V}O_2$max 10 mi (16 km) w/ 5 × 800 m @ 5K race pace; jog 50 to 90% interval time between
Wednesday	Recovery 5 mi (8 km) a.m. Medium-long run 15 mi (24 km) p.m.	Recovery 5 mi (8 km) a.m. $\dot{V}O_2$max 10 mi (16 km) w/ 6 × 1,200 m @ 5K race pace p.m.; jog 50 to 90% interval time between	Medium-long run 13 mi (21 km)
Thursday	Recovery 5 mi (8 km) a.m. General aerobic + speed 8 mi (13 km) w/ 8 × 100 m strides p.m.	Recovery 4 mi (6 km) a.m. Medium-long run 15 mi (24 km) p.m.	Recovery 4 mi (6 km) a.m. General aerobic + speed 8 mi (13 km) w/ 8 × 100 m strides p.m.
Friday	Recovery 6 mi (10 km)	Recovery 4 mi (6 km) a.m. General aerobic 10 mi (16 km) p.m.	Recovery 6 mi (10 km)
Saturday	8K-15K tune-up race (total 9-13 mi/13-21 km)	Recovery 4 mi (6 km) a.m. General aerobic + speed 8 mi (13 km) w/ 8 × 100 m strides p.m.	8K-10K tune-up race (total 9-11 mi/14-18 km)
Sunday	Long run 18 mi (29 km)	Long run 21 mi (34 km)	Long run 17 mi (27 km)
Weekly volume	92-96 mi/147-154 km	102 mi/163 km	78-80/125-129 km

Mesocycle 4—Taper and Race

	WEEKS TO GOAL	
	1	**Race week**
Monday	Recovery 6 mi (10 km)	Recovery 6 mi (10 km)
Tuesday	General aerobic + speed 10 mi (16 km) w/ 10 × 100 m strides	Recovery 6 mi (10 km) a.m. 4 mi (6 km) p.m.
Wednesday	Recovery 6 mi (10 km) a.m. 4 mi (6 km) p.m.	Dress rehearsal 9 mi (14 km) w/ 2.5 mi (4 km) @ marathon race pace
Thursday	V̇O₂max 9 mi (14 km) w/ 3 × 1,600 m @ 5K race pace; jog 50 to 90% interval time between	Recovery 6 mi (10 km)
Friday	Recovery 6 mi (10 km)	Recovery + speed 5 mi (8 km) w/ 6 × 100 m strides
Saturday	General aerobic + speed 8 mi (13 km) w/ 8 × 100 m strides	Recovery 4 mi (6 km)
Sunday	Medium-long run 13 mi (21 km)	Goal marathon
Weekly volume	62 mi/100 km	40 mi/64 km (6 days prerace)

Mesocycle 5—Recovery

	WEEKS TO GOAL				
	1	**2**	**3**	**4**	**5**
Monday	Rest or cross-training	Rest or cross-training	Rest or cross-training	Rest or cross-training	Recovery 6 mi (10 km)
Tuesday	Rest or cross-training	Recovery 5 mi (8 km)	Recovery 6 mi (10 km)	General aerobic 8 mi (13 km)	General aerobic 8 mi (13 km)
Wednesday	Recovery 4 mi (6 km)	Recovery 6 mi (10 km)	Recovery 7 mi (11 km)	General aerobic 10 mi (16 km)	General aerobic + speed 10 mi (16 km) w/ 10 × 100 m strides
Thursday	Rest or cross-training	Rest or cross-training	Rest or cross-training	Rest or cross-training	Rest or cross-training
Friday	Recovery 6 mi (10 km)	Recovery 7 mi (11 km)	General aerobic + speed 8 mi (13 km) w/ 8 × 100 m strides	General aerobic + speed 9 mi (14 km) w/ 8 × 100 m strides	Lactate threshold 10 mi (16 km) w/ 4 mi (6 km) @ 15K to half marathon race pace
Saturday	Rest or cross-training	Recovery 5 mi (8 km)	Recovery 6 mi (10 km)	Recovery 6 mi (10 km)	Recovery 6 mi (10 km)
Sunday	Recovery 8 mi (13 km)	General aerobic 10 mi (16 km)	Medium-long run 11 mi (18 km)	Medium-long run 12 mi (19 km)	Medium-long run 14 mi (23 km)
Weekly volume	18 mi/29 km	33 mi/53 km	38 mi/62 km	45 mi/72 km	54 mi/88 km

12

Multiple Marathoning

This chapter is for those occasions when, for whatever perverse reason, you've decided to do two marathons with 12 weeks or less between. Though doing two (or more) marathons in rapid succession generally isn't the best way to go after a personal best time, this chapter focuses on structuring your training to maximize your likelihood of success. It includes five schedules, covering 12, 10, 8, 6, and 4 weeks between marathons.

These schedules are substantially different from the schedules in chapters 9 through 11; the schedules in chapter 12 must start with helping you recover from marathon number 1 and then help you train and taper for marathon number 2. The number of weeks between marathons dictates how much time you devote to recovery, training, and tapering. For example, the 12-week schedule allows a relatively luxurious 4 weeks for recovery, whereas the 6-week schedule can allocate only 2 weeks to recovery.

The schedules in this chapter are written for marathoners who typically build to 60 to 70 miles (97 to 113 km) per week during marathon preparation. The 10- and 12-week schedules build to a peak weekly mileage of 67 (108 km), whereas the 8-, 6-, and 4-week schedules peak at 66(106 km), 60 (97 km), and 48 miles (77 km), respectively. If your mileage during marathon preparation is typically more than 70 miles (113 km) per week, then scale up the volume in these schedules moderately. Similarly, if your mileage typically peaks at less than 60 miles (97 km) per week, then scale the training back proportionately.

The schedules assume that you want to do your best in your second marathon. Though this might not mean running a personal best or even running as fast as in the first race in your double (or triple, or whatever), it does mean toeing the line with the intention of running as fast as you can that day. If your multiple-marathoning goal is to cruise comfortably through a second or third marathon soon after a peak effort, then ignore these schedules. Simply focus on recovering from your first race while interspersing enough long runs to maintain your endurance until your next one.

Why Multiple Marathoning?

Olympic gold medalist Frank Shorter said that you can't run another marathon until you've forgotten your last one. If that's so, then a lot of runners out there have short memories.

Although statistics in this area are hard to come by, anecdotal evidence suggests that many runners choose to circumvent the conventional wisdom—which is to do, at most, a spring and a fall marathon—and are running three, four, or more marathons a year. Some run a marathon a month. And we're not just talking about middle-of-the-packers here. Gete Wami won the Berlin Marathon in September 2007. Five weeks later, she was back at it, battling Paula Radcliffe for victory at the New York City Marathon and fading only in the last few hundred meters. Still, she hung on for second and followed her Berlin time of 2:23:17 with a 2:23:32 on the much tougher New York City course.

Of course, Wami ran both so that she could win the $500,000 World Marathon Majors jackpot. You probably won't have that financial incentive. So should you be a multiple marathoner? We can't answer that question for you other than to describe why some people are drawn to multiple marathoning.

Unmet Goals

It's rare to finish a marathon and—after the obligatory utterance of "Never again"—not think you could have run at least a little faster, if only X, Y, and Z hadn't occurred. If you've run a less-than-satisfying marathon, but it didn't seem to take too much out of you, and if another likely site for a good race looms several weeks ahead, then you might want to consider drawing on your horse-remounting skills.

Building Blocks

A marathon run at a controlled but honest pace a few months before a peak effort can provide a significant training boost and a good measure of your fitness. If you run a race too hard or too close to your real goal race, of course, this is akin to pulling up roots to see how your carrots are growing. Certainly these are excellent opportunities to test your marathon drink, shoes, and the like in battle conditions.

Travel

As the growing popularity of destination marathons shows, a special knowledge of an area comes from covering it at length on foot. Many runners plan vacations around a scenic marathon for a chance to view the scenery in a way you can't experience from a tour bus. When you combine such trips with a standard marathon schedule, you're likely to run into instances of short turnaround times.

Variety

Some runners simply like to run marathons and to experience them in all their permutations, from intimate affairs such as the Green River Marathon (no entry fee and 52 finishers in 2007) in Kent, Washington; to medium-size marathons such as Napa Valley (1,800 runners traversing California wine country) and Twin Cities (8,000 runners along the Mississippi River at peak fall foliage); on up to the mega-events such as Chicago and Berlin. Even though marathons are held throughout the year, the traditional spring and fall clustering can mean that sampling the marathon world requires becoming a multiple marathoner.

A Foolish Consistency

How can we put this gently? Some runners are drawn to challenges for no better reason than because they sound good. This would include such undertakings as running a marathon a month for a year, running a marathon in all 50 U.S. states plus the District of Columbia, running one in every province and territory in Canada, and completing a marathon on every continent. The marathon-a-month goal obviously requires scant time between efforts, but so can the geographically based ones, given that you'll be at the mercy of marathon planners.

Why Not?

"Normal" marathoners should check the amount of glass in their houses before throwing stones at multiple marathoners. After all, the bulk of this book has been devoted to detailing how to maximize your chances of success at an activity that the human body isn't really suited for. So if some runners want to give the standard reason for undertaking such a challenge—"Because it's there"—several times a year, well, it's not as if they're clubbing seals.

Reading the Schedules

The schedules are presented in a day-by-day format. This is in response to requests from readers of our first book, *Road Racing for Serious Runners*, to provide schedules that specify what to do each day of the week.

The main limitation with this approach is that it's impossible to guess the myriad of outside factors that may influence your day-to-day nonrunning life. Work schedules, family life, relationships, school commitments, and Mother Nature all play their part in determining when you get to do your long runs and other aspects of marathon preparation. You'll no doubt require some flexibility in your training and will need to juggle days around from time to time. That's expected, and as long as you don't try to make up for lost time by doing several hard days in a row, you should be able to avoid injury and overtraining.

The schedules express each day's training in miles and kilometers; use whichever you're accustomed to. The mile and kilometer figures for each day (and the weekly total) are rough equivalents of each other, not a conversion from one to the other accurate to the third decimal point.

Because of the large variation between runners in the time required for marathon recovery, you should approach these schedules with a high degree of flexibility. Also, if, in your first marathon, the weather was hot, you became severely dehydrated, or you became unusually hobbled, then your recovery is likely to take longer than usual. When a conflict arises between what the schedule says to do and what your body indicates it's willing to do, listen to your body. With these tight time frames between marathons, your best strategy is first to focus on recovery and then to worry about the other aspects of training. If you're not able to follow the schedules closely for one reason or another, then follow the priorities discussed later in this chapter in choosing which workouts to do and which to miss.

For all the schedules in this chapter, remember that in the first few weeks after marathon number 1, recovery is your primary objective, and that during the last 3 weeks, tapering to consolidate your energy reserves is paramount. If you're worn out or injured going into marathon number 2, then any extra workouts you've squeezed in won't have been worth the effort.

One way to ensure that you don't run too hard during the first few weeks after your previous marathon is to use a heart rate monitor. As discussed in chapter 4, a heart rate monitor can help prevent you from going too fast on your easy days. During the first few weeks after the marathon, keep your heart rate below 76 percent of your maximal heart rate or 70 percent of your heart rate reserve to help speed your recovery.

■ Pete's 1983 Trifecta

In 1983, I ran three high-quality marathons in 17 weeks. Nine weeks after winning the San Francisco Marathon in 2:14:44, I finished second in the Montreal Marathon in 2:12:33. Eight weeks after that, I won the Auckland Marathon in 2:12:19. At the time, the last two races were personal bests.

I did a few things wrong between San Francisco and Montreal but was able to hold my body together through a combination of luck, enthusiasm, and youth (I was 26). After San Francisco, I was remarkably stiff for several days. I'm not sure whether that was from standing around in the cold for a couple of hours after the race or because it was my first marathon in almost 2 years because of surgery on my plantar fascia. I hobbled a 2-miler (3 km) 2 days after the race and racked up 46 miles (74 km) for the week. Regular massage helped bring my legs around.

Fortunately, my body bounced back really well after that first week, and I was up to 100 miles (161 km) in the third week after, including a session of eight 800-meter repeats on the track. My mileage climbed to 116 (187) and 122 (196) for the fourth and fifth weeks, which was about as high as I used to get back then. (I hadn't made an Olympic team yet, so I was working full time.) There was just enough time to fit in two tune-up races, a 5-miler (8 km) in 23:35 and a third-place finish in the New Haven 20K, and then it was time to taper again. Eight days before Montreal, I went to the track and did two repeats of 1,600 meters in 4:24 and 4:23, which was really fast for me and a good omen. The last 2 weeks before the race I tried to get caught up on sleep, and I felt really ready going into Montreal.

The night after Montreal, I stayed out until 5:00 a.m., took an 8:00 a.m. flight back to Boston, and caught a cab directly to work. This didn't help my recovery. After that, though, I settled down, and in the first 3 weeks after Montreal covered 48, 72, and 97 miles (77, 116, and 156 km). Lots of sleep and weekly massage kept me injury free, and, except for the occasional "Felt like hell" notation in my diary, training went pretty well.

Three weeks before the Auckland Marathon, I started my leave of absence from work at New Balance to prepare for the Olympic trials and flew to New Zealand with my training partner, Tom Ratcliffe, who was also running Auckland. We got a bit carried away with the excitement and probably overtrained the first week there. The second week in New Zealand, I ran a 10K tune-up race in 29:12, which I was very pleased with. During the last week before the marathon, however, I could tell that my body was on a fine edge, and I decided to back right off. Three days before the race, I was still feeling pretty tired. Fortunately, on race day, I felt strong and broke away after 17 miles (27 km). It had been a very positive experience in multiple marathoning that was excellent practice for the following year's Olympic trials and marathon.

—Pete Pfitzinger

Following the Schedules

Each column of the schedules represents a week's training. For example, in the 10-week schedule, the column for 9 weeks to goal indicates that at the end of that week you have 9 weeks until your second marathon. The schedules continue week by week until race week.

We have included the specific workout for each day as well as the category of training for that day. For example, in the 10-week schedule, on the Friday of the 5-weeks-to-go column, the specific workout is a 9-mile (14 km) run, and the category of training for that day is general aerobic conditioning. This aspect of the schedules allows you to quickly see the balance of training during each week and the progression of workouts from week to week. Look again at the 10-week schedule—it's easy to see that with 5 weeks to go until the marathon, there are three recovery days that week along with a $\dot{V}O_2$max session, a long run, a medium-long run, and a general aerobic conditioning run. Looking at the row for Sunday, it's easy to see how the long runs progress and then taper in the last few weeks before the marathon.

The workouts are divided into the following eight categories: long runs, medium-long runs, marathon-pace runs, general aerobic runs, lactate threshold runs, recovery runs, $\dot{V}O_2$max intervals, and speed training. Each of these categories is explained in depth in chapter 7, and the physiology behind the training is explained in chapter 1.

Multiple-Marathoning Priorities

The following sections explain the priorities for the training schedules in this chapter. But what if you don't have 12, 10, 8, 6, or 4 weeks between marathons?

If you have less than 4 weeks between marathons, you're on your own. Your main concern should be recovery, recovery, and more recovery, not only from your first marathon but also from the lobotomy that led you to come up with this plan.

For other amounts of time between marathons, follow these guidelines:

- For 11 weeks between, do the 12-week schedule, but skip the week "6 weeks to goal."
- For 9 weeks between, do the 10-week schedule, but skip the week "5 weeks to goal," and with 35 days to go, increase the distance of the run to 18 miles (29 km).
- For 7 weeks between, do the 8-week schedule, but skip the week "3 weeks to goal," and with 21 days to go, increase the distance of the run to 18 miles (29 km).
- For 5 weeks between, do the 6-week schedule, but skip the week "2 weeks to goal," and with 14 days to go, increase the medium-long run to 16 miles (26 km).

■ Pete's 1984 Dynamic Double

On May 26, 1984, I ran 2:11:43 to win the Olympic marathon trials, and then on August 12, I placed 11th in 2:13:53 in the Olympics. Here's how I approached the 11 weeks in between.

I was on a bit of a high after winning the trials, to say the least. I took the next day off and went for a relaxed swim and a pathetic 3-mile (5 km) shuffle 2 days after the race. The next day, I had my weekly massage, and my muscles weren't too bad. Building toward the Olympics, massage each week helped keep me injury free despite the short recovery. I ran 45 miles (72 km) the week after the trials. Using the philosophy that I needed to get the training in as quickly as possible to be able to taper again and be in top form for the Olympics, I initially ran as I felt and got in 112 miles (180 km) the second week and 151 miles (243 km) the third week. During the second week after the trials, I started doing a few strideouts every couple of days to try to get my legs turning over. This seemed to help quite a bit.

In retrospect, I should have run 80 to 90 miles (129 to 145 km) the second week and 110 to 120 miles (177 to 193 km) the third week. Doing the amount I did showed a lack of confidence because I wouldn't have lost fitness by doing fewer miles. In fact, if I had run a bit less mileage right after the trials, I probably would have performed better at the Olympics. But I didn't understand that at the time.

The problem I faced was that in 11 weeks I couldn't very well do a 4-week recovery and a 3-week taper because that would have left only 4 weeks to train to compete against the best runners in the world. I got around that by cutting back the recovery and getting back into fairly high-quality long intervals by the fourth or fifth week posttrials. The beauty of the short recovery after the trials was that I was fit enough to do my long intervals at a good clip right away, so I didn't need as long to build into them. For example, in the fifth week posttrials, I did a 3-mile (5 km) time trial on the track in 14:02.

I did continue, however, to train according to how I felt, with flexibility both ways. For example, one day I headed out for a 15-miler (24 km), felt good, and wound up going 26 miles (42 km). On other days, I would postpone a track workout for a day or two until my legs felt as if they could give a good effort without getting injured.

I tapered more for the Olympics than for the trials. This was somewhat necessitated by tightness that I developed in my back during the last 3 weeks before the race. It was also out of a realization that I had trained a bit too hard in the weeks after the trials and that my energy level needed time to come up a notch. This is a very subjective matter, but I could tell during my training runs that a bit of zip was missing and that it was better to cut back and regain my strength. I did this by making my easy days—in terms of speed and distance—easier. I also trimmed the volume of my long runs and my speed workouts. This taper became the model that I followed for the rest of my racing career.

—Pete Pfitzinger

12-Week Schedule

A period of 12 weeks between marathons isn't too bad. There's a real risk, however, of either taking it too easy and gradually losing marathon-specific fitness or overdoing it and finding yourself at the starting line of marathon number 2 feeling tired and wondering why you're there. You need to find the perfect balance for your individual situation. The best strategy is to really take it easy for the first 3 or 4 weeks after your previous marathon to ensure that your body is fully recovered. That leaves 8 or 9 weeks until the next marathon, including 5 or 6 weeks of solid training and a 3-week taper.

The key training time is the 6-week period lasting from 7 weeks to go through 2 weeks until the second marathon. The most important workouts during those weeks are the tune-up races with 29 and 15 days to go; the marathon-specific run with 42 days to go; the long runs with 49, 35, 28, and 21 days to go; the $\dot{V}O_2$max sessions with 39, 33, and 25 days to go; and the medium-long runs with 52, 44, 38, 32, and 24 days until marathon number 2.

10-Week Schedule

Allowing 10 weeks between marathons is almost reasonable, and the schedule reflects this by providing 3 weeks of solid recovery, 4 weeks of solid training, and a 3-week taper.

The key training weeks are those that end with 6, 5, 4, 3, and 2 weeks until your second marathon. The most important workouts during those weeks are the tune-up races with 29 and 15 days to go; the long runs with 35, 28, 21, and 14 days to go; the lactate threshold session with 44 days to go; the $\dot{V}O_2$max sessions with 39 and 25 days to go; and the medium-long runs with 38, 32, and 24 days until marathon number 2. The only word of caution concerning a 10-week time frame between marathons is to allow yourself to recover fully from your previous marathon before training too intensely for the next one.

8-Week Schedule

The 8-week schedule allows you to recover thoroughly from your previous marathon, train well for about 3 weeks, and then taper for marathon number 2. A period of 8 weeks between marathons is far less risky than 4 or 6 weeks. Even if your first marathon was in hot weather, or if you came out of it with a minor injury, with a bit of luck you should still be okay for marathon number 2.

The key training weeks are those that end with 4, 3, and 2 weeks until the second marathon. The most important workouts during those weeks are the tune-up race with 15 days to go; the long runs with 28, 21, and 14 days to go; the lactate threshold session with 30 days to go; and the medium-long runs with 24 and 18 days until the marathon. Try to avoid doing more than the schedules call for because 8 weeks between marathons is still brief enough that you don't have much room for error.

6-Week Schedule

The 6-week schedule was difficult to put together because 6 weeks is just enough time to start to lose fitness if you don't train enough, but it is also just barely enough time to recover from marathon number 1 before you need to taper for marathon number 2. The most important training weeks are those that end 3 weeks and 2 weeks before marathon number 2. Those weeks provide a small window during which you can train fairly hard without wearing yourself out for the second marathon.

The key workouts during those weeks are the tune-up race with 15 days to go, the long run with 14 days to go, the $\dot{V}O_2$max sessions with 23 and 19 days to go, and the medium-long runs with 21 and 18 days until the marathon. This brief training stimulus will keep you in peak marathon fitness so that after tapering, you should be close to your best.

4-Week Schedule

The 4-week schedule is about as compact as you can get. This program consists of 2 weeks of recovery merging into 2 weeks of taper. The objective is to get you to the starting line injury free, fully recovered from your previous marathon, and still in top shape. The mileage for this program starts at 25 miles (40 km) and builds to 48 miles (77 km) during the third week. Unfortunately, that's also the penultimate week before the marathon, so mileage and intensity building abruptly halt and merge into a taper.

The most important workouts in this schedule are the medium-long runs with 14 and 10 days until marathon number 2 and the $\dot{V}O_2$max session with 12 days to go. If you need to do two marathons just 4 weeks apart (and *need* is a relative term), then this schedule should maximize your chances of success.

Racing Strategies

Don't do it!

Just kidding. You should definitely set a clear goal for the second (or third, or fourth, . . .) marathon you're running within a brief time frame. Otherwise, you might very well find yourself a few miles into it already wondering, *What am I doing here?* Being able to state what you want to accomplish in your multiple marathoning will provide en route direction and motivation. The longer you've allowed between marathons, the more precisely you should be able to state your goals for marathon number 2 (beyond "to get through it").

Once you've picked your goal, map out the splits you'll need to hit. Throughout this book, we've stressed the merits of showing restraint early in the marathon to maximize your chances of being able to run a strong second half. That advice is especially pertinent if you've already finished one marathon in the last 12 weeks or sooner. Your multiple-marathoning experience will almost certainly become a self-fulfilling death march if you run too fast early in the race in the hope of building a cushion against an inevitably slower second half.

Wait until the week before your second marathon to decide on a time goal. Be realistic, taking into account how your recovery from your first race went; the quality of your long runs, tempo runs, and interval sessions in the interim; and whether you've felt your energy level rise during your taper for marathon number 2.

Also consider the circumstances of your previous marathon. For example, if you ran a huge personal record (PR) off of negative splits, then there's probably room for improvement this time around. Or say you wilted over the last 10K the last time around and realize in retrospect that this was because of a too-aggressive first 10 miles (16 km); you should be able to make another attempt at your goal time for the first marathon. If, however, you prepared with monk-like devotion for 24 weeks for your previous marathon and shaved 3 seconds off your lifetime best, and your second marathon is 4 weeks later, well, sorry, but this probably isn't the time to try for a 10-minute PR.

If you've never consciously tried to run a marathon with negative splits, this might be the occasion to do so. Give yourself the first several miles to get an accurate feel for how your body is responding to the challenge you've set for it, and pick up the pace only when you're fairly confident that you can sustain it to the end.

After the Marathon

If you've just run two or more marathons within a brief time span, your best strategy for future success is to take a well-deserved break. A few weeks of no running or easy training will help your body to recover and your mind to develop new challenges. You have little to gain by rushing back into training, and your risk of injury is exceptionally high at this point, owing to the reduced resiliency of your muscles and connective tissue after running multiple marathons. If you choose to keep training, then the 5-week recovery schedule (mesocycle 5) in chapter 10 will help you recover and rebuild your training safely.

	WEEKS TO NEXT MARATHON			
	11	**10**	**9**	**8**
Monday	Rest or cross-training	Rest or cross-training	Rest or cross-training	Rest or cross-training
Tuesday	Rest or 5 mi (8 km)	Recovery 6 mi (10 km)	Recovery 6 mi (10 km)	General aerobic + speed 8 mi (13 km) w/ 10 × 100 m strides
Wednesday	Recovery 5 mi (8 km)	Recovery 5 mi (8 km)	General aerobic 9 mi (14 km)	Medium-long run 12 mi (19 km)
Thursday	Rest or cross-training	Rest or cross-training	Rest or cross-training	Recovery 4 mi (6 km)
Friday	Recovery 5 mi (8 km)	General aerobic + speed 7 mi (11 km) w/ 8 × 100 m strides	General aerobic + speed 9 mi (14 km) w/ 8 × 100 m strides	Lactate threshold 9 mi (14 km) w/ 5 mi (8 km) @ 15K to half marathon race pace
Saturday	Recovery 5 mi (8 km)	Recovery 5 mi (8 km)	Recovery 5 mi (8 km)	Recovery + speed 5 mi (8 km) w/ 6 × 100 m strides
Sunday	Recovery 7 mi (11 km)	General aerobic 10 mi (16 km)	Medium-long run 13 mi (21 km)	Long run 16 mi (26 km)
Weekly volume	22-27 mi/35-43 km	32 mi/53 km	42 mi/67 km	54 mi/86 km

	WEEKS TO NEXT MARATHON			
	7	6	5	4
Monday	Rest or cross-training	Rest or cross-training	Rest or cross-training	Rest or cross-training
Tuesday	$\dot{V}O_2$max 9 mi (14 km) w/ 6 × 800 m @ 5K race pace; jog 50 to 90% interval time between	General aerobic + speed 8 mi (13 km) w/ 10 × 100 m strides	Recovery 6 mi (10 km)	$\dot{V}O_2$max 9 mi (14 km) w/ 6 × 600 m @ 5K race pace; jog 50 to 90% interval time between
Wednesday	Recovery 6 mi (10 km)	Medium-long run 15 mi (24 km)	$\dot{V}O_2$max 10 mi (16 km) w/ 4 × 1,200 m @ 5K race pace; jog 50 to 90% interval time between	Medium-long run 11 mi (18 km)
Thursday	Medium-long run 13 mi (21 km)	Recovery 6 mi (10 km)	Medium-long run 15 mi (24 km)	Recovery + speed 6 mi (10 km) w/ 6 × 100 m strides
Friday	General aerobic + speed 8 mi (13 km) w/ 10 × 100 m strides	Medium-long run 13 mi (21 km)	General aerobic 9 mi (14 km)	Recovery 5 mi (8 km)
Saturday	Recovery 6 mi (10 km)	Recovery + speed 7 mi (11 km) w/ 6 × 100 m strides	Recovery 6 mi (10 km)	8K-15K tune-up race (total 9-13 mi/14-21 km)
Sunday	Long run 18 mi (29 km)	Marathon-pace run 15 mi (24 km) w/ 12 mi (19 km) @ marathon race pace	Long run 20 mi (32 km)	Long run 17 mi (27 km)
Weekly volume	60 mi/97 km	64 mi/103 km	66 mi/106 km	57-61 mi/91-98 km

	WEEKS TO NEXT MARATHON			
	3	**2**	**1**	**Race week**
Monday	Rest or cross-training	Rest or cross-training	Rest or cross-training	Rest
Tuesday	Recovery 6 mi (10 km)	$\dot{V}O_2$max 9 mi (14 km) w/ 6 × 600 m @ 5K race pace; jog 50 to 90% interval time between	General aerobic + speed 8 mi (13 km) w/ 8 × 100 m strides	Recovery 6 mi (10 km)
Wednesday	$\dot{V}O_2$max 11 mi (18 km) w/ 6 × 1,000 m @ 5K race pace; jog 50 to 90% interval time between	Medium-long run 11 mi (18 km)	Recovery 5 mi (8 km)	Dress rehearsal 7 mi (11 km) w/ 2 mi (3 km) @ marathon race pace
Thursday	Medium-long run 15 mi (24 km)	Recovery + speed 6 mi (10 km) w/ 6 × 100 m strides	$\dot{V}O_2$max 9 mi (14 km) w/ 3 × 1,600 m @ 5K race pace; jog 50 to 90% interval time between	Recovery 6 mi (10 km)
Friday	General aerobic 9 mi (14 km)	Recovery 5 mi (8 km)	Recovery 5 mi (8 km)	Recovery + speed 5 mi (8 km) w/ 6 × 100 m strides
Saturday	Recovery 6 mi (10 km)	8K-10K tune-up race (total 9-11 mi/14-18 km)	General aerobic + speed 7 mi (11 km) w/ 10 × 100 m strides	Recovery 4 mi (6 km)
Sunday	Long run 20 mi (32 km)	Long run 17 mi (27 km)	Medium-long run 13 mi (21 km)	Second marathon
Weekly volume	67 mi/108 km	57-59 mi/91-95 km	47 mi/75 km	28 mi/45 km (6 days prerace)

	WEEKS TO NEXT MARATHON				
	9	**8**	**7**	**6**	**5**
Monday	Rest or cross-training	Rest or cross-training	Rest or cross-training	Rest or cross-training	Rest or cross-training
Tuesday	Rest or cross-training	Recovery 5 mi (8 km)	Recovery 6 mi (10 km)	General aerobic + speed 8 mi (13 km) w/ 10 × 100 m strides	Recovery 6 mi (10 km)
Wednesday	Recovery 5 mi (8 km)	Recovery 5 mi (8 km)	General aerobic 9 mi (14 km)	Medium-long run 12 mi (19 km)	$\dot{V}O_2$max 10 mi (16 km) w/ 4 × 1,200 m @ 5K race pace; jog 50 to 90% interval time between
Thursday	Rest or cross-training	Rest or cross-training	Rest or cross-training	Recovery 4 mi (6 km)	Medium-long run 15 mi (24 km)
Friday	Recovery 5 mi (8 km)	General aerobic + speed 7 mi (11 km) w/ 8 × 100 m strides	General aerobic + speed 9 mi (14 km) w/ 8 × 100 m strides	Lactate threshold 9 mi (14 km) w/ 5 mi (8 km) @ 15K to half marathon pace	General aerobic 9 mi (14 km)
Saturday	Recovery 5 mi (8 km)	Recovery 5 mi (8 km)	Recovery 5 mi (8 km)	Recovery + speed 5 mi (8 km) w/ 6 × 100 m strides	Recovery 6 mi (10 km)
Sunday	Recovery 7 mi (11 km)	General aerobic 10 mi (16 km)	Medium-long run 13 mi (21 km)	Long run 17 mi (27 km)	Long run 19 mi (31 km)
Weekly volume	22 mi/35 km	32 mi/53 km	42 mi/64 km	55 mi/87 km	65 mi/105 km

Multiple Marathoning 10-Week Schedule

	WEEKS TO NEXT MARATHON				
	4	3	2	1	Race week
Monday	Rest or cross-training	Rest or cross-training	Rest or cross-training	Rest or cross-training	Rest
Tuesday	$\dot{V}O_2$max 9 mi (13 km) w/ 6 × 600 m @ 5K race pace; jog 50 to 90% interval time between	Recovery 6 mi (10 km)	$\dot{V}O_2$max 9 mi (14 km) w/ 6 × 600 m @ 5K race pace; jog 50 to 90% interval time between	General aerobic + speed 8 mi (13 km) w/ 8 × 100 m strides	Recovery 6 mi (10 km)
Wednesday	Medium-long run 11 mi (18 km)	$\dot{V}O_2$max 11 mi (14 km) w/ 6 × 1,000 m @ 5K race pace; jog 50 to 90% interval time between	Medium-long run 11 mi (18 km)	Recovery 5 mi (8 km)	Dress rehearsal 7 mi (11 km) w/ 2 mi (3 km) @ marathon race pace
Thursday	Recovery + speed 6 mi (10 km) w/ 6 × 100 m strides	Medium-long run 15 mi (24 km)	Recovery + speed 6 mi (10 km) w/ 6 × 100 m strides	9 mi (14 km) w/ 3 × 1,600 m @ 5K race pace; jog 50 to 90% interval time between	Recovery 6 mi (10 km)
Friday	Recovery 5 mi (8 km)	General aerobic 9 mi (14 km)	Recovery 5 mi (8 km)	Recovery 5 mi (8 km)	Recovery + speed 5 mi (8 km) w/ 6 × 100 m strides
Saturday	8K-15K tune-up race (total 9-13 mi/14-21 km)	Recovery 6 mi (10 km)	8K-10K tune-up race (total 9-11 mi/14-18 km)	General aerobic + speed 7 mi (11 km) w/ 10 × 100 m strides	Recovery 4 mi (6 km)
Sunday	Long run 17 mi (27 km)	Long run 20 mi (32 km)	Long run 17 mi (27 km)	Medium-long run 13 mi (21 km)	Second marathon
Weekly volume	57-61 mi/90-97 km	67 mi/104km	57-59 mi/92-95 km	47 mi/75 km	28 mi/45 km (6 days prerace)

	WEEKS TO NEXT MARATHON			
	7	6	5	4
Monday	Rest or cross-training	Rest or cross-training	Rest or cross-training	Rest or cross-training
Tuesday	Rest or cross-training	Recovery 5 mi (8 km)	Recovery 6 mi (10 km)	General aerobic + speed 8 mi (13 km) w/ 10 × 100 m strides
Wednesday	Recovery 5 mi (8 km)	Recovery 5 mi (8 km)	General aerobic 9 mi (14 km)	Medium-long run 12 mi (19 km)
Thursday	Rest or cross-training	Rest or cross-training	Rest or cross-training	Recovery 4 mi (6 km)
Friday	Recovery 5 mi (8 km)	General aerobic + speed 7 mi (11 km) w/ 8 × 100 m strides	General aerobic + speed 9 mi (14 km) w/ 8 × 100 m strides	Lactate threshold 9 mi (14 km) w/ 5 mi (8 km) @ 15K to half marathon race pace
Saturday	Recovery 5 mi (8 km)	Recovery 5 mi (8 km)	Recovery 5 mi (8 km)	Recovery + speed 5 mi (8 km) w/ 6 × 100 m strides
Sunday	Recovery 7 mi (11 km)	General aerobic 10 mi (16 km)	Medium-long run 13 mi (21 km)	Long run 17 mi (27 km)
Weekly volume	22 mi/35 km	32 mi/52 km	42 mi/63 km	55 mi/87 km

（側）Multiple Marathoning 8-Week Schedule

	WEEKS TO NEXT MARATHON			
	3	**2**	**1**	**Race week**
Monday	Rest or cross-training	Rest or cross-training	Rest or cross-training	Rest
Tuesday	Recovery 6 mi (10 km)	$\dot{V}O_2$max 9 mi (14 km) w/ 6 × 600 m @ 5K race pace; jog 50 to 90% interval time between	General aerobic + speed 8 mi (13 km) w/ 8 × 100 m strides	Recovery 6 mi (10 km)
Wednesday	$\dot{V}O_2$max 10 mi (16 km) w/ 5 × 1,000 m @ 5K race pace; jog 50 to 90% interval time between	Medium-long run 11 mi (18 km)	Recovery 5 mi (8 km)	Dress rehearsal 7 mi (11 km) w/ 2 mi (3 km) @ marathon race pace
Thursday	Medium-long run 15 mi (24 km)	Recovery + speed 6 mi (10 km) w/ 6 × 100 m strides	$\dot{V}O_2$max 9 mi (14 km) w/ 3 × 1,600 m @ 5K race pace; jog 50 to 90% interval time between	Recovery 6 mi (10 km)
Friday	General aerobic 9 mi (14 km)	Recovery 5 mi (8 km)	Recovery 5 mi (8 km)	Recovery + speed 5 mi (8 km) w/ 6 × 100 m strides
Saturday	Recovery 6 mi (10 km)	8K-10K tune-up race (total 9-11 mi/14-18 km)	Recovery + speed 6 mi (10 km) w/ 8 × 100 m strides	Recovery 4 mi (6 km)
Sunday	Long run 20 mi (32 km)	Long run 17 mi (27 km)	Medium-long run 13 mi (21 km)	Second marathon
Weekly volume	66 mi/106 km	57-59 mi/91-95 km	46 mi/74 km	28 mi/45 km (6 days prerace)

	WEEKS TO NEXT MARATHON		
	5	**4**	**3**
Monday	Rest or cross-training	Rest or cross-training	Rest or cross-training
Tuesday	Rest or cross-training	Recovery 6 mi (10 km)	General aerobic + speed 7 mi (11 km) w/ 8 × 100 m strides
Wednesday	Recovery 5 mi (8 km)	General aerobic 8 mi (13 km)	Medium-long run 12 mi (19 km)
Thursday	Rest or cross-training	Rest or cross-training	Recovery 4 mi (6 km)
Friday	Recovery 6 mi (10 km)	General aerobic + speed 8 mi (13 km) w/ 8 × 100 m strides	$\dot{V}O_2$max 9 mi (14 km) w/ 6 × 800 m @ 5K race pace; jog 50 to 90% interval time between
Saturday	Recovery 5 mi (8 km)	Recovery 5 mi (8 km)	Recovery 5 mi (8 km)
Sunday	General aerobic 8 mi (13 km)	General aerobic 10 mi (16 km)	Medium-long run 15 mi (24 km)
Weekly volume	24 mi/39 km	37 mi/60 km	52 mi/82 km

	WEEKS TO NEXT MARATHON		
	2	**1**	**Race week**
Monday	Rest or cross-training	Rest or cross-training	Rest
Tuesday	V̇O₂max 9 mi (14 km) w/ 6 × 600 m @ 5K race pace; jog 50 to 90% interval time between	General aerobic + speed 8 mi (13 km) w/ 8 × 100 m strides	Recovery 6 mi (10 km)
Wednesday	Medium-long run 11 mi (18 km)	Recovery 5 mi (8 km)	Dress rehearsal 7 mi (11 km) w/ 2 mi (3 km) @ marathon race pace
Thursday	Recovery + speed 6 mi (10 km) w/ 6 × 100 m strides	V̇O₂max 9 mi (14 km) w/ 3 × 1,600 m @ 5K race pace; jog 50 to 90% interval time between	Recovery 6 mi (10 km)
Friday	Recovery 5 mi (8 km)	Recovery 5 mi (8 km)	Recovery + speed 5 mi (8 km) w/ 6 × 100 m strides
Saturday	8K-10K tune-up race (total 9-11 mi/14-18 km)	Recovery + speed 6 mi (10 km) w/ 8 × 100 m strides	Recovery 4 mi (6 km)
Sunday	Long run 18 mi (29 km)	Medium-long run 13 mi (21 km)	Second marathon
Weekly volume	58-60 mi/93-97 km	46 mi/74 km	28 mi/45 km (6 days prerace)

	WEEKS TO NEXT MARATHON			
	3	2	1	Race week
Monday	Rest or cross-training	Rest or cross-training	Rest or cross-training	Rest
Tuesday	Rest or cross-training	Recovery 6 mi (10 km)	$\dot{V}O_2$max 8 mi (13 km) w/ 5 × 800 m @ 5K race pace; jog 50 to 90% interval time between	Recovery 6 mi (10 km)
Wednesday	Recovery 5 mi (8 km)	General aerobic 8 mi (13 km)	Recovery 5 mi (8 km)	Dress rehearsal 7 mi (11 km) w/ 2 mi (3 km) @ marathon race pace
Thursday	Rest or cross-training	Rest or cross-training	Medium-long run 15 mi (24 km)	Recovery 6 mi (10 km)
Friday	Recovery 6 mi (10 km)	General aerobic + speed 8 mi (13 km) w/ 8 × 100 m strides	Recovery 4 mi (6 km)	Recovery + speed 5 mi (8 km) w/ 6 × 100 m strides
Saturday	Recovery 5 mi (8 km)	Recovery 5 mi (8 km)	Recovery + speed 5 mi (8 km) w/ 8 × 100 m strides	Recovery 4 mi (6 km)
Sunday	General aerobic 8 mi (13 km)	Medium-long run 11 mi (18 km)	Medium-long run 11 mi (18 km)	Second marathon
Weekly volume	24 mi/39 km	38 mi/62 km	48 mi/77 km	28 mi/45 km (6 days prerace)

Marathon Race-Pace Chart

Goal	Pace per mile	5 mi	10K	10 mi	20K	Halfway
2:10:00	4:57.5	24:47	30:48	49:35	1:01:36	1:05:00
2:15:00	5:09.0	25:45	32:00	51:30	1:04:00	1:07:30
2:20:00	5:20.4	26:42	33:11	53:24	1:06:22	1:10:00
2:25:00	5:31.8	27:39	34:22	55:18	1:08:44	1:12:30
2:30:00	5:43.2	28:36	35:33	57:12	1:11:06	1:15:00
2:35:00	5:54.7	29:33	36:44	59:07	1:13:28	1:17:30
2:40:00	6:06.1	30:30	37:55	1:01:01	1:15:50	1:20:00
2:45:00	6:17.6	31:28	39:06	1:02:56	1:18:12	1:22:30
2:50:00	6:29.0	32:25	40:17	1:04:50	1:20:34	1:25:00
2:55:00	6:40.5	33:22	41:28	1:06:45	1:22:56	1:27:30
3:00:00	6:51.9	34:19	42:39	1:08:39	1:25:18	1:30:00
3:05:00	7:03.3	35:16	43:50	1:10:33	1:27:40	1:32:30
3:10:00	7:14.8	36:14	45:02	1:12:28	1:30:04	1:35:00
3:15:00	7:26.2	37:11	46:13	1:14:22	1:32:26	1:37:30
3:20:00	7:37.7	38:08	47:24	1:16:17	1:34:48	1:40:00
3:25:00	7:49.1	39:05	48:35	1:18:11	1:37:10	1:42:30
3:30:00	8:00.5	40:02	49:46	1:20:05	1:39:32	1:45:00
3:35:00	8:12.0	41:00	50:57	1:22:00	1:41:54	1:47:30
3:40:00	8:23.4	41:57	52:08	1:23:54	1:44:16	1:50:00
3:45:00	8:34.9	42:54	53:19	1:25:49	1:46:38	1:52:30
3:50:00	8:46.3	43:51	54:30	1:27:43	1:49:00	1:55:00
3:55:00	8:57.8	44:49	55:41	1:29:38	1:51:22	1:57:30
4:00:00	9:09.2	45:46	56:53	1:31:32	1:53:46	2:00:00

15 mi	30K	20 mi	40K	25 mi	Finish
1:14:22	1:32:24	1:39:10	2:03:12	2:03:57	2:10:00
1:17:15	1:36:00	1:43:00	2:08:00	2:08:45	2:15:00
1:20:06	1:39:33	1:46:48	2:12:44	2:13:30	2:20:00
1:22:57	1:43:06	1:50:36	2:17:28	2:18:15	2:25:00
1:25:48	1:46:39	1:54:24	2:22:12	2:23:00	2:30:00
1:28:40	1:50:12	1:58:14	2:26:56	2:27:47	2:35:00
1:31:31	1:53:45	2:02:02	2:31:40	2:32:32	2:40:00
1:34:24	1:57:18	2:05:52	2:36:24	2:37:20	2:45:00
1:37:15	2:00:51	2:09:40	2:41:08	2:42:05	2:50:00
1:40:07	2:04:24	2:13:30	2:45:52	2:46:52	2:55:00
1:42:58	2:07:57	2:17:18	2:50:36	2:51:37	3:00:00
1:45:49	2:11:30	2:21:06	2:55:20	2:56:22	3:05:00
1:48:42	2:15:06	2:24:56	3:00:08	3:01:10	3:10:00
1:51:33	2:18:39	2:28:44	3:04:52	3:05:55	3:15:00
1:54:25	2:22:12	2:32:34	3:09:36	3:10:42	3:20:00
1:57:16	2:25:45	2:36:22	3:14:20	3:15:27	3:25:00
2:00:07	2:29:18	2:40:10	3:19:04	3:20:12	3:30:00
2:03:00	2:32:51	2:44:00	3:23:48	3:25:00	3:35:00
2:05:51	2:36:24	2:47:48	3:28:32	3:29:45	3:40:00
2:08:43	2:39:57	2:51:38	3:33:16	3:34:32	3:45:00
2:11:34	2:43:30	2:55:26	3:38:00	3:39:17	3:50:00
2:14:27	2:47:03	2:59:16	3:42:44	3:44:05	3:55:00
2:17:18	2:50:39	3:03:04	3:47:32	3:48:50	4:00:00

Lactate-Threshold Workout Charts

The training schedules in this book call for doing lactate-threshold workouts between your current 15K and half marathon race pace, in tempo runs of 4 to 7 miles (6 to 11 km). The charts that follow give per-mile and split times for tempo runs based on these parameters. The charts include roughly equivalent race times—for example, a 58:00 15K is roughly equivalent to a 1:24 half marathon—so you should be able to find the narrow range of paces to run to provide the greatest stimulus to improve your lactate threshold.

Slower runners should run closer to their 15K race pace on tempo runs. Faster runners should run closer to their half marathon race pace during these workouts. Remember, though, that it's important to run your tempo runs at an even pace. Doing so provides a greater stimulus for boosting your lactate threshold than doing a 5-miler (8 km) in which you finish with the same time but during which you start fast, lag in the middle, and finish fast.

If you'll be doing your tempo runs on a track, bear in mind that on a 400-meter track, four laps at a given pace will be short a few seconds per mile. For example, 20 laps at 85 seconds per lap take 28:20. During this time, you'll have covered 8K, which is almost 50 meters short of 5 miles, so you haven't quite averaged 5:40 per mile on this tempo run.

Current 15K race time	Fast end of lactate threshold pace/ mile	Split of 2 mi on tempo run at this pace	Split of 3 mi on tempo run at this pace	Split of 4 mi on tempo run at this pace	Split of 5 mi on tempo run at this pace	Split of 6 mi on tempo run at this pace	Split of 7 mi on tempo run at this pace
44:00	4:43	9:26	14:10	18:53	23:36	28:19	33:02
45:00	4:49	9:39	14:29	19:19	24:08	28:58	33:48
46:00	4:56	9:52	14:48	19:44	24:40	29:37	34:33
47:00	5:02	10:05	15:08	20:10	25:13	30:16	35:18
48:00	5:09	10:18	15:27	20:36	25:45	30:54	36:03
49:00	5:15	10:31	15:46	21:02	26:17	31:32	36:48
50:00	5:21	10:44	16:06	21:28	26:49	32:11	37:33
51:00	5:28	10:57	16:25	21:53	27:21	32:50	38:18
52:00	5:34	11:09	16:44	22:19	27:53	33:28	39:03
53:00	5:41	11:22	17:04	22:45	28:26	34:07	39:48
54:00	5:47	11:35	17:23	23:10	28:58	34:46	40:33
55:00	5:54	11:48	17:42	23:36	29:30	35:25	41:19
56:00	6:00	12:01	18:01	24:02	30:02	36:03	42:03
57:00	6:06	12:14	18:21	24:28	30:34	36:41	42:48
58:00	6:13	12:27	18:40	24:54	31:07	37:20	43:34
59:00	6:19	12:40	18:59	25:19	31:39	37:59	44:19
1:00:00	6:26	12:52	19:19	25:45	32:11	38:37	45:03
1:01:00	6:32	13:05	19:38	26:11	32:43	39:16	45:49
1:02:00	6:39	13:18	19:57	26:36	33:15	39:55	46:14
1:03:00	6:45	13:31	20:17	27:02	33:48	40:34	47:19
1:04:00	6:52	13:44	20:36	27:28	34:20	41:12	48:04
1:05:00	6:58	13:57	20:55	27:54	34:52	41:50	48:49
1:06:00	7:04	14:10	21:15	28:20	35:24	42:29	49:34
1:07:00	7:11	14:23	21:34	28:45	35:56	43:08	50:19
1:08:00	7:17	14:35	21:53	29:11	36:28	43:46	51:04
1:09:00	7:24	14:48	22:13	29:37	37:01	44:25	51:49
1:10:00	7:30	15:01	22:32	30:02	37:33	45:04	52:34
1:11:00	7:37	15:14	22:51	30:28	38:05	45:43	53:20
1:12:00	7:43	15:27	23:10	30:54	38:37	46:21	54:04
1:13:00	7:49	15:40	23:30	31:20	39:09	46:59	54:49
1:14:00	7:56	15:53	23:49	31:46	39:42	47:38	55:35
1:15:00	8:02	16:06	24:08	32:11	40:14	48:17	56:20
1:16:00	8:09	16:18	24:28	32:37	40:46	48:55	57:04
1:17:00	8:15	16:31	24:47	33:03	41:18	49:34	57:50
1:18:00	8:22	16:44	25:06	33:28	41:50	50:13	58:35

Current half marathon race time	Slow end of lactate threshold pace/ mile	Split of 2 mi on tempo run at this pace	Split of 3 mi on tempo run at this pace	Split of 4 mi on tempo run at this pace	Split of 5 mi on tempo run at this pace	Split of 6 mi on tempo run at this pace	Split of 7 mi on tempo run at this pace
1:04:00	4:53	9:46	14:39	19:32	24:24	29:17	34:10
1:06:00	5:02	10:04	15:06	20:08	25:10	30:13	35:15
1:08:00	5:11	10:22	15:34	20:45	25:56	31:07	36:18
1:10:00	5:20	10:41	16:01	21:22	26:42	32:02	37:23
1:12:00	5:29	10:59	16:28	21:58	27:27	32:57	38:26
1:14:00	5:38	11:17	16:56	22:35	28:13	33:52	39:31
1:16:00	5:47	11:36	17:23	23:11	28:59	34:47	40:35
1:18:00	5:57	11:54	17:51	23:48	29:45	35:42	41:39
1:20:00	6:06	12:12	18:18	24:24	30:30	36:37	42:43
1:22:00	6:15	12:31	18:46	25:01	31:16	37:32	43:47
1:24:00	6:24	12:49	19:13	25:38	32:02	38:26	44:51
1:26:00	6:33	13:07	19:41	26:14	32:48	39:22	45:55
1:28:00	6:42	13:25	20:08	26:51	33:33	40:16	46:59
1:30:00	6:51	13:44	20:36	27:28	34:19	41:11	48:03
1:32:00	7:01	14:02	21:03	28:04	35:05	42:07	49:08
1:34:00	7:10	14:20	21:31	28:41	35:51	43:01	50:11
1:36:00	7:19	14:39	21:58	29:18	36:37	43:56	51:16
1:38:00	7:28	14:57	22:25	29:54	37:22	44:51	52:19
1:40:00	7:37	15:15	22:53	30:31	38:08	45:46	52:24
1:42:00	7:46	15:34	23:20	31:07	38:54	46:41	54:28
1:44:00	7:56	15:52	23:48	31:44	39:40	47:36	55:32
1:46:00	8:05	16:10	24:15	32:20	40:25	48:31	56:36
1:48:00	8:14	16:29	24:43	32:57	41:11	49:26	57:40
1:50:00	8:23	16:47	25:10	33:34	41:57	50:20	58:44
1:52:00	8:32	17:05	25:38	34:10	42:43	51:16	59:48
1:54:00	8:41	17:23	26:05	34:47	43:28	52:10	1:00:52
1:56:00	8:50	17:42	26:33	35:24	44:14	53:05	1:01:56
1:58:00	9:00	18:00	27:00	36:00	45:00	54:00	1:03:00
2:00:00	9:09	18:18	27:28	36:37	45:46	54:55	1:04:04

V̇O₂max Workout Chart

The training schedules in this book call for doing $\dot{V}O_2$max workouts at your current 5K race pace, in repeat segments of 600 meters to 1,600 meters. By current 5K race pace, we mean a race run on a reasonable course in good conditions—not, say, a hilly 5K on a cold, windy day.

The chart that follows gives lap and split times on a standard 400-meter track for workouts based on 5K race times of 14:00 to 24:30. (One mile is almost 10 meters longer than four laps of a 400-meter track, so the 1,600-meter splits are slightly faster than the per-mile pace for a given 5K time.)

Current 5K race time	Per-mile pace for $\dot{V}O_2$max workouts	Split of 400 m at this pace	Split of 600 m at this pace	Split of 800 m at this pace	Split of 1,000 m at this pace	Split of 1,200 m at this pace	Split of 1,600 m at this pace
14:00	4:30.4	1:07.2	1:40.8	2:14.4	2:48.0	3:21.6	4:28.8
14:30	4:40.0	1:09.6	1:44.4	2:19.2	2:54.0	3:28.8	4:38.4
15:00	4:49.7	1:12.0	1:48.0	2:24.0	3:00.0	3:36.0	4:48.0
15:30	4:59.3	1:14.4	1:51.6	2:28.8	3:06.0	3:43.2	4:57.6
16:00	5:09.0	1:16.8	1:55.2	2:33.6	3:12.0	3:50.4	5:07.2
16:30	5:18.6	1:19.2	1:58.8	2:38.4	3:18.0	3:57.6	5:16.8
17:00	5:28.3	1:21.6	2:02.4	2:43.2	3:24.0	4:04.8	5:26.4
17:30	5:38.0	1:24.0	2:06.0	2:48.0	3:30.0	4:12.0	5:36.0
18:00	5:47.6	1:26.4	2:09.6	2:52.8	3:36.0	4:19.2	5:45.6
18:30	5:57.3	1:28.8	2:13.2	2:57.6	3:42.0	4:26.4	5:55.2
19:00	6:06.9	1:31.2	2:16.8	3:02.4	3:48.0	4:33.6	6:04.8
19:30	6:16.6	1:33.6	2:20.4	3:07.2	3:54.0	4:40.8	6:14.4
20:00	6:26.2	1:36.0	2:24.0	3:12.0	4:00.0	4:48.0	6:24.0
20:30	6:35.9	1:38.4	2:27.6	3:16.8	4:06.0	4:55.2	6:33.6
21:00	6:45.6	1:40.8	2:31.2	3:21.6	4:12.0	5:02.4	6:43.2
21:30	6:55.2	1:43.2	2:34.8	3:26.4	4:18.0	5:09.6	6:52.8
22:00	7:04.9	1:45.6	2:38.4	3:31.2	4:24.0	5:16.8	7:02.4
22:30	7:14.5	1:48.0	2:42.0	3:36.0	4:30.0	5:24.0	7:12.0
23:00	7:24.2	1:50.4	2:45.6	3:40.8	4:36.0	5:31.2	7:21.6
23:30	7:33.8	1:52.8	2:49.2	3:45.6	4:42.0	5:38.4	7:31.2
24:00	7:43.5	1:55.2	2:52.8	3:50.4	4:48.0	5:45.6	7:40.8
24:30	7:53.1	1:57.6	2:56.4	3:55.2	4:54.0	5:52.8	7:50.4

Glossary

This glossary is purposefully short. It contains only the main physiological terms used in this book that are highly pertinent to marathon training and racing. It's provided here for easy reference if you're reading the book other than from cover to cover.

biomechanics—How the various parts of your body work together to create your running form. Although some features of your biomechanics, such as the structure of your bones, are primarily genetically determined, stretching and strengthening exercises may improve your running biomechanics and therefore improve your marathon performance.

capillaries—The smallest blood vessels; several typically border each muscle fiber. With the correct types of training, you'll increase the number of capillaries per muscle fiber. By providing oxygen directly to the individual muscle fibers, increased capillary density allows your rate of aerobic energy production to increase. Capillaries also deliver fuel to the muscle fibers and remove waste products such as carbon dioxide.

fast-twitch muscle fibers—Muscle fibers that contract and fatigue rapidly to power intense short-term exercise such as sprinting. They're classified into two categories, A and B; fast-twitch A fibers have more of the characteristics of slow-twitch fibers than do fast-twitch B. Although your fast-twitch muscle fibers can't be converted to slow-twitch fibers, with general endurance training your fast-twitch A fibers gain more of the characteristics of slow-twitch fibers. These adaptations are beneficial because your fast-twitch fibers then become better at producing energy aerobically.

glycogen—The storage form of carbohydrate in your muscles and the main source of energy during running. Endurance training reduces your body's need to burn glycogen at a given pace and teaches your body to store more glycogen.

hemoglobin—A red blood cell protein that carries oxygen in the blood. The higher your hemoglobin content, the more oxygen that can be carried (per unit of blood) to your muscles to produce energy aerobically.

lactate threshold—The exercise intensity above which your rate of lactate production is substantially greater than your rate of lactate clearance. At effort levels above your lactate threshold, the lactate concentration rises in your muscles and blood. The hydrogen ions associated with lactate production inactivate the enzymes for energy production and may interfere with the uptake of calcium, thereby reducing the muscles' ability to contract. You can't, therefore, maintain a pace faster than your lactate-threshold pace for more than a few miles. For well-trained runners, lactate threshold usually occurs at 15K to half marathon race pace.

maximal heart rate—The highest heart rate you can attain during all-out running. Your maximal heart rate is determined genetically. In other words, it doesn't increase with training. Successful marathoners don't have particularly high maximal heart rates, so it isn't a factor in determining success.

maximal oxygen uptake—Commonly referred to as $\dot{V}O_2$max; the maximal amount of oxygen your heart can pump to your muscles and your muscles can then use to produce energy. The combination of your training and your genetics determines how high a $\dot{V}O_2$max you have.

mitochondria—The only part of your muscle fibers in which energy can be produced aerobically. Think of them as the aerobic energy factories in your muscle fibers. The right types of training increase the size of your mitochondria (i.e., make bigger factories) and the number of mitochondria (i.e., make more factories) in your muscle fibers.

running economy—How fast you can run using a given amount of oxygen. If you can run faster than another athlete while using the same amount of oxygen, then you have better running economy. Running economy can also be looked at as how much oxygen is required to run at a given speed. If you use less oxygen while running at the same speed as another runner, then you're more economical.

slow-twitch muscle fibers—Muscle fibers that contract and tire slowly and that power sustained submaximal exercise such as endurance running. Slow-twitch muscle fibers naturally resist fatigue, and they have a high aerobic capacity, high capillary density, and other characteristics that make them ideal for marathon running. The proportion of slow-twitch fibers in your muscles is determined genetically and is believed not to change with training.

$\dot{V}O_2$max—See maximal oxygen uptake.

References and Recommended Reading

Alter, M. 1998. *Sport stretch* (2nd ed.). Champaign, IL: Human Kinetics.

Armstrong, L.E., A.C. Pumerantz, M.W. Roti, D.A. Judelson, G. Watson, J.C. Dias, B. Sokmen, D.J. Casa, C.M. Maresh, H. Lieberman, and M. Kellogg. 2005. Fluid, electrolyte and renal indices of hydration during 11 days of controlled caffeine consumption. *International Journal of Sports Nutrition and Exercise Metabolism* 15:252-265.

Beck, K. 2005. *Run strong*. Champaign, IL: Human Kinetics.

Bompa, T.O. 2005. *Periodization training for sports* (2nd ed.). Champaign, IL: Human Kinetics.

Brittenham, G., and D. Brittenham. 1997. *Stronger abs and back*. Champaign, IL: Human Kinetics.

Burke, L.M. 2007. Nutrition strategies for the marathon: Fuel for training and racing. *Sports Medicine* 37(4/5):344-347.

Cavanagh, P.R., and K.R. Williams. 1982. Effect of stride length variation on oxygen uptake during distance running. *Medicine and Science in Sports and Exercise* 14(1):30-35.

Chapman, R., and B.D. Levine. 2007. Altitude training for the marathon. *Sports Medicine* 37(4/5):392-395.

Cheuvront, S.N., S.J. Montain, and M.N. Sawka. 2007. Fluid replacement and performance during the marathon. *Sports Medicine* 37(4/5):353-357.

Clark, N. 2008. *Nancy Clark's sports nutrition guidebook* (4th ed.) Champaign, IL: Human Kinetics.

Cochrane, D.J. 2004. Alternating hot and cold water immersion for athlete recovery: A review. *Physical Therapy in Sport* 5:26-32.

Coyle, E.F. 2007. Physiological regulation of marathon performance. *Sports Medicine* 37(4/5):306-311.

Daniels, J. 2005. *Daniels' running formula* (2nd ed.). Champaign, IL: Human Kinetics.

Eberle, S.G. 2007. *Endurance sports nutrition* (2nd ed.). Champaign, IL: Human Kinetics.

Eyestone, E.D., G. Fellingham, J. George, and A.G. Fisher. 1993. Effect of water running and cycling on maximum oxygen consumption and 2-mile run performance. *American Journal of Sports Medicine* 21(1):41-44.

Farrell, P.A., J.H. Wilmore, E.F. Coyle, J.E. Billing, and D.L. Costill, 1979. Plasma lactate accumulation and distance running performance. *Medicine and science in sports and exercise* 11:338-344.

Flynn, M.G., K.K. Carroll, H.L. Hall, B.A. Bushman, P.G. Brolinson, and C.A. Weideman. 1998. Cross training: Indices of training stress and performance. *Medicine and Science in Sports and Exercise* 30(2):294-300.

Foster, C. 1998. Monitoring training in athletes with reference to overtraining syndrome. *Medicine and Science in Sports and Exercise* 30(7):1164-1168.

Foster, C., L.L. Hector, R. Welsh, M. Schrager, M.A. Green, and A.C. Snyder. 1995. Effects of specific versus cross-training on running performance. *European Journal of Applied Physiology and Occupational Physiology* 70(4):367-372.

Foster, C., and A. Lucia. 2007. Running economy: The forgotten factor in elite performance. *Sports Medicine* 37(4/5):316-319.

Gellish, R.L., B.R. Goslin, R.E. Olson, A. McDonald, G.D. Russi, and V.K. Moudgil. 2007. Longitudinal modeling of the relationship between age and maximal heart rate. *Medicine and Science in Sports and Exercise* 39(5):822-829.

Goldenberg, L., and P. Twist. 2007. *Strength ball training* (2nd ed.). Champaign, IL: Human Kinetics.

Hawley, J.A., and F.J. Spargo. 2007. Metabolic adaptations to marathon training and racing. *Sports Medicine* 37(4/5):328-331.

Hickson, R.C., B.A. Dvorak, E.M. Gorostiaga, T.T. Kurowski, and C. Foster. 1988. Potential for strength and endurance training to amplify endurance performance. *Journal of Applied Physiology* 65(5):2285-2290.

Janssen, P. 2001. *Lactate threshold training*. Champaign, IL: Human Kinetics.

Kenefick, R., S. Cheuvront, and M. Sawka. 2007. Thermoregulatory function during the marathon. *Sports Medicine* 37(4/5):312-315.

Lambert, M. 1998. Is a heart rate monitor worth it? *Marathon and Beyond* 2(6):10-18.

Larson-Meyer, D.E. 2006. *Vegetarian sports nutrition*. Champaign, IL: Human Kinetics.

Martin, D. 1997 *Better training for distance runners*. Champaign, IL: Human Kinetics.

Mujika, I. 1998. The influence of training characteristics and tapering on the adaptation in individuals: A review. *International Journal of Sports Medicine* 19(7):439-446.

Nieman, D.C. 2007. Marathon training and immune function. *Sports Medicine* 37(4/5):412-415.

Noakes, T. 2003. *Lore of running* (4th ed.). Champaign, IL: Human Kinetics.

Noakes, T. 2007. Hydration in the marathon: Using thirst to gauge safe fluid replacement. *Sports Medicine* 37(4/5):463-466.

Pfitzinger, P., and S. Douglas. 1999. *Road racing for serious runners*. Champaign, IL: Human Kinetics.

Sawka, M.N., L.M. Burke, E.R. Eichner, R.J. Maughan, S.J. Montain, and N.S. Stacherfield. 2007. ACSM position stand: Exercise and fluid replacement. *Medicine and Science in Sports and Exercise* 39:377-390.

Spriet, L. 2007. Regulation of substrate use during the marathon. *Sports Medicine* 37(4/5):332-336.

Svedenhag, J., and J. Seger. 1992. Running on land and in water: Comparative exercise physiology. *Medicine and Science in Sports and Exercise* 24(10):1155-1160.

Tanaka, H. 1994. Effects of cross-training. Transfer of training effects on $\dot{V}O_2$ max between cycling, running and swimming. *Sports Medicine* 18(5):330-339.

Wilber, R.L. 2004. *Altitude training and athletic performance*. Champaign, IL: Human Kinetics.

Wilber, R.L., R.J. Moffatt, B.E. Scott, D.T. Lee, and N.A. Cucuzzo. 1996. Influence of water run training on the maintenance of aerobic performance. *Medicine and Science in Sports and Exercise* 28(8):1056-1062.

Williams, M. 1998. *The ergogenics edge*. Champaign, IL: Human Kinetics.

Index

Note: The italicized *f* and *t* following page numbers refer to figures and tables, respectively.

About the Authors

Pete Pfitzinger ran in the 1984 and 1988 Olympic marathons, both times finishing as the top American. With a personal best of 2:11:43, Pfitzinger is a two-time winner of the San Francisco Marathon and placed third in the 1987 New York City Marathon. He was ranked the top American marathoner in 1984 by *Track & Field News*, and he is a member of the Road Runners Club of America's Hall of Fame. Currently the chief executive of the New Zealand Academy of Sport in Auckland, he has written all or parts of two other books on running and was a senior writer for *Running Times* from 1997 to 2007, in which his popular column, "The Pfitzinger Lab Report," appeared.

© Stacey Cramp

Scott Douglas is a freelance writer and editor with more than 15 years of professional journalism experience related to running. A former editor of *Running Times*, he is a regular contributor to *Runner's World* and *Running Times* and has coauthored four books on running, including two with running legend Bill Rodgers.